PRAISE FOR

ELLIOTT WAVE TECHNIQUES SIMPLIFIED

"On my radio program, Bennett McDowell made a bold, unpopular prediction for the 2008 stock market, saying it could fall dramatically. And, then it happened. What alerted Ben to the upcoming crash was expressed in patterns of market behavior which have reoccurred throughout market history. With this book, *Elliott Wave Techniques Simplified*, you can learn how Bennett McDowell's system can help increase your odds for success, by harnessing the power of probability forecasting."

—GABRIEL WISDOM, Host of the "Financial Wisdom" Radio Program

"As always, Ben McDowell does an excellent job of explaining a complicated subject, plus Ben adds a new dimension to the analysis with his Probability Matrix—taking some of the vagueness out of the analysis. Whether or not you rely on Elliott Wave analysis, this book will explain it in such a way that you'll be able to decide it if belongs in your arsenal of technical "weapons" or not."

—LAWRENCE G. MCMILLAN, President McMillan Analysis, author of *Options as a Strategic Investment*

"I've always felt that applying Elliott wave principles could be very helpful in analyzing the market, but felt overwhelmed when I tried to make sense of it. Bennett presents a well written book on both the classic Elliott wave theories and adds some great tips on how to check or confirm your wave counts. This is a great place to start for anyone interested in this methodology."

—CAROLYN BORODEN, aka "Fibonacci Queen", Author of *Fibonacci Trading: How to Master the Time and Price Advantage*

"I love this book! It provides an excellent understanding of using the Elliott Wave. It goes into the history of Elliott Wave from the founder of Elliott Wave theory, Ralph Nelson Elliott, to Robert Prechter who kept the wave alive. The book also explains how manias, panics, bubbles and crashes work with the five waves using psychology. This book is a must for anyone who believes there is a method of trading using chart patterns in terms of Elliott Wave.

—LARRY JACOBS, Editor *Traders World Magazine*

"A Japanese proverb says, 'If you wish to know the road, inquire of those who have traveled it.' My friend Bennett McDowell clearly knows the Elliott Wave road. His book fuses together his years of real world experience with his skills at computerized trading. *Elliott Wave Techniques Simplified* does exactly what the title says, it truly simplifies the principles of Elliott Wave. For those new to Elliott or those who have been using it for years, this is a resource that you must have."

—STEVE NISON, CMT, Founder and CEO of Candlecharts.com and the first to reveal candlesticks to the Western world

"Elliott Waves are all about forecasting but to be able to forecast as well as Ralph Nelson Elliott is a challenge. In *Elliott Wave Techniques Simplified* Bennett McDowell clearly explains how you can combine Elliott Waves with other techniques to identify tops and bottoms in the markets. Readers will be able to eliminate some of the uncertainties of using Elliott Waves and will be more confident in their entries and exits. Applying the methods discussed in this book will sharpen your forecasting skills."

—JAYANTHI GOPALAKRISHNAN, Editor Technical Analysis of *Stocks & Commodities Magazine*

"R.N. Elliott developed his wave theory based on harmonious patterns within the laws of nature. Now Bennett McDowell has taken Elliott Wave analysis to a new watermark, sharing his Probability Matrix to provide traders and investors with an objective framework to evaluate any stock or market in detail. Newer traders and market veterans alike will enjoy the many lessons shared by a real-world trader and renowned educator to guide them though the many facets of successful trading. "

— PRICE HEADLEY, CFA, CMT, Founder of BigTrends.com

"Throughout *Elliott Wave Techniques Simplified*, Bennett is mindful of providing both sound theory and practical applications. While he helps decode the "secret language" of Elliotticians, he never forgets that it is critically important to understand how to employ Elliott Wave interpretation in today's markets. Having worked closely with Bennett for many years—and having heard him present his work directly to traders on countless occasions—his passion for his subject and respect for his audience are always apparent. *Elliott Wave Techniques Simplified* is no exception."

—STANLEY DASH, CMT, VP, Applied Technical Analysis, TradeStation Securities

ELLIOTT WAVE TECHNIQUES SIMPLIFIED

BENNETT A. McDOWELL

McGraw Hill Education

New York Chicago San Francisco Athens London Madrid
Mexico City Milan New Delhi Singapore Sydney Toronto

1 2 3 4 5 6 7 8 9 0 DOC/DOC 1 2 1 0 9 8 7 6

ISBN: 978-0-07-181930-5
MHID: 0-07-181930-4

e-ISBN: 978-0-07-181931-2
e-MHID: 0-07-181931-2

Library of Congress Cataloging-in-Publication Data

Names: McDowell, Bennett A., 1957- author.
Title: Elliott wave techniques simplified : how to use the probability matrix to profit on more trades / Bennett A. McDowell.
Description: New York : McGraw-Hill, [2016] | Includes bibliographical references and index.
Identifiers: LCCN 2015038268| ISBN 9780071819305 (alk. paper) | ISBN 0071819304 (alk. paper)
Subjects: LCSH: Elliott wave principle. | Stock price forecasting. | Stocks—Charts, diagrams, etc. | Technical analysis (Investment analysis)
Classification: LCC HG6041 .M3834 2016 | DDC 332.63/2042—dc23 LC record available at http://lccn.loc.gov/2015038268

This book is dedicated with affection to my wife, Jean.
I am thankful for her guidance, love, and support, and for
inspiring me to always shoot for the stars.

CONTENTS

Thank You

Ralph Nelson outlined an approach that works for me, and I'm grateful to him for sharing his vision with the world in 1938.

I've been trading waves for years. The Wave Principle has such accuracy and clarity for me. And, in 2008, my charts so clearly predicted the 1,000 point one-day drop in the DJIA—my students and colleagues were amazed. Now there's not a day that I don't use waves.

Many of my students share my passion for Elliott Wave analysis, and I'd like to thank several of them here for their years of friendship and mutual passion for "wave counting."

Yves Pitteloud and Dr. Scott Ricke were instrumental in the manuscript development, giving their valuable insights from a student's perspective. And special thanks go out to Dean Jenkins for contributing his personal story in Chapter 9 of this book.

And of course, thanks to my good friend Stanley Dash, VP, Applied Technical Analysis, of TradeStation Securities for writing the foreword to this book. Stan is the ultimate professional, and I'm honored to know him.

Finally, thanks to my wife Jeannie and my kids Brady and Heather Frances for reminding me every day that home is where the heart is.

Bennett A. McDowell
San Diego, California
December 2015

Past Performance Does Not Guarantee Future Results

The information in this book, *Elliott Wave Techniques Simplified*, is intended for educational purposes only. Traders and investors are strongly advised to do their own research and testing to determine the validity of any trading idea or system.

Trading in the financial markets involves substantial risk, and TradersCoach.com®, Bennett A. McDowell, or affiliates assume no responsibility for your success or failure in trading or investing in the markets. For this reason you should use only money you can afford to risk.

Past performance does not guarantee future results and, even if you were successful with your trading and investing in the past, you may not be successful in the future. Traders coach.com and Bennett A. McDowell make no performance representation or guarantee of any kind. TradersCoach.com encourages you to engage in numerous practice trades prior to risking any actual money.

Hypothetical or simulated performance results have certain inherent limitations. Unlike an actual performance record, simulated results do not represent actual trading. Also, since trades have not actually been executed, results may have undercompensated or overcompensated for the impact, if any, of certain market factors, such as lack of liquidity.

Simulated trading programs and ideas are subject to the fact that they are designed with the benefit of hindsight. No representation is being made that any account will, or is likely to, achieve results similar to those discussed in this book.

A Three of a Three is a Thing of Beauty

Technical analysis of financial markets is predicated on using market data—price, time and volume—to identify price direction and critical price levels. Historians of the field have noted many landmarks such as Japanese candlesticks and the work done by Charles Dow on the economy and stock markets.

As the twentieth century progressed, we witnessed an expansion in the use of technical analysis including new applications of statistical concepts, aided by the power of computers. This blended many seemingly disparate ideas and perspectives into the art and craft as we know it today.

Gann, Edwards and Magee, Appel and Wilder are names familiar to every student of technical analysis. It was their pioneering work that propelled technical analysis to recognition as a viable and accepted discipline.

Another name that should be familiar to anyone who aspires to an understanding of technical analysis is that of Ralph Nelson Elliott and his eponymous wave.

Early in my own journey, I was mystified by discussions of Elliott Wave. Jargon such as "it's a *3* of an *a* of a *2*" seemed like a code impossible to crack. I'd come to grips with technical analysis, but this was a secret language and I wasn't in the loop.

R. N. Elliott's statement of the "Wave Principle" still stands as a benchmark 80 years after he formally organized his thoughts. In the ensuing decades, Elliott Wave has been accorded its proper place in the modern canon of technical analysis.

Bennett McDowell's "Elliott Wave Techniques Simplified" pays due homage to this pioneering work and brings it into the twenty-first century; this book is a notable contribution to the modern era of Elliott Wave analysis.

In all candor, Elliott's work may be among the most controversial of technical methods. It seems to divide technicians into believers and doubters.

Yet, doubters notwithstanding, even a novice chart reader who never heard of R. N. Elliott will agree that prices display patterns of ebb and flow. And just that simple agreement is all that's needed to open the door, and the mind, to Elliott.

Throughout "Elliott Wave Techniques Simplified," Bennett is mindful of providing both sound theory and practical applications. While he helps decode the "secret language" of Elliotticians, he never forgets that it is critically important for you, the reader, to understand how to employ Elliott Wave interpretation in today's markets.

So let this be an invitation to you to bring an open mind and explore how Elliott Wave analysis can help you interpret price action. You'll be able to judge for yourself whether your view of market action becomes clearer. After all, the goals with Elliott Wave remain the same as the ones I mentioned at the outset: identify price direction and critical price levels. Don't give in to the temptation to make complex what should be simple.

Having worked closely with Bennett for many years—and having heard him present his work directly to traders on countless occasions—his passion for his subject and respect for his audience are always apparent. "Elliott Wave Techniques Simplified" is no exception.

There's an expression I heard years ago, the attribution now lost, that sums up the perspective of every Elliottician—"A three of a three is a thing of beauty." If that sounds like gibberish now, fear not; it will make perfect sense after you read this book.

Stanley Dash, CMT
VP, Applied Technical Analysis, TradeStation
New York City, NY
December 2015

Let's Have Fun Counting Waves

In talking with traders around the world, one of the biggest complaints I hear when they are attempting to use Elliott Wave analysis is that many feel it is subjective, making it unreliable. Others have voiced concerns that it is overly complex, making it difficult to learn and too cumbersome to use.

I'm here to tell you that when you use Elliott Wave analysis correctly, it is neither overly complex nor cumbersome. And when you employ the techniques covered in the following chapters, Elliott Wave analysis becomes reliable because you know how to identify the wave counts with the highest probabilities.

I've designed this book to simplify the process and make it easy for the novice and experienced trader alike to learn how to use the Elliott Wave count without having to resort to head-spinning calculations. And doing so will help you remove the subjectivity you may have experienced in the past.

You will learn how to quickly and easily identify Wave 3 of the Elliott Wave pattern. This ability in itself will improve your trading skills immensely, since it is Wave 3 that the savvy professional traders use to generate the bulk of their profits.

Here you'll also see how to place a numerical probability percentage on Elliott Wave counts using the McDowell Probability Matrix, thereby separating stronger wave counts from weaker wave counts.

Plus, you'll learn how to apply what is known as the classical approach to Elliott wave analysis in conjunction with a more modern approach that yields higher probability wave counts and goes a long way in removing the subjectivity in your analysis.

REMEMBER: The guessing game is now over.

From this point on you will have a systematic and straightforward mathematical approach to learning and then implementing the Elliott Wave count. Now you will have a "road-map of the markets" to help anticipate and then prepare for future price action rather than having to react to significant events that have already happened—so you will no longer be reacting to these events after the fact.

The methods you will learn in this book do not require any specialized software other than a good quality charting platform and market data feed, which you are probably already using.

If you need guidance on trading platforms and software, there's lots of information at the back of this book. In fact, you can utilize some excellent technical analysis trading platforms at absolutely no cost. Typically, these free charting platforms provide end-of-day data, but if you are a position trader, that is all you need.

Depending on which broker(s) you have an account with, you may even be able to get a quality real-time market data feed at no cost. Again, at the back of this book there are a variety of quality solutions for you to choose from once you know what kind of trading or investing you will be involved in and once you know what markets are best suited for your needs.

Maintain an open mind as you begin reading about this new approach and let the material sink in. If you have had a bad experience with Elliott Wave previously, it is not your fault, and it is no wonder you had a hard time using price structure alone to count Elliott Waves. This book will give you the knowledge and tools needed to provide a winning edge that you may have been missing in your previous Elliott Wave encounters.

Having relied on the Elliott Wave for the last 20 years, I can tell you from personal trading experience that it truly is the "road map of the markets" on all markets and all time frames.

It has rewarded me time and time again with information and a true edge in the markets.

In order to become armed with this valuable information, though, you must understand how to properly apply a numerical probability percentage to every wave count. You will learn how to do this in the following chapters by implementing the McDowell Probability Matrix.

This matrix will guide you and assign probabilities to price events, multiple time frame analysis, price and volume relationships, etc., used to formulate an Elliott Wave high-probability wave count. And the beauty is that it's really not difficult to learn. You'll see step-by-step how to count Elliott Waves so by the time you have digested this material, you will be proficient.

In addition to learning how to use my matrix, you'll also learn how to utilize my "Trust and Verify" systematic approach where price support and resistance levels are constantly established in trends and corrections in order for the Elliott Wave count to be confirmed.

The concepts are easy to learn, straightforward, yet structured so that they can be applied on any time frame and any market you want to trade. This formula leads to consistency and puts the probabilities on your side for the edge you need to be successful in trading the markets.

Don't be concerned if you're completely new to Elliott Wave or new to trading. This book is written with the assumption that the reader is starting at the beginning knowing very little about the markets.

And there is no need to worry if you have never even heard of the Elliott Wave. If you can count to five, that is all the math skill you will need.

HTTP://ELEVATEYOURTRADING.COM/BOOKMEMBERSHIP/

Plus, I've set up a complete support system at the link http://elevateyourtrading.com/bookmembership/ where you can get ongoing information on using and implementing the techniques you will be learning in this book. Just go to this link and sign up.

And if you have any difficulty with the link, you can also call my team in San Diego, California, using the telephone number (858) 695-0592 or e-mail me at support@traderscoach.com.

I want you to enjoy the process of learning as you read this book and practice the principles until they become second nature. I suggest that until you become proficient in the use of these Elliott Wave methods and develop a good solid track record you should practice trading in a simulated "paper trading" environment while you learn.

Let's get started and have some fun counting waves.

Bennett A. McDowell
http://elevateyourtrading.com/bookmembership/

CHAPTER 1

Who Is Ralph Nelson Elliott?

He's the Man Who Discovered a Connection Between Market Patterns and Human Emotion

Ralph Nelson Elliott (1871–1948) is my hero (Figure 1.1). Well, one of my heroes. I say this because if it weren't for his discovery and development of the Elliott Wave Principle back in the 1930s, my work as a trader and financial market analyst today would be far less successful and far less fascinating. In the spirit of honoring heroes, it seems fitting to begin this book with a chapter devoted to the man with a unique vision that, at the time, no one else could see.

FIGURE 1.1 Photograph of Elliott around 1924 at the age of 53. His passport applications state that he was five feet, eight inches tall, had blue eyes and brown hair, and wore glasses.

The Elliott Wave Principle

A form of technical analysis, the Elliott Wave Principle (also known as Elliott Wave theory or just plain Elliott Wave), discovered by Ralph Nelson Elliott in the United States during the 1930s, states that financial market prices unfold in specific patterns that are referred to as waves. The principle provides a comprehensive structure as to where price patterns in the market are most *likely* to go.

The concept of waves is borrowed from the natural phenomenon of waves in the ocean, which are subject to the overriding force of tidal patterns driven by the moon orbiting around the earth and the gravitational pull between the two.

In the financial markets, rather than the moon's orbit around the earth, the overriding force is sometimes said to be human emotion and human crowd behavior. Many, including myself, believe that it is human emotion that moves financial markets in the same way that the force of the moon orbiting around the earth moves the ocean's tides.

The beauty of the Elliott Wave is that it creates a clear structure with which to forecast future price movement based on historical prices and patterns. Although there is no way to predict the future with *absolute* certainty, the Elliott Wave Principle can predict the most *probable* future regarding the direction of market prices.

In my experience, the Elliott Wave is the most powerful forecasting tool I have ever seen. And now that you are learning to use this approach, or if you are already a seasoned Elliottician, rather than just guessing where the market is headed, you have a tool available to you to help you "see into the future" of what the most *likely* direction of the market will be.

You will find that the Elliott Wave has an uncanny and mystical way of behaving like a crystal ball in predicting future market price activity. When you master this tool, the *probable* direction of future price will be clear. What won't be clear is the actual fundamental cause of the impending price action.

Not until after the fact will your predicted price action be defined and explained by world economic and behavioral aspects of the environment. Global events like war, economic depressions, political developments, and so-called acts of God like earthquakes, fires, and tidal waves have all consistently been forecasted by the Elliott Wave before they happened.

Said in another way, if you predict and then observe a dramatic move in price, there is usually a fundamental underlying trigger or reason that accounts for this move. You as an analyst will have no idea what the trigger will be when you are creating the forecast. It will only be after you observe your forecast develop into an actuality that you will know the entire story.

ROBERT R. PRECHTER JR. RESEARCHED ELLIOTT'S LIFE

It should be noted here that the bulk of information that exists on Elliott's biography was beautifully researched and documented by Robert R. Prechter Jr., author of *Elliott Wave Principle: Key to Market Behavior*, around 1980. Prior to this, little or no information on R. N. Elliott the man and his life was available in an accessible format.

The world, including myself in particular, is grateful to Prechter for diligently searching out every written document in existence (such as passport records, Library of Congress files, birth and death certificates, along with Elliott's personal and professional correspondence), thereby piecing together the revealing story that led up to Elliott's discovery of the wave principle.

Prechter left no stone unturned, and with the help of other Elliott enthusiasts, including (but not limited to) Peter Kendall, Howard Fay, Brenda Taylor, George A. Schade Jr., Michael Buettner, and most important Charles J. Collins, a colorful and rich tapestry of Elliott's life was exposed.

A fitting quote that Prechter includes in his book *R. N. Elliott's Masterworks* on page 17 sums up the importance of understanding Elliott's entire life as it relates to his discovery:

> "A man's life, like a piece of tapestry, is made up of many strands, which interwoven make a pattern; to separate a single one and look at it alone not only destroys the whole, but gives the strand itself a false value."
>
> —**Learned Hand**

Ralph Nelson Elliott Born and Raised in 1871

On July 28, 1871, Ralph Nelson Elliott was born in Marysville, Kansas. His parents' names were Franklin Elliott and Virginia Nelson, and his only sibling was his older sister Anna May Elliott. Marysville was a small community by the Big Blue River in the northeastern part of Kansas. It was also a stop for the Pony Express and travelers on the Oregon Trail.

Professionally, Elliott had dual influences: his mother was from a wealthy farming family in Philadelphia, and his father worked as a merchant on the frontier. Shortly after Elliott's birth, the family moved from Marysville, Kansas, to Fairbury, Illinois, a small and prosperous farming community about 100 miles southwest of Chicago. This location was better for his father's work as a merchant.

Then in 1880 the family discovered a completely new climate when they moved south to San Antonio, Texas, near the Mexican border. Elliott visited Mexico during his youth, sometimes for long periods, and he embraced the Spanish language and Mexican culture. Certainly by the time he was 10 or 11, he had become a seasoned traveler and had experienced a variety of climates and cultures ranging from the frozen tundra of the Midwest to the sunshine and warmth of the Southwest. Traveling would prove to be one of his lifelong passions.

The Beginning of Elliott's Career in 1891

At the age of 20, in 1891 Elliott ventured out on his own leaving his mother, father, and sister in San Antonio, Texas. He set out to work on railroads in Mexico at the height of North America's railroad boom. His ability to speak and write Spanish and English made him a great asset to his employers, and he worked in many positions including that of a railroad lineman, train dispatcher, stenographer, telegraph operator, and station agent.

Around 1896 he entered the accounting profession, and because he knew the railroad industry inside and out, it was natural for him to develop a niche in railroad accounting. For the following 25 years, Elliott worked for a number of companies, primarily railroad companies, in Mexico, Central America, and South America.

Elliott had great affection for this Latin American region that he resided in for decades. He sometimes commented on the contrast between wealth and poverty in this part of the world. Robert R. Prechter Jr. found a quote from one of Elliott's manuscripts that is illuminating as to Elliott's insights and perceptions about the environment around him: "Latin America is a land of extremes. Riches and poverty, health and sickness, enlightenment and direst ignorance, virtue and vice rub shoulders continually, presenting contrasts perhaps as striking as in any other part of the world."[1]

His observations about the Latin American people and culture indicate that he had an ability to understand and connect with the psychological and emotional structure of the region. Perhaps his ability to clearly observe people and their personal human condition enabled him to realize later on that it is people and emotions that move financial markets.

He Was Much More Than an Accountant

Suffice it to say that no matter what Elliott became involved in professionally, he dedicated himself to it completely, heart and soul. His responsible nature drove him to serve superiors and subordinates with nothing less than excellence.

Prechter describes Elliott's progression from accountant to high-level business consultant in the following passage:

> As Elliott practiced his profession, his corporate positions became more and more important. The main reason was that his expertise proved much broader than simply accounting. As later documents reveal, his value to a company was primarily in the area of business restructuring. As he put it in a book in 1926, "Accounting, like everything else, is undergoing very radical steps in evolution; it is becoming serviceable in a vastly broader sense." Fulfilling that vision, Elliott financially reorganized numerous corporations by installing new systems of record keeping, anticipating future expenditures, and applying a principle of percentage allocation of revenues.[2]

It is probable that Elliott's skills in restructuring, organization, monetary analysis, and problem solving made him uniquely able to find meaningful patterns amongst apparent chaos. Much like the chaos he found in many struggling Latin American railroad companies that he worked with during a turbulent time in history, the seemingly random chaos of stock prices were inviting to him rather than intimidating. These skills carried over for him later in life when he was developing the Elliott Wave Principle.

Love and Money in 1903

In September 1903 Ralph Nelson Elliott married Mary Elizabeth Fitzpatrick (1869–1941). He was 31 and she was 34 years old. They met in Mexico, and we can gather that she was an adventurous type, as was Elliott, since she trekked down to Mexico from her comfortable Irish-Catholic roots in New York. At the time they met she probably was working with a team of United Sates currency reform advisors to the Mexican government. No doubt Ralph and Mary shared a love of adventure, exploration, and travel.

They never had children, but they did provide support and companionship to each other in their 38 years of marriage. She was by his side for most of his Latin American travels and professional assignments, with the exception of a few periods including one in 1919 when the potential danger from the revolutionary sentiment in Mexico forced her to reside in Asheville, North Carolina, while he remained in Tampico, Mexico, from June to December.

Economically, the couple lived a comfortable life both in Mexico and later in the United States due to Elliott's distinguished career. They socialized with the well-to-do, and by today's standards Elliott's salary was above average, affording them the ability to travel and live in pleasant surroundings. For example, Prechter found that Elliott's annual salary was $9,000 in 1925,[3] which by today's standards is approximately $122,316 (after taxes).[4]

RALPH AND MARY ELLIOTT LEAVE MEXICO IN 1916

During the Mexican Revolution (1910–1920), during which nearly two million people died, Mexico experienced turbulent times. Ralph and Mary Elliott were living in Mexico during the revolution, but:

> In June 1916, when President Woodrow Wilson "ordered all Americans out of Mexico," Elliott complied. He moved to Los Angeles where he cared for his elderly father who died within a year. His mother Virginia had died in 1909.[5]
>
> Even after his forced departure, Elliott's passion for Latin America remained unabated. Between 1917 and 1920, Elliott tried to establish an American paper company's export business in Mexico (1918); was an auditor for the Pierce Oil Corporation in Tampico, Mexico (1919); and, passed up an offer of employment from the Cuba Railroad Company (1920).[6]

Tea Room and Gift Shop Magazine in 1924

In 1920 Elliott obtained a residence at 142 West 82nd Street in New York City. He then applied for a passport to investigate a position in Cuba with the Cuba Railroad Company. His abilities were widely known and highly regarded in Latin America, and obtaining this position was basically guaranteed for Elliott if he wanted to take it.

Prechter describes what happened next:

> Then came an abrupt change in Elliott's life. For whatever reason, he suddenly called off his trip and ceased his efforts to find employment and residence in Latin America. Perhaps the reason was simply that in his fortuitous move to New York City he had found another place that suited his adventurous nature.[7]

For the first time in his career, he no longer was seeking a position in Latin America; instead he wanted to remain in New York City. Prechter may be right that Elliott had found another place that was as adventurous as Latin America.

Or, another theory could be that Elliott's wife Mary preferred the safety of a New York City stateside residence as opposed to the turbulent environment of Latin America. In any event, the couple enjoyed their new home in the bustling city of New York.

During this New York period, Elliott maintained a busy schedule including travels to Canada, Germany, England, and France. He also completed his largest company reorganization outside the railroad industry for Amsinck & Company.

Then, in the summer of 1924, he accepted a position with a monthly business magazine based in New York City as a columnist for *Tea Room and Gift Shop*. Compared to Elliott's exotic Latin American adventures, writing a column for a business journal on tea room management sounds like it would be rather mundane and ordinary.

But in the roaring 1920s tea rooms were a booming business, and Elliott's arrival at the magazine was marked with much excitement. The November 1924 cover of the magazine is quaint, with typography and layout distinctly from this period. The cover has a photograph of the interior of a beautiful 1920s tea room, and below the photograph is listed "Mr. Elliott's Column" as a feature of the magazine.

Here is an excerpt from the announcement that the magazine released upon Elliott's arrival:

> Mr. Elliott Joins Our Staff
>
> We are glad to be able to make good so soon some of the promises of a "bigger and better" *Tea Room and Gift Shop* made in the August number. One of the very important steps made toward increased service to our readers is the addition of Mr. R. N. Elliott to the corps of experts in the various problems of our field. . . . Mr. Elliott will conduct a department devoted to the financial phases of tea room operation. . . . Mr. Elliott in his consulting practice, has been able to locate the financial leaks and the violations of administrative principles, which have prevented an adequate return. . . . Mr. Elliott has the accounting background, and what is exceedingly important the business acumen, to be of great service to our subscribers.[8]

As you can imagine, Elliott did not disappoint his readers, and his column became a smashing success. Each month he gave sound advice on how to run a business profitably with tips on essentials such as record keeping. He also emphasized the importance of avoiding debt, a lesson he learned while observing the challenges that many Latin American countries he worked with faced as a result of their struggles related to this issue.

The December 1924 column that Elliott wrote was complete with his photograph and the title of his column, which was "Mr. Elliott's Column." The topic for this particular month was "Incorporation Versus Individual" and was in response to a question that had been sent in by a reader of the magazine. Elliott was in essence the "Dear Abby" of the restaurant business in 1924, and below his photograph in the column the text read, "Our readers are invited to submit their problems to this department. Write fully and frankly to Mr. Elliott, care of *Tea Room and Gift Shop*, and your question will be answered. Your name will not be printed."

At one point, he even offered a novel concept to his readers suggesting they first work for a successful restaurant in every aspect of every job to "learn the business" before opening their own restaurant, or tea room. This very technique was drawn from his own experience as a young man working at every job possible in a number of Mexican railroads before becoming the most successful and sought-after business consultant to railroads in that region. This was extremely sound and timeless advice coming from Elliott. This concept could be relevant in any field or profession and could be applied in any era from 1924 to the present day.

All in all, Elliott spoke from the heart and from his own business and personal experience, and the readers were all the more enriched because of it.

Nicaragua's Chief Accountant in 1925

Just as the popularity of Elliott's *Tea Room and Gift Shop* monthly magazine column was skyrocketing, Elliott and his wife set sail for Nicaragua from New York City in January 1925.

President Calvin Coolidge's secretary of state, Charles Evans Hughes, appointed Elliott chief accountant of Nicaragua in Central America, at the recommendation of Dr. Jeremiah Whipple Jenks. At this time, Nicaragua was under American military governance.

The mode of written communication in the 1920s was much different than it is today. Rather than e-mail or fax or FedEx as the fastest way to communicate, telegrams were used. The telegram correspondence that led to Elliott's departure in January 1925 occurred on December 15, 1924.

Jenks was a distinguished lawyer, academician, political advisor, and author of nearly two dozen books on politics, social issues, religion, and business. It was Jenks's influential status that opened the door to this prestigious position for Elliott. For many reasons, this was a position Elliott could not refuse, so he swiftly accepted the offer, packed his bags, and set out "to revise the banking and financial laws of Nicaragua."[9]

Originally scheduled to stay for as long as two years, Elliott served in his official government position in Managua, the capital of Nicaragua, only from February 1925 to June 1925. At that time the United States removed itself from Nicaragua and recalled all State Department appointees as well as the U.S. Marines under the belief that calm and order had been sufficiently restored.

Politically, as history proved later, calm and order had not been restored in Nicaragua in 1925. The ruling coalition immediately collapsed under rebel pressure when the United States withdrew its resources from the region. Within months civil war was raging. The U.S. Marines were sent back to Nicaragua after less than a year's absence and stayed until 1933, completing a 21-year span of occupation.

This Nicaraguan experience was significant for Elliott; it opened his eyes to the political side of his potential influence. Intimately familiar with the Latin American condition, having lived and worked in the region since 1891, over 30 years of his adult life, Elliott had specific ideas and solutions for reducing if not eliminating the unrest that the Latin American people had suffered from for so long.

Elliott's View on the Future of Latin America

Elliott was eager and willing to offer these insights to those in power, and around 1926 he wrote a 100-page document that he submitted to the U.S. State Department in which he proposed a broad economic plan for the United States to implement in Latin America.

As Prechter explains, "Elliott noted that talks were then underway between the State Department and Nicaraguan President Adolfo Diaz 'On lines proposed in my memorandum.' Apparently, ideas that Elliott had formulated during and after his brief tenure in Nicaragua were already substantially shaping U.S. economic policy in the region."[10]

One of the primary obstacles to Latin American economic progress mentioned in Elliott's memorandum was the staggering burden of debt and a somewhat casual attitude toward its repayment. Elliott said, "The financial history of almost all of these nations, is one long tale of default."[11] According to Prechter, Elliott attributed this condition in part or in whole to "a political process that allowed unrelenting plunder and favoritism and a citizenry that allowed it."[12]

Steadfast about his thoughts on Latin America's economic health, Elliott contacted a New York City publisher regarding the possibility of publishing a book entitled *The Future of Latin America*. Half of the proposed book was planned to include the 100-page memorandum he had sent to the U.S. State Department.

The publisher agreed to the book proposal provided that the U.S. State Department approved the text. When Elliott contacted Secretary of State Frank Billings Kellogg in 1927, the department's reply "was pointedly noncommittal, thanking Elliott for his courtesy in bringing it to their attention, but declined further comment. If indeed the Department had been engaged in talks with President Diaz, it may have preferred to present the ideas as those of the State Department rather than of one individual."[13]

In one passage of *The Future of Latin Americ*a, Elliott states:

> The preceding chapters may have led the reader to the conclusion that the problems of the United Sates and of Latin

> America lend themselves to a mutual solution. By a seeming coincidence, but what may well be a provision of nature working in accordance with laws not yet properly understood, all those things which the United States lacks are to be found in profusion in Latin America, and the needs of Latin America are such as the United States is best fitted to provide for.[14]

In this passage Prechter feels there is evidence of Elliott's ability to see meaningful patterns in the nature of things. And that nature tends toward a compensatory balance, in which scarcity of one sort is countered by abundance of another sort. These ideas directly correlate with the rhythmic, or dynamic, balance that he later found in the stock market.

TEA ROOM AND GIFT SHOP MAGAZINE CLOSES

The monthly publication of *Tea Room and Gift Shop* ceased operations in June 1925. The closing may very well have been triggered by the fact that Elliott had suddenly taken his overseas position in Nicaragua, and the disappearance of his popular column from the magazine may have impacted readership. This is conjecture, but in theory it has merit.

At this point Elliott applied for an executive position with the International Railway of Central America, a U.S. company based in New York City whose stock was traded on the New York and London Stock Exchanges.

He was hired immediately as its general auditor, upon which Elliott and his wife set out on a nine-day voyage from New York City to the company's center of operations in Guatemala City, the capital of Guatemala. He served in this position from August 1925 to October 1926.

In this position records show that Elliott earned $9,000 USD in salary per year, which amounts to about $122,316 USD after taxes in today's buying power.[15]

Elliott's Tea Room Book Published in 1926

While living in Guatemala, Elliott wrote a 176-page book entitled *Tea Room and Cafeteria Management*, published in August 1926 by the New York City publisher Little, Brown & Company.

The book focuses on the economic aspects of the preparation of food as a business. Giving great attention to the importance of organization in arranging, analyzing, and planning a business, Elliott also cautioned readers about the absolute necessity of obtaining adequate capital for start-up purposes. By all accounts, the book was very well received.

The cover of this book had charming 1920s illustrations, and the book was priced at $1.50 USD in 1926. In today's dollars that price would be about $20.00 USD.[16] Back in Guatemala, according to International Railway of Central America records, an "interim" general auditor had been appointed by November 1926, by which time Elliott had already returned to New York City, indicating that he had resigned from this position.

With Elliott's return to New York City and the publication of his new book, clearly he decided to resume his career as a restaurant management specialist. His primary goal was to promote the book with his publisher Little, Brown & Company and build his stature as the leading expert in the food service and restaurant management field.

Suddenly, on the Brink of Death in 1929

Seemingly out of nowhere, Elliott developed an illness caused by an organism known as *Entamoeba histolytica*, which he most likely contracted during decades of living in Latin America. The organism may have been in fact lying dormant in his system for many years, but it did not begin to show symptoms until around 1926 when he was 55 years old.

The pathogenic nature of *E. histolytica* was first reported in 1875, but it was not given its Latin name until Fritz Schaudinn described it in 1903. *E. histolytica*, as its name suggests (*histo* + *lytic* = "tissue destroying") is pathogenic; the infection can be asymptomatic or can lead to amoebic dysentery or amoebic liver abscess.[17]

Prechter describes the onset of Elliott's condition:

> Unfortunately, the illness stubbornly persisted during the month or two that he was developing book promotion strategy in New York. By January 1927, Elliott had left New York City and taken up residence in Los Angeles, his old home base from ten years previous, in an apartment hotel suite at 548 South Spring Street. Having left behind all his old business contacts, he concentrated every effort toward relocating his consulting business while attempting to recover from the malady that had stricken him.[18]
>
> In December 1927, . . . just when Elliott's future appeared its brightest, his independence and financial security seemingly assured, disaster struck. Instead of recovering from his illness, Elliott's condition worsened. By 1929, his affliction had developed into a debilitating case of pernicious anemia, involving chronic fever, dysentery and weight loss, leaving him bedridden. . . . Several times over the next five years, he came extremely close to death. Each time he managed to recover."[19]

Elliott Studies the Stock Market in 1932

With time on his hands due to the severity of his illness, Ralph Nelson Elliott became interested in studying patterns of stock market behavior. He had not been involved in the stock market before, but when forced into retirement from his prior careers, he focused his time and talents on examining yearly, monthly, weekly, daily, hourly, and even half-hourly charts of the various indexes covering 75 years of stock market behavior dating back to 1857.

Sometime around 1932, Elliott read Robert Rhea's 1932 book *The Dow Theory* and was one of the first subscribers to Rhea's stock market service, Dow Theory Comment (1932–1937). The total sum of Rhea's subscribers, as described by Rhea himself, amounted to "perhaps fifty correspondents."[20] This involvement with Rhea marked Elliott's shift from previous careers to his new endeavor of studying the stock market.

Causality and the Elliott Wave Principle

The Merriam-Webster's dictionary definition of *causality* is "the relationship between something that happens or exists and the thing that causes it" (www.merriam-webster.com).

When considering the physics and causality of the Elliott Wave Principle discovery, and what caused it to exist, one has to wonder a number of things: (1) Had Elliott not become severely ill, would he have discovered the principle? (2) If Elliott had not found something like the stock market that he was passionate about, would he have died earlier? (3) If Elliott had been born today instead of in 1871, would he have discovered the principle at all?

Who is to say that if Elliott had never come down with this debilitating condition, he would still have pursued studying the stock market? Had he been healthy and not bedridden, he might have gone along in New York City with his consulting business helping restaurant owners manage their businesses instead and never made this important contribution.

Then I wonder how he had the tenacity to come close to death so many times and still bounce back. Could it have been his sense of purpose and determination that gave him the will to live, to see his vision of the wave principle to its successful completion? His sense of purpose may have been the one thing that enabled him to fight off death time after time.

Current medical journals state that left untreated, the condition that caused Elliott's illness would likely to lead to death. Given that today's medications and treatments did not exist in 1926 through 1934, it is a miracle that Elliott survived. In effect, the only treatment available to him was bed rest, which is close to no treatment at all. Had he been given access to the medications of our day, he might have recuperated quickly, never pursued studying the stock market at all, and we might not now be enjoying the benefits of his discovery.

TAOIST PARABLE

There is a parable called the "Old Man at the Fort," written by the great Taoist philosopher Lieh Tse in the fourth century BC. The story of Ralph Nelson Elliott and his discovery of the Elliott Wave Principle resembles the story in the parable. It goes something like this:

> An Old Man was living with his Son at an abandoned fort on the top of a hill, and one day he lost a horse. The neighbors came to express their sympathy for his misfortune, and the Old Man asked, "How do you know this is bad luck?" A few days afterwards, his horse returned with a number of wild horses, and his neighbors came again to congratulate him on this stroke of good fortune, and the Old Man replied, "How do you know this is good luck?" With so many horses around, his son began to take to riding, and one day he broke his leg. Again the neighbors came around to express their sympathy, and the Old Man replied, "How do you know this is bad luck?" The next year, there was a war, and because the Old Man's son was crippled, he did not have to go to the front.

The parable also resembles the ebb and flow of the ocean's waves, the constant ebb and flow of luck, fortunes, and how they are all connected in some way and repeat themselves in ever-changing fluid cycles.

Elliott Is the Comeback Kid in 1934

> Around May 1934, just two months after his final brush with death, Elliott's mission began to be fulfilled. His numerous observations of general stock market behavior began falling together into a general set of principles that applied to all degrees of wave movement in the stock price averages. Today's scientific term for a large part of Elliott's observation about the markets is that they are "fractal," thereby coming under the umbrella of what is today called chaos science, although he went further than most studies today in actually describing the component patterns and how they link together.[21]

As you can imagine, after being ill for so many years, Elliott's personal finances were severely depleted. In addition to the monetary losses from lack of income and the expenses of medical care, he also suffered losses to his savings in the 1929–1932 bear market.

Although never fully recovering from his illness, Elliott finally began to regain some of his energy at this point in his life. It seems probable that his success in studying the stock market energized him and gave him purpose in the face of his financial and physical challenges.

Charles J. Collins Meets Elliott in 1934

On November 28, 1934, from his home in Los Angeles, California, Elliott mailed his first letter to Charles J. Collins, president of Investment Council, Inc. in Detroit, Michigan. This was Collins's first introduction to Elliott.

Elliott had subscribed for some time to Collins's stock market publication and was very impressed with it. He felt he could trust Collins and decided to share with him his discovery. Elliott even requested that Collins pay for travel expenses so that he could personally show Collins how these theories worked.

Collins denied this request and replied with a standard form letter that in effect said he would monitor Elliott's market calls for one complete market cycle to see if they had any merit. If they proved to be accurate, then Collins would consider further steps.

This form letter procedure had been put into place because Collins frequently received unsolicited materials from individuals who claimed they had a system that could beat the market. As it turns out, the majority of these systems were failures, with the exception of Elliott's.

Upon receiving Collins's reply, Elliott began to send Collins a series of letters and charts outlining the basis of what he referred to as "wave theory." It wasn't until January 4, 1935, that Collins began to personally respond to Elliott's "flood of letters," as Elliott himself put it. Prior to this date, an associate of Collins had handled the replies.

SEVENTEEN PAGES OUTLINE "THE WAVE PRINCIPLE"

"On February 19, 1935, Elliott mailed Collins seventeen pages of a hastily organized yet meticulously detailed treatise entitled 'The Wave Principle.' He sent twelve more pages and five additional charts over the next two months along with his regular correspondence."[22]

After receiving "The Wave Principle" in this raw format, Collins was hooked and began to personally write Elliott more frequently. He also sent him several books, recommendations, and articles of interest. This correspondence indicates that it was Collins who introduced Elliott to the concept of Fibonacci numbers and their occurrence in nature. Fibonacci numbers of course eventually became an integral part of Elliott's work.

Elliott's Famous Telegram to Collins in 1935

On Wednesday, March 13, 1935, Elliott sent a telegram to Collins and stated the following: "NOTWITHSTANDING BEARISH (DOW) IMPLICATIONS ALL AVERAGES ARE MAKING FINAL BOTTOM."

> Two months later, Elliott's call had proved so precisely and dramatically correct as the market continues on its upward climb that Collins, "impressed by his dogmatism and accuracy," wrote and proposed that "Investment Counsel" subscribe for payment to Elliott's forecasts and commented, "we are of the opinion that the Wave Principle is by far the best forecasting approach that has come to our attention."[23]

The Wave Principle Published in 1938

Elliott regarded Collins as a talented writer, and in 1935 he made a proposal to Collins asking him to write the book that would later be known as *The Wave Principle*. The copyright was to be in both their names, but Elliott was to receive full credit for the discovery and development of the Wave Principle. Elliott felt that Collins's name as the author of the book would be effective in giving the book wider acceptance and distribution.

The proposal also included a provision that Collins's company, Investment Counsel, pay to subscribe to Elliott's market timing service for two years. After that time, if Elliott's market timing service was successful and accurate, then Collins would indeed write the book. Collins accepted Elliott's offer, and in the summer of 1935, Elliott went to Collins's house in Michigan for three days to bring him up to speed on the working details of the Wave Principle.

"For the next two years, pursuant to their agreement, Collins received and monitored Elliott's calls on the market. His accuracy remained true, and at the end of the second year, in March 1937, Collins began working on Elliott's first monograph "The Wave Principle," which was based on Elliott's original treatise."[24]

The final book was published on August 31, 1938, with an estimated 500 copies printed. The size was 8½ by 11 inches, and it had a dark blue softcover with no text on the cover.

12 Articles for *Financial World* in 1939

The now famous 12 articles that Elliott wrote for *Financial World* magazine spanned from April 1939 to July 1939. Elliott asked Collins, who had been writing regular feature articles for this publication, to introduce him to the editors. Collins obliged, and as a result, Elliott was given the assignment to write 12 articles on his wave principle.

Elliott reached a much broader audience with this series of articles than he did with his book *The Wave Principle*, which only had the original 500 copies in print at the time. His magazine articles resonated with financial analysts far and wide.

Mary Elizabeth Elliott Dies in 1941

Elliott's wife of 38 years, Mary Elizabeth Elliott, died on December 30, 1941, at the age of 72 in Brooklyn, New York. She was Elliott's constant companion and was by his side during his Latin American travels and during his illness. It must have been a difficult time for Elliott.

Nature's Law Published in 1946

Elliott's final work was published on June 10, 1946, and was entitled *Nature's Law: The Secret of the Universe*. It was printed on 8½-by-11-inch paper with a buff-colored softcover and spiral binding. The 1,000 copies that were printed sold out quickly to members of the New York financial community.

This work was less organized and not as well written as his prior work, which can be attributed to the fact that he was 75 years old and suffering from medical issues including anemia at the time. He no doubt felt that he was in a race with time and wanted to get his final discoveries on record.

Elliott Dies in New York in 1948

At the age of 77, on January 15, 1948, Elliott died in King's Park, New York. At the time of his death he lived in a leading hospital for the mentally ill in New York that also served as a home for the elderly. He was coherent and rational to the end and continued occasional correspondence and meetings with Collins.

He was survived only by his sister May Elliott, who died in Los Angeles, California, five years later in 1953. Elliott's wife, Mary Elizabeth Elliott, had died six years earlier.

Though there is no record of Ralph Nelson and Mary Elizabeth having children, we can say that Elliott is the father of the Elliott Wave Principle, which he raised and protected as any conscientious parent would.

Prechter and Frost Keep the Wave Alive in 1978

Thirty years after Elliott's death, Robert R. Prechter Jr. and A. J. Frost published the book *Elliott Wave Principle: Key to Market Behavior*, published by New Classics Library in 1978.

The collaboration of Prechter and Frost undoubtedly brought the Elliott Wave into the limelight, especially since Prechter became quite the superstar in the early 1980s with a number of on-the-mark forecasts that only brought more attention to the wave principle and to their book.

As a result, a number of young "Elliotticians" were born in the years following 1978, resulting in a variety of new interpretations of the wave principle. To this day there continues to be much debate on how to best use and interpret Ralph Nelson Elliott's original theory. Of course the best interpretations of the theory are the ones that when applied to the financial markets yield the most significant and most consistent profits.

Prechter Reprints Elliott's Work in 1980

In 1980, Robert Prechter (who by the way owns the largest collection of Ralph Nelson Elliott memorabilia of anyone on earth) took on the monumental task of reprinting all of Elliott's original manuscripts and writings to share with the world. The first book containing this collection is titled *The Major Works of R. N. Elliott* and was published by New Classics Library.

Contained in this 1980 volume are: (1) *The Wave Principle*, 1938; (2) the *Financial World* articles, 1939; and (3) *Nature's Law: The Secret of the Universe*, 1946.

A later book with similar material to the 1980 edition is entitled *R. N. Elliott's Masterworks: The Definitive Collection* and was published by New Classics Library in 1994. This version is similar to the 1980 book but seems to have more updated material. The biography of Elliott in this volume is thorough and has great detail. Elliott's works contained in this 1994 edition are: (1) *The Wave Principle*, 1938; (2) the *Financial World* articles, 1939; (3) *Nature's Law: The Secret of The Universe*, 1946; and (4) selected essays, 1940–1942.

The value of studying the original works of Elliott is that they have not been altered, filtered, or edited. By studying the original work in combination with studying current interpretations of the Elliott Wave, we can draw more useful conclusions on how to implement this theory into our own system and set of rules.

My approach is a combination of what I call the *classic* and *modern* Elliott Wave analysis. The book you have in your hands is an instruction manual on how to blend the two methods for optimal results.

CHAPTER 2

Manias, Panics, Bubbles, and Crashes

Everything You Need to Know About the Psychology That Creates Financial Market Events

The Elliott Wave Principle states that bullish and bearish crowd psychology moves in five waves. At the end of Wave 5, the crowd shifts in mood causing a change in trend.

Optimism and Pessimism Are What Drive the Markets

Usually the crowd's mood shifts between optimism and pessimism in predictable patterns, or waves. Typically the crowd will linger in a state of optimism longer than it should, feeding on itself and causing irrationally inflated bubbles and inflated prices. At some point, the crowd will eventually move into pessimism, where it then feeds on itself again causing extreme panics that generate irrationally deflated prices, or crashes. Following that, the cycle repeats itself over and over.

The seemingly manic nature of crowd behavior that moves between optimism and pessimism and back again is very often completely irrational. At the same time these mood swings can be predictable when using the Elliott Wave Principle to make sense out of the chaos.

These mood swings are also called *fractals* or changes in psyche and are part of our biology. We have good feeling days and bad feeling days sometimes without a rational reason.

This same type of irrational mood swing occurs in the markets, and bullish and bearish trends are simply a natural result of events in the collective human psyche and not necessarily the operative effect from some form of "news." Instead, news can be a trigger that initiates a mood swing much like "spilled milk," as they say, can cause a good day to swing into a bad day.

The former chairman of the Federal Reserve, Alan Greenspan, understood this fact well as he noted that the idea that the Fed can prevent recessions is a "puzzling notion." Rather, the stock market is "driven by human psychology" and "waves of optimism and pessimism."

Markets don't go straight up or down—instead they zigzag like a lightning bolt. And for an Elliottician, this lightning bolt is made up of five waves. In fact, all human progression and regression comes in waves, not straight linear movements. Human progress is sometimes said to follow a pattern of two steps forward and one step backward. Most of mankind experiences life in this way. An Elliottician might expand on the two steps forward, one step backward idea by seeing the sequence as one step forward (Wave 1), one step back (Wave 2), one big step forward (Wave 3), another step back (Wave 4), and then one final step forward (Wave 5).

This is the basis of the Elliott Wave Principle. This mass form of progression and regression seems to be hardwired deep within the psyche of all living creatures, and that is what we have come to know today as the "herding principle," which is what gives the Elliott Wave Principle its ultimate power. The importance of the herd has been discussed time and time again throughout history and is the foundation of the Elliott Wave Principle. Analysis of "herd behavior" is further enhanced by using Fibonacci ratios found in nature.

The value of Fibonacci ratios was understood by many great minds such as Plato, Pythagoras, Bernoulli, da Vinci, and Newton. In addition, architects of many famous historic structures such as the Greek Parthenon, and even as far back as the Great Pyramid of Giza in Egypt, recorded their knowledge of

Fibonacci ratios as the building blocks. So it is no surprise that Elliott found them useful when developing his wave approach.

Irrational Thought Among the Masses Has a Dramatic Effect on the Markets

Irrational thought for an individual creates certain outcomes for the individual and possibly those around that individual. Just imagine irrational thought on a global scale, and how it can create a frenzy of either optimism or pessimism that can move the financial markets either up or down.

One example of an irrational thought is "fear of failure" since failure has not yet actually occurred. However the fear itself may be so intense that it can lead to irrational actions that actually can create failure. Fear itself can get out of balance and distort reality for an individual and among the masses as well.

Another example of an irrational thought is "greed," which can also get out of balance and distort reality for an individual and among the masses. During market tops it is staggering how quickly the mood can change from one of optimism-based irrational exuberance to pessimism-based irrational fear. And during market bottoms the opposite occurs.

The stages building up to market tops and market bottoms occur in waves known as Elliott Waves with market tops and bottoms occurring after bullish or bearish Wave 5 has completed. It is important to understand this concept of impulses and corrections found in nature as well as in humans to understand the Elliott Wave model and its reasons for use in the markets.

Without this understanding the Elliott Wave model seems mystical and void of scientific validity. However it is well documented that markets move in impulsive waves and corrective waves based on the human psyche being part of a universe that moves in a rhythmical series of impulses and corrections on all levels.

There will be times when you notice during a strong uptrend that the market will ignore bad news. This is the essence of an Elliott Wave impulsive trend. During these times it's amazing that the market continues to trend upward, but actually this is very common.

It is due to the underlying collective mindset of investors and traders that have chosen to ignore the bad news—rather than seeing reality for what it is—that markets are driven upward from an emotional standpoint. Likewise, when sentiment changes to pessimism and the trend is down or bearish, good news is often overlooked as traders' and investors' pessimistic views drive the markets.

Thus in an uptrending bullish market, market participants focus only on the good news and discard the bad news, and in a downtrending market, market participants focus only on the bad news and discard the good news. Trends change when reality becomes so unmistakably clear that it forces the market participants to let go of their irrational expectations and pay attention to reality.

Exploiting Crowd Psychology with the Elliott Wave

As previously noted, the Elliott Wave unfolds in wave patterns based on mass psychology, also known as crowd psychology. In essence the Elliott Wave allows us to see this psychology unfolding as five wave price patterns in the markets, and therefore we can devise a plan to exploit mass psychology by properly trading these wave patterns.

This book will outline a plan to do just that, but first let's take a look at psychology and what drives traders to behave in certain ways that result in these predictable and repetitive patterns called Elliott Waves.

Personal psychology and interpretation of reality based on their own personal beliefs is why two different traders might "see" the same market differently. We ultimately all trade our own belief systems, which is a reflection of human behavior and may explain why the Elliott Wave works and has been present in the markets since the beginning of time. Mass psychology can influence our personal psychology and can create beliefs that cause market bubbles, induce herd mentality, and distort reality. In trends, prices usually go to levels destined by crowd psychology and are represented as Elliott Wave patterns.

When looking at market psychology and especially our own personal psychology in relation to the markets, it is important to understand how greed and fear create emotions that supersede rational thought. This fuels market bubbles with crowd psychology that can drive markets in an irrational way.

To understand how this works, let's take a look at psychology on a micro level as it applies to us individually and on a macro level as it applies to the masses.

There are three significant factors that affect our psychology:

1. Visual perception—illusion or reality?
2. Emotional perception—your mood: fearful or confident?
3. Environment—past and present

All three of these factors affect our personal trading every day and affect the markets on a global level every day. We must completely understand both the personal and micro effects of these factors along with the global and macro effects before we can reach our full potential in our trading.

1. VISUAL PERCEPTION—ILLUSION OR REALITY?

Our minds are capable of more than we realize. And sometimes our minds can play tricks on us when we least expect it. This can be costly to the trader who has misinterpreted a chart or a market based on visual assumptions, and in this chapter the goal is to make you aware that visual illusions are possible. Being armed with that knowledge alone puts you ahead of the game since you will know to look at your charts and your analysis from a number of perspectives to determine if you are seeing reality or if you are seeing an illusion.

Visual examples illustrate how our minds can create illusions we may not even be aware of. Figures 2.1 and 2.2 show visual examples of illusions.

In Figure 2.1, the lines look angled or sloped, but they are actually straight. The illusion is created by the alternating white and black colored squares between the lines. I've got to say that unless you get a ruler out to check this example, it is really hard to believe that the lines are straight.

Now try to focus on the black dots in Figure 2.2 and see what happens. You will find that the black dots that appear in the white circles are an optical illusion.

These two examples clearly illustrate how our visual perception can be distorted. The key is to be aware of the fact that your mind and your eyes can play tricks on you. And then, develop cross checks to identify the visual illusions before they cloud your decision making.

My goal is to give you the awareness of these illusions so that you can avoid them. Later in this book you'll also learn about technical tools that can assist you in determining reality versus illusion. These technical tools can guide you in the same way that a pilot is guided by his instrument panel even in foggy weather when visibility is clouded.

FIGURE 2.1 Café wall illusion with wavy lines. Get your ruler out and you will see that these lines are all perfectly straight even though they look wavy.

FIGURE 2.2 Black dots illusion. Those darn black dots keep moving—just try and count them, and you will see that when you focus on them, they disappear.

Now let's apply these visual illusion concepts to trading. Figures 2.3 and 2.4 are examples of chart illusions. Does chart A in Figure 2.3 seem volatile to you? Or does chart B in Figure 2.4 seem more volatile?

FIGURE 2.3 **Illusion chart A. Does this chart look like it is a volatile or quiet market?**

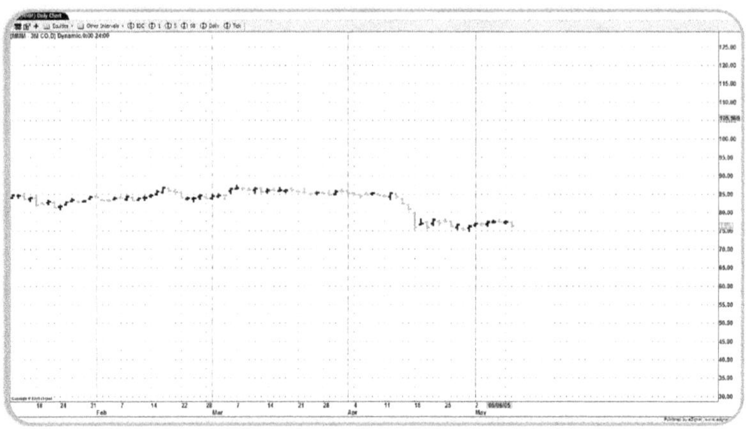

FIGURE 2.4 **Illusion chart B. Does this chart look like it is a volatile or quiet market?**

Actually, both charts are of the same market, but chart B in Figure 2.4 is zoomed in and appears more volatile to most viewers and usually creates more anxiety and emotion. Other viewers might instead see chart B as one that offers more profit potential because it appears to be more volatile. In any event, this shows how manipulating chart appearances can lead to emotional responses that are irrational at times and not based in reality.

Figure 2.5 shows charts A and B side by side. When you see these two charts side by side, and you know that they are the same market, same time frame, and same everything, it is easier to see the reality. The only reason the charts don't look the same is that the *x* and *y* axes on the charts are sized differently. This makes me realize I must carefully size my charts so I can see the reality of the current market when placing trades.

FIGURE 2.5 **Illusion charts A and B side by side. Both charts A and B are the same market and the same time frame.**

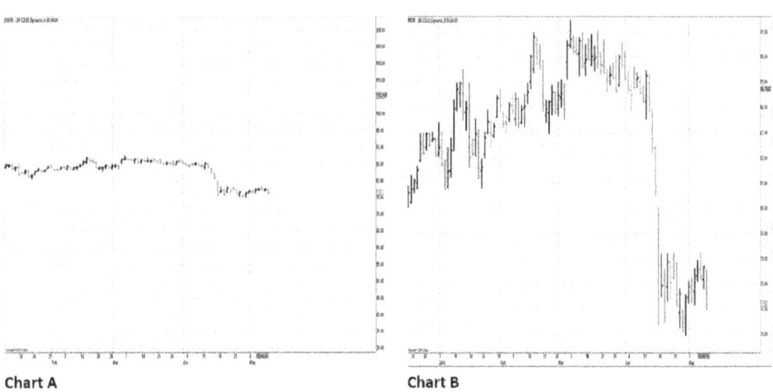

Since visual examples illustrate how our minds and our eyes can create illusions, this leads us to ask: Are we seeing the market as it really is from a visual point of view?

Now let's look at emotional perception. Emotional perception can also be an illusion created by the mind and more specifically created by our current mood.

2. EMOTIONAL PERCEPTION—YOUR MOOD: FEARFUL OR CONFIDENT?

Often our emotions can be created by our thoughts. Emotions when attached to thoughts "energize" those thoughts to help manifest the outcome. Here is an example of revealing a subconscious thought of what the market represents to you.

EXERCISE: Without thinking, write down what animal the market signifies to you.

Your answer will tell you much about your beliefs about the market. If the market is threatening or tricky to you, you will most likely choose an animal that could hurt or deceive you—like a lion, tiger, snake, etc. If the market is a threatening and hostile place, you will trade from a fearful mindset. The usual outcome of trading from a fearful mindset is emotional trading. Usually, fearful traders exit the market too quickly or hesitate and cannot "pull the trigger" at the right time.

If the market is a fun and safe place for you, you will most likely choose an animal that is nonthreatening—like a cuddly bear, or a favorite pet.

However, taken to the extreme, this will lead to a lackadaisical and unstructured trading approach leading to poor risk control and eventual loss. Remember, some fear is good. You could even consider that a healthy respect for the market. The key is to find a balance where you are not paralyzed with fear and not completely lackadaisical.

This exercise is useful in helping you see if the market feels like a dangerous or a safe place to you. If you determine that you have excessive fear of the market and feel it is a dangerous place to be in, you can work on finding out where that thought, belief, and attitude came from. And then you can create a plan to change that fearful attitude so that you avoid negative behaviors that may result from it.

THOUGHTS, BELIEFS, ATTITUDES, AND BEHAVIORS

What is the difference between a thought, a belief, an attitude, and a behavior? The relationship between these things can be enlightening and can help us understand our own personal trading psychology.

- **Thought:** Thoughts (subconscious and conscious) go through your mind, but none of them have any power except those that are energized by emotions.
- **Belief:** A belief is an energized thought that you make real, or accept as true.
- **Attitude:** Beliefs create attitudes, and these attitudes can influence our actions and reactions.
- **Behavior:** The result of thoughts, beliefs, and attitudes set into action is behaviors. Emotions that are attached to our thoughts thus ultimately create behavior.

HOW CAN THOUGHTS, BELIEFS, ATTITUDES, AND BEHAVIORS AFFECT YOUR TRADING?

Thoughts are powerful, and becoming more aware of the thoughts you choose to focus on and energize can improve your trading and profitability. The secret is to create a strategy to increase your positive thoughts and decrease your negative thoughts.

As a trader, how much emotion do you attach to:

- **Losing:** When you have a loss, do you energize it?
- **Winning:** When you have a win, do you energize it?

What are your core beliefs?

- **About yourself:** Do you perceive yourself as a winner or loser?
- **About money:** Is money good or bad?
- **About trading:** Is it possible to trade successfully?
- **About success:** Do you deserve it?

Here is an area of self-discovery, and you really have to take a close look at yourself and find out what your true thoughts, beliefs, attitudes, and behaviors are.

Then figure out which are helping and which are hurting your trading results. If you find your behavior is self-sabotaging by not using risk control or not adhering to your stops, it's a matter of figuring out where that behavior is coming from. Once you answer that question, you can work on changing it.

HOW BELIEFS FORM AND HOW TO CHANGE THEM

Let's say your belief system says that "the love of money is the root of all evil." The first thing you want to do is to identify and face that belief. Is it empowering or disempowering? If you feel that it is disempowering, then you must change it.

You can do this by understanding where you got this belief about money being evil. Give me some examples of money being evil.

Now come up with some new thoughts about the love of money that don't support it being the root of all evil. Think of how in some situations money is used for good. Give me some examples.

Which belief is true? Before one can adopt a new belief, the previous belief must be disavowed as being "not true."

Now replace the old belief with a new belief. Adopt the new empowering belief and get rid of the old one since you have now determined that the old belief is "not true." There is no need to place conflicting beliefs inside your mind.

The new belief may be "money can do wondrous things in this world," or maybe, "people with money are generous." Think of examples that support this new belief. Find evidence for this in your life.

You are now ready to move on into creating what you desire. Remember that what you can *conceive* and *believe* you can *achieve*.

NO TWO TRADERS "SEE" THE MARKET IN THE SAME WAY

We are all unique individuals and come from different environments and are preprogrammed with different beliefs, so it is natural that we all see the world and the market differently. With this in mind, let's look at how we process information we are receiving to get a better understanding of how it can affect our trading results.

There are five phases of perception:

- **Source:** Chart—the actual message
- **Perception:** "Source" plus beliefs—how you perceive or see the message
- **Interpretation:** Your unique opinion of what the reality of the source is
- **Processing:** Analysis—biased by your unique interpretation
- **Conclusion:** Your new perceived unique message!

This is why traders "see" the same market differently and why we ultimately trade our own belief system, which is a reflection of human behavior and may explain why the Elliott Wave works.

THE SCIENCE OF QUANTUM PHYSICS AND CROWD PSYCHOLOGY

Is it possible that prices in the markets represent moments of mass consciousness generated by highly energized emotional thoughts that become beliefs that create physical realities, and is this why markets can be irrational at times? In other words, do mass irrational beliefs influence prices? The answer is *yes*!

Since this can happen on a mass scale, we also know that this can happen on a personal level. Your beliefs will influence your trading results. And this is what makes traders losers or winners. Traders manifest their beliefs in their choices and behaviors, and that results in winning or losing. So choose your thoughts very carefully.

People's perceptions of the markets can be compared to the question asked in Figure 2.6: Is the glass half full or half empty? The answer may be different for each of us depending on two major factors:

- Visually the shape of the glass may influence your answer.
- Emotionally your current mood may influence your answer.

FIGURE 2.6 **Does this glass look half full or half empty to you?**

Each of us is wired differently: some of us are eternal optimists, while others are forever pessimists. The challenge is to know yourself and what your tendencies are so that you can manage them while trading. Looking at Figure 2.6, the pessimist might answer, "The glass is half empty," and the optimist might answer, "The glass is half full."

For you, knowing if you are a pessimist or an optimist is useful information. This will assist you in managing impulses in one direction or another and this will assist you in managing your psychology.

3. ENVIRONMENT—PAST AND PRESENT

Your environment is the world around you, past and present. It's the house you grew up in, the house you live in now, your parents, your friends, your health, your job, your spouse, your kids, your social status, your financial status, your everything.

This environment past and present most certainly has a big impact on much of what you do in your life. Understanding the impact your environment has on you is essential in strengthening your psychology.

Everyone has a unique and different environment. Your environment will impact your belief system. Think about your past and how that influences your beliefs. Think about your present and how that influences your beliefs. The result is your unique journey.

HOW TO ACHIEVE AWARENESS OF YOUR "TRIGGERS"

We all have triggers, things that set us off and derail us. For each of us these triggers will be different, maybe even opposite. For example, for some traders a large winning trade will set them off into a self-sabotaging streak. A large win may actually make them feel uncomfortable and create anxiety. For other traders, a series of small losses or drawdown may be the trigger. Whatever they may be, make a promise to yourself to become more aware of your triggers.

Take the following action steps to achieve awareness of the beliefs and emotional factors that affect your trading:

- Stop denial: don't run from your fear, your past, or your present.
- Seek the truth in yourself and your environment.
- Face your problems head-on.
- Become aware of your "emotional triggers" and realize how they can affect you and your relationship with reality.

EMOTIONAL MINDSET AND TRADING PERFORMANCE

Studies have proved a clear link between intense emotional feelings and trading performance. Intense emotions equal worse performance. For example, consider the pressure of *having to* make money at trading versus having fun trading without monetary pressure.

One of the ways to take the pressure out of trading is to enjoy the process of trading in a simulated environment ("paper trade") until you have a profitable set of trading rules and to learn to live in the present moment, thus reducing the emotions that can be created by worry about past or future outcomes.

LEARN TO LIVE AND TRADE IN THE PRESENT MOMENT

Learn to stop your fear!

Many professions can be stressful, but some have consequences that could rattle most. In these professions the key has always been to practice in a safe environment until the skill is mastered, then, when applying the skill, live in the present moment. Below is a list of professions that require the practitioner to not think about the outcome of the event but instead live in the present moment with "no mind" so reactions are automatic and split-second decisions are made without emotional thought:

- Emergency room doctors
- Samurai warriors
- Combat fighter pilots
- Race car drivers
- *Traders!*

TIP: Try to live in the present moment. It is hard to do, but keep trying and you will begin to see the benefits of less stress and anxiety and better performance in all you do. Do not confuse living in the moment with not being prepared. Living in the moment applies to executing your skills without any emotional baggage.

FEAR AND GREED

Which is more powerful, fear or greed? Question: Doesn't greed also have an element of fear in it? For example, if you fear you will miss the move, is that greed to get in or fear that you will miss out? Both are intertwined, but are they equal in intensity?

Your goal is to see fear and greed for what they are—emotions!

Be able to spot these emotions in the markets and exploit them. Emotions create volatility, increased volume, fast markets, and "fractals" or "pivot points" representing behavior changes.

ONE KEY TO SUCCESSFUL TRADING IS TO BELIEVE IN YOURSELF

Believing in yourself is a matter of choosing your thoughts carefully. For some it is easier to believe in themselves because they had parents or mentors that believed in them from the beginning. For others that were not so lucky, they must learn to have faith in their own ability and choices. And in time, the confidence will come.

But remember that everyone makes mistakes, so believing in yourself does not mean that you won't make mistakes or be faced with challenges. It means that you will persevere and focus on solutions and problem solving.

Ask yourself these questions:

- Do you believe in yourself?
- Do you believe you can be successful?
- Do you believe successful trading is possible?
- Do you believe you can make a living trading?
- "If you don't *believe* it, that is why you *fail*!"

A successful trading psychology requires balance and full awareness:

- Learn the correct balance between fear and greed.
- Learn skills to build confidence.
- Learn to trade the markets with the belief that you will succeed and in full awareness without fear, anxiety, or despair.

This allows a balance that manifests itself into a positive reality creating a feeling of abundance and goodwill.

IT ALL STARTS WITH A THOUGHT!

Your thoughts shape your beliefs. And your beliefs in turn shape your thoughts. Your beliefs shape your emotions such as fear and greed. Emotions such as fear and greed are relative, based on your unique beliefs. Fear and greed drive markets and life itself. Ultimately, you live your beliefs, which create your reality. Trading is nothing more than a vehicle you choose to create your reality by trading your beliefs. So choose and protect your thoughts carefully!

YOUR MIND AND PSYCHOLOGY MAY AFFECT YOUR TRADING PERFORMANCE

Thus, your mind is creating illusions you may not even be aware of. Illusions may be visual or may be created subconsciously by emotions created by beliefs.

Are your emotions such as fear distorting what is real and how you interpret and act in the markets? How your mind sees and interprets the markets may be affecting your trading—without you even being aware of it!

CHAPTER 3

Classic Elliott Wave

Elliott's 1938 Classic Rules Based Purely on Price Patterns

In this book we'll be looking at two different approaches to Elliott Wave analysis. Both work hand in hand to deliver to you the highest probability wave counts and potential for profit in the markets.

The first approach is the Classic Elliott Wave Approach and consists of a set of rules first discovered by Ralph Nelson Elliott back in the 1930s when he observed wave price patterns that correlated with Fibonacci numbers representing extension and retracement levels and price target zones.

The second approach is the Modern Elliott Wave Approach. In this approach we are able to use computerized tools to aid in the confirmation of wave counts determined by the classic approach, which uses price structure only. Also part of the modern approach is to "connect the dots" between a series of unique computerized indicators to confirm or deny the Elliott Wave price structure analysis established using the classic approach.

When both the classic and modern analyses are in confirmation or agreement, this leads to a highly accurate Elliott Wave count. The McDowell Probability Matrix assigns probabilities to both classic and modern readings to achieve a numerical confirmation of the two. The key to learning my method is to properly combine the modern and classic approaches to identify high probability Elliott Wave counts that can be traded for profit.

When you've finished reading this book, you'll know how to do this. In this chapter we will look at the classic approach as it is applied to price structure only, while in the next chapter we will look at the classic approach that includes Fibonacci analysis. Fibonacci analysis is considered part of the classic approach since it deals with price structure and was part of Ralph Nelson Elliott's original theory.

Now let's take a look at classic Elliott Wave rules. Remember in classic Elliott Wave counting the trader focuses on price, volume, price patterns, price statistics, wave lengths, and Fibonacci price levels.

COUNTING ELLIOTT WAVES USING THE CLASSIC APPROACH

Elliott five-wave patterns represent the main trends in the market. Because no trend goes straight up or straight down, each five-wave pattern creates a shape that looks like a zigzag line or a lightning bolt. There is significant meaning associated with each of the individual five waves, and in order to effectively use these patterns to profit in the markets you must first understand the meaning of each wave.

THERE ARE THREE IMPULSIVE WAVES AND TWO CORRECTIVE WAVES IN EVERY TREND

In a five-wave sequence, there are three waves that always point in the same direction of the current trend. Elliott called these *impulsive waves* (Figures 3.1 and 3.2). The other two waves are called *corrective waves* and "correct" or "retrace" in the opposite direction of the current trend. The impulsive waves are numbered, 1, 3, and 5. The corrective waves are numbered 2 and 4.

Although the corrective Waves 2 and 4 are in opposition to the impulsive waves, they do not signal an end to the current trend. They are temporary, and as soon as they are over, the current trend continues in the same direction as before, either to the upside or to the downside.

The corrective waves usually have three waves inside them. These waves are not labeled with a number but instead are labeled with a letter, A, B, and C.

If the corrective wave has just three of these subwaves, it is called a *simple correction*. It can also be called a zigzag or an ABC correction. Sometimes, however, there are more than three waves. If there are more than three waves in the correction, we call that a *complex correction*. We will go into more detail outlining the characteristics of simple versus complex corrections later in this chapter.

TIP: Corrective waves can also be referred to as pullbacks or retracements.

Typically, corrective waves are not tradeable. Corrective waves present higher trade risk than impulsive waves, and their risk-to-reward-ratio is very low. Simply put, for the most part, it is best to stay out of Waves 2 and 4.

ELLIOTT FIVE-WAVE PATTERN

Following are descriptions of each wave in a typical Elliott five-wave pattern (Figures 3.1 and 3.2).

FIGURE 3.1 Bear five-wave trend with ABC corrections

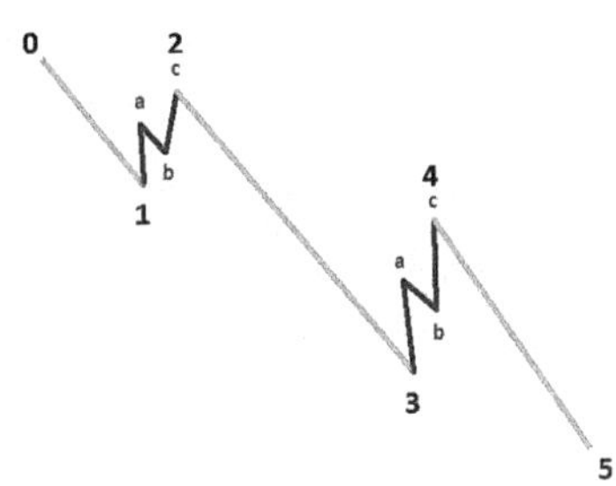

FIGURE 3.2 **Bull five-wave trend with ABC corrections**

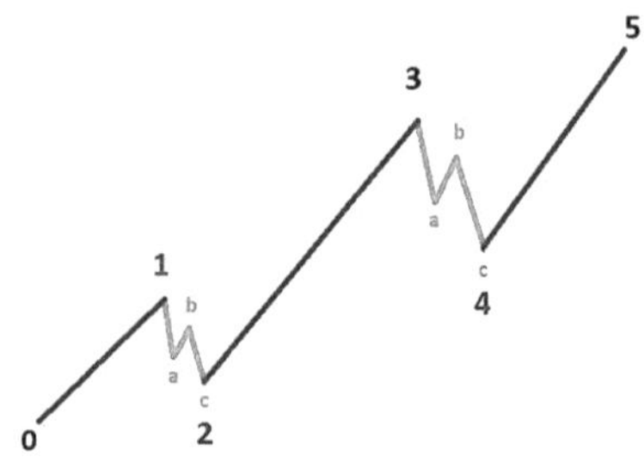

WAVE 1

Wave 1 is an impulsive wave and is rarely obvious at its inception. One of the best ways to identify the beginning of Wave 1 is to determine what the target zone is for the previous trend and determine when Wave 5 of the previous trend is complete.

For example, when the first wave of a new bull market begins, the fundamental news is almost universally negative. The previous trend is considered still strongly in force. Fundamental analysts continue to revise their earnings estimates lower; the economy probably does not look strong. Sentiment surveys are decidedly bearish, put options are in vogue, and implied volatility in the options market is high.

This new bullish impulsive Wave 1 will break the previous downtrend and marks the beginning of a new uptrend. You want to start watching for a pullback when Wave 1 starts. This first pullback will be Wave 2. When you see this pullback you will be able to identify the end of Wave 1.

The opposite is true for a bearish Wave 1. fundamental news is positive, the previous trend is still strong and sentiment is still bullish. Wave 1 is identified when Wave 5 of the previous trend has completed.

Wave 1 often consists of "profit-taking" where traders are exiting their previous positions from the previous trend.

WAVE 2

Wave 2 is a corrective wave. It can be either simple or complex. Here is where you want to start looking for a trade entry, and this sets up your *first pullback* scenario. You are hopping on board at the beginning of a new trend, either bullish or bearish.

Wave 2 corrects Wave 1 but can never extend beyond the starting point of Wave 1. Volume should be lower during Wave 2 than during Wave 1, and in Wave 2 prices will retrace 23.6 percent to 100 percent from the start of Wave 1. (Rule for Wave 2: Wave 2 never retraces more than 100 percent of the length of Wave 1.)

TIP: As a general rule, do not trade in the direction of corrections—they tend to be messy and create losses.

WAVE 3

Wave 3 of an Elliott Wave cycle is an impulsive wave and is the steepest and the strongest of all five waves. It also has the highest volume. While it can be, it is not always the longest wave in terms of time. That is why we want to get ready during Wave 2 (the pullback) so we can jump in immediately as Wave 3 is beginning to unfold.

You must wait for Wave 3 to exceed the final price level of Wave 1. That is your signal that Wave 2 is over, and any price bar that goes beyond the final price level of Wave 1 must be Wave 3. Wave 3 is usually the largest and most powerful wave in a trend (although some research suggests that in commodity markets, Wave 5 is the largest).

In a bull market news is now positive, and fundamental analysts start to raise earnings estimates. Prices rise quickly, and corrections are short-lived and shallow. Wave 3 often exceeds Wave 1 by a ratio of 1.618:1. This is helpful to know because you can draw a Fibonacci extension from the start of Wave 1 to the end of Wave 1, then to the end of Wave 2.

Look for 1.618. That is your target for prices to reach in Wave 3. And yes, prices can go beyond 1.618, but this will give you a target zone for taking profits. You want to get out sometime during Wave 3 because Wave 4 is sure to follow, and time may run out. You don't want to be stuck losing all your profits as the market sinks back into Wave 4. Some of my students exit the trade with a sure profit at the 1.618 mark and do not lament those occasions when Wave 3 extends higher than that.

> TIP: When you can get into a trade in the beginning of a Wave 3, hold on to your position for as long as possible. Don't treat it as a little swing trade—instead, treat it as a trend trade. You want to ride this powerful wave to completion. Why? Because you will make the largest amount of money in the least amount of time with a Wave 3 trade. Wave 3 is powerful and is the most tradeable wave in this pattern.

WAVE 4

Wave 4 is a corrective wave and can be either simple or complex. If Wave 2 was simple, then Wave 4 will be complex and vice versa.

Prices may create a simple Elliott Wave *ABC zigzag* corrective pattern, which can easily be seen. This is the most common. Or instead prices may meander sideways for an extended period, forming a complex correction that is not as easily seen and represents chaos as prices move in pennants and channels with hard-to-follow volatility.

Typically, Wave 4 prices retrace 38.2 percent to 61.8 percent. This wave is pretty disappointing for those that got in too late at the end of Wave 3. Wave 4 is a signal that the best part of the trend is over—which was Wave 3.

> TIP: As I've said before, do not trade in the direction of corrections—they tend to be messy and create losses. However, there is an exception to this "Caution Rule" for Wave 4 trading. You will see complete details on this set up later in this chapter under the heading "Exception to the Caution Rule for Corrective Waves."

WAVE 5

Wave 5 is an impulsive wave. This wave moves in the direction of the overall trend but is usually sluggish and not nearly as dynamic as the third wave of an Elliott Wave cycle. Wave 5 marks the last burst of buying (in a bull trend) or selling (in a bear trend)before a new trend starts. Wave 5 is the is the final leg in the direction of the dominant trend.

In a bullish scenario, the news is almost universally positive and everyone is bullish during Wave 5. Unfortunately, this is when many unknowing investors finally buy in, right before the top. Volume is lower in Wave 5 than in Wave 3, and many momentum indicators start to show divergences (prices reach a new high, but the indicator does not reach a new peak).

At the end of a major bull market, bear forecasters may be ridiculed. I experienced this in the late 1990s when I released a forecast stating that a major Wave 3 bull market top was near; no one wanted to hear it, and instead I often heard those that disagreed with me say that the market is different now and "this time would be different." Of course we all know that the market lost a significant percent of its value between the years 2000 and 2003.

THE MOST PROFITABLE AND TRADEABLE WAVES IN THE FIVE-WAVE PATTERN

Having reviewed the characteristics in each of the five waves, let's summarize which are the best waves to trade. The highest probability trades are going to be the impulsive waves: Wave 1, Wave 3, and Wave 5. There is also opportunity for profit when trading the corrective Wave C in Wave 4, but this is an advanced technique and you should proceed with caution if you are not experienced with this setup.

ELLIOTT WAVE CORRECTIVE PATTERN BASICS FOR WAVE 2 AND WAVE 4

Elliott Wave corrective patterns are represented by Waves 2 and 4 in an Elliott Wave five-wave sequence. There are a number of terms that describe a correction—all of them mean the same thing. The most common of these are: *correction*, *pullback*, and *retracement*. Throughout this book all of these terms are used, but you will notice that I primarily refer to this move as a correction. Let's take a look at the different types of corrections that can occur in Wave 2 and in Wave 4.

THERE ARE TWO TYPES OF ELLIOTT WAVE CORRECTIVE PATTERNS

Corrections can be difficult to master. Most experienced Elliott traders earn the bulk of their profit trading during an impulse pattern (Waves 1, 3, and 5) and stay away from the corrections. Less experienced traders tend to give back all their winnings to the market during corrective cycles (Waves 2 and 4).

Corrective patterns fall under two categories:

1. **Simple corrections**—known as a zigzag or an ABC correction
2. **Complex corrections**—There are three types: flat, irregular, and triangle

In simple corrections, there are three moves within the wave that are labeled A, B and C. This is the most common correction and is relatively clear and simple to identify.

In complex corrections there are more than three moves in the wave and they are labeled with an A, B, C, D, and E structure. These complex corrections cause channels and pennants and can be confusing and unclear and extremely difficult to trade.

ALTERNATION RULE FOR CORRECTIVE WAVES

If Wave 2 is a simple correction, expect Wave 4 to be a complex correction. And, if Wave 2 is a complex correction, you can expect Wave 4 to be a simple correction.

CAUTION RULE FOR CORRECTIVE WAVES

I do not recommend trading Wave 2 or Wave 4 corrections, since you are technically counter-trend trading, which is hard to do profitably.

If you choose to trade Wave 2 and/or Wave 4 stay away from complex corrections, or messy markets since they lack clarity and are difficult to read. These scenarios can whipsaw you and generate quick losses.

EXCEPTION TO THE CAUTION RULE FOR CORRECTIVE WAVES

One exception to this caution rule is to trade Wave C of the Wave 4 pattern. If done correctly it can be profitable.

When the Fibonacci Wave 4 price target zone creates an opportunity in which you can get in to a trade immediately after Wave B and still make significant profit on the Wave C move, this is a trade that has potential. This opportunity occurs when Wave B completely retraces to the final Wave 3 price level.

This is an exception to the rule. It's an advanced technique and you must be experienced in identifying these patterns before trading with real money.

SIMPLE CORRECTIONS

The *simple* corrective pattern is called a zigzag correction or an ABC correction (Figure 3.3) and is made up of three-waves. This is the most common and easy-to-spot correction.

THREE-WAVE ABC PATTERN AS IT APPEARS IN A SIMPLE CORRECTION

The underlying structure of a simple corrective Wave 2 or Wave 4 is an ABC zigzag pattern. You will notice that Wave A looks like a minor pullback in a current trend, but instead it is the first leg of a significant correction.

Wave A and Wave C of a zigzag correction always consist of five subwaves. In contrast, Wave B consists of only three sub-waves. The subwaves of this ABC pattern illustrate the fractal symmetry of the wave structure that we will investigate later in this chapter.

FIGURE 3.3 **Simple ABC zigzag corrective patterns**

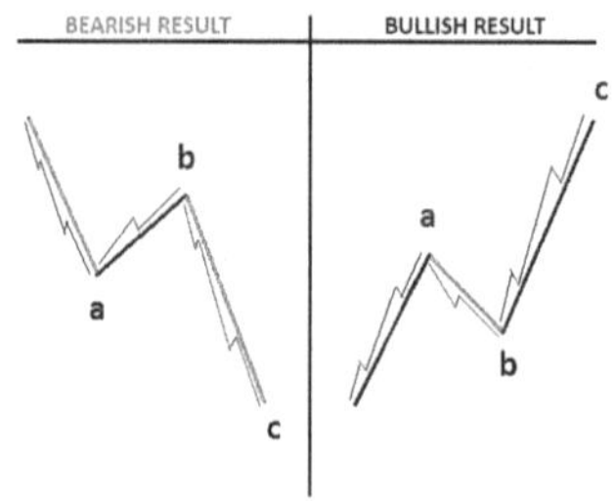

SIMPLE ABC WAVE STATISTICS

Wave A: There are five subwaves in Wave A. It is the first leg of a swing in the opposite direction of the previous impulsive trend.

Wave B: There are three subwaves in Wave B. The length of Wave B is usually 50 percent of Wave A and should not exceed 76.4 percent of Wave A.

Wave C: There are five subwaves in Wave C. The length of Wave C is likely to be 1 times Wave A, or 1.618 times Wave A, or 2.618 times Wave A. These are Fibonacci extension numbers.

Complex Corrections

Complex corrections usually unfold as *triangular* or even *diagonal triangular* corrections that are represented by ABC channel corrections or ABCDE wave structures that can cause confusion.

These types of corrections are known to form channels, pennants, and flags used in technical analysis. As a general rule, if you find Wave 3, followed by Wave 4, but Wave 4 is confusing and not clear, then chances are it is a complex correction. Complex corrections can also occur in Wave 2.

Complex corrections usually last longer than simple ABC corrections. There are three types of complex corrections:

1. Flat
2. Irregular
3. Triangular

Each of these complex corrections has unique characteristics, which are outlined in great detail in the following sections.

FLAT COMPLEX CORRECTIONS

In a flat complex correction, the length of each wave is identical (Figure 3.4); this creates a *channel.* After an impulse pattern, the market begins its correction in Wave A. It then reverses and begins Wave B. Finally, the market corrects one last time in Wave C to the Wave A start. Then the market breaks into the next impulsive wave.

FIGURE 3.4 **Flat complex corrective patterns**

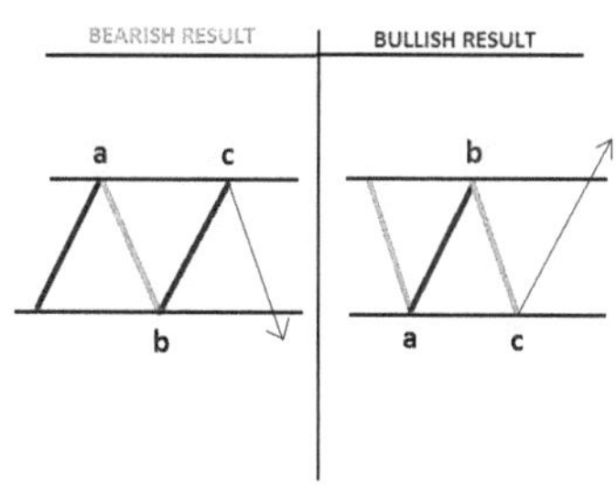

IRREGULAR COMPLEX CORRECTIONS

In irregular complex corrections (Figure 3.5), Wave B makes a new low when this type of correction occurs in a bearish impulsive trend and a new high in a bullish impulsive trend. Also, the final Wave C may rise to the beginning of Wave A in a bearish impulsive trend and vice versa in a bullish impulsive trend.

FIGURE 3.5 **Irregular complex corrective patterns**

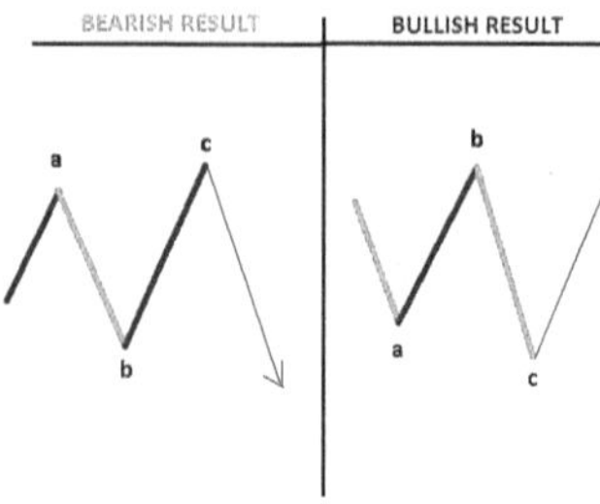

You will find more detail in the next chapter on Fibonacci, but these ratios are useful here:

Wave B = 1.15 to 1.272 longer than Wave A

Wave C = 1.618 to 2.618 longer than Wave A

TRIANGULAR COMPLEX CORRECTIONS

In addition to the three-wave corrective patterns, there is another complex corrective pattern that appears at times. It is called the *triangle pattern* (Figure 3.6). The five subwaves of a triangle pattern are designated A, B, C, D, and E in sequence. These triangle patterns are where *pennants* form. Pennants are a form of technical analysis marking price compression followed by a significant move when the pennant pattern is broken. There are bullish and bearish triangular corrections.

FIGURE 3.6 **Triangle complex corrective patterns**

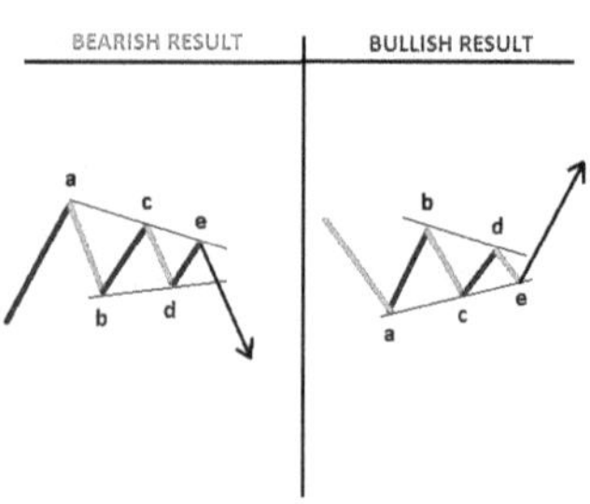

Triangles are, by far, most common in fourth waves. One can sometimes see a triangle pattern as Wave B of a three-wave correction. Triangles are very tricky and confusing. One must study the pattern very carefully prior to taking action. Prices tend to shoot out of the triangle formation in a swift thrust coming out of a correction and can be an excellent place for a trade entry.

PRICE SYMMETRY IN ELLIOTT WAVES

Price symmetry is present in all Elliott Waves. Figure 3.7 illustrates the concept of waves within waves as they are examined on different time frames. This price pattern symmetry occurs in all Elliott waves on all time frames.

It is similar in concept to the symmetry found in nature. For example, if you put a snowflake under a microscope, you will see its crystal structure go deeper at higher magnification and will see crystal structure within crystal structure. This is how the Elliott Wave works as well. Notice how the waves within waves are all part of a larger scheme of symmetry.

FIGURE 3.7 **Waves within waves illustrating fractal symmetry in the markets**

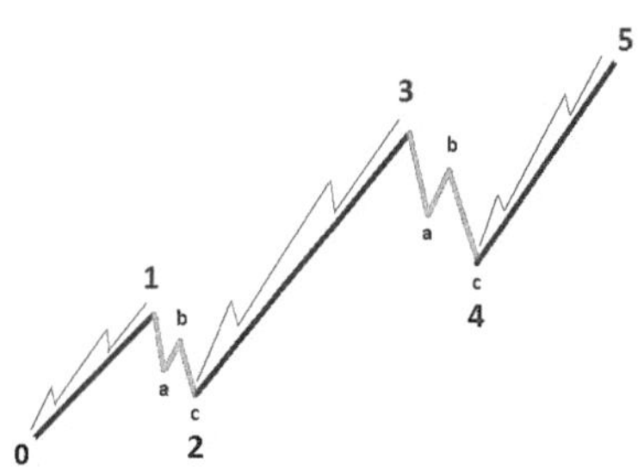

Are You Ready to Count Waves?

Start looking at charts and try counting Waves 1 through 5 until you can start to "see" the price structures that make sense. Not all charts will be clear; if a chart is not clear, move to another chart. Also try to see the ABC pattern in the corrective Waves 2 and 4.

My suggestion to you is, only place trades when you find charts that are clear and where you can find a pattern. If it is a messy chart, don't try to force a pattern on to it. Just move on.

Question: Figure 3.8 is a chart that shows waves within waves. Can you count the Elliott Waves on this chart using the classic approach?

> TIP: Locate Elliott Wave 3, which is the steepest Elliott Wave in the trend. At times a chart may also have a "gap" in prices in the direction of the trend. After identifying a possible Wave 3 using the classic approach to price structure, locate the correction after Wave 3 called Wave 4. See if you can find an ABC pattern in Wave 4 followed by Wave 5, which resumes in the direction of the trend. The answer is in Figure 3.9.

Answer: The larger numbers in Figure 3.9 represent the dominant trend, while the smaller numbers and letters represent the waves inside the larger waves. This bullish uptrend will complete after Wave 5 ends.

FIGURE 3.8 **Question: In the chart shown here, can you count Elliott Waves using the classic approach?**

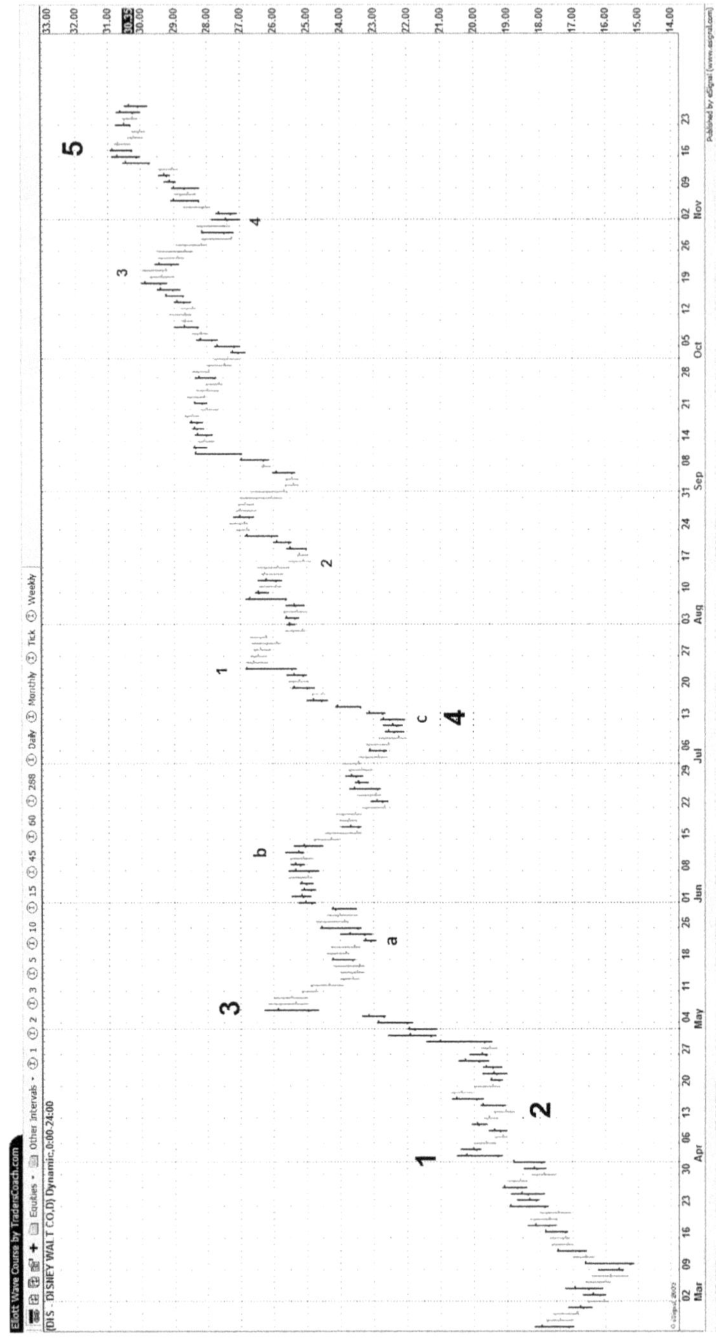

FIGURE 3.9 Answer: Here are Elliott Waves correctly counted using the classic approach.

McDowell's Elliott Wave Guidelines

My Elliott Wave guidelines are based on years of experience in using the Elliott Wave. While these guidelines work for me in my trading, you should test them to see how they work with your style of trading.

Some of these rules are Ralph Nelson's classic Elliott Wave rules, and he designed many rules that make up the Elliott Wave Principle. Wave length, volume, Fibonacci retracements, extensions, and time intervals are part of these rules.

- The Elliott Wave pattern consists of five waves and alternates between bullish and bearish market cycles.
- Wave 1 appears at the beginning of a trend, and Wave 5 appears at the end.
- Impulsive waves are Waves 1, 3, and 5.
- Corrective waves are Waves 2 and 4.
- Tradable waves are Waves 1, 3, and 5 and Wave C of a Wave 4 correction.
- Wave 3 is the steepest and most dramatic of all the waves and occurs on the highest volume.
- Wave 3 has the highest histogram indicator of all waves.
- Wave 3 is the dominant wave of a five-wave pattern and offers the greatest potential for profit.
- Waves 1, 3, and 5 are made up of five subwaves.
- Waves 2 and 4 are made up of three subwaves unless they are a complex correction, in which case they will have more than three subwaves.
- There are two types of corrections: simple and complex.
- Most corrections are simple ABC zigzag corrections.
- There are three types of complex corrections: flat, irregular, and triangular.
- If Wave 2 is a simple correction, you can expect Wave 4 to be a complex correction.
- If Wave 2 is a complex correction you can expect Wave 4 to be a simple correction.

- Wave 5 will usually exceed Wave 3 on lower volume than the Wave 3 high.
- Wave 5 can fail and just form a double top (or a double bottom) with Wave 3 instead of going to higher price levels.
- Always base your trade entries and exits using your own set of trading entry and exit signals.
- Most traders get whipsawed and lose money in Wave 4.
- Don't assume Wave 4 is over until you can clearly see an ABC wave pattern with Wave 4 ending at Fibonacci levels of 38.2 percent to 61.8 percent of Wave 3 length.

ELLIOTT WAVE STATISTICS FOR ALL FIVE WAVES

Following are characteristics of each Elliott Wave.

Impulsive Wave 1 statistics: Wave 1 will begin after Wave 5 of the preceding trend ends. Wave 1 will usually be steep and short. Depending on market conditions, Wave 1 may break out of a narrowing channel.

Corrective Wave 2 statistics: Only 15 percent retrace between 23.6 and 38.2 percent of Wave 1; 70 percent retrace between 38.2 and 61.8 percent, and 15 percent retrace between 61.8 percent and 100 percent of Wave 1.

Impulsive Wave 3 statistics: 45 percent of the time Wave 3 extends from 161.8 to 175 percent of Wave 1; 30 percent of the time Wave 3 extends 175 to 261.8 percent of Wave 1; 15 percent of the time it extends from 100 to 161.8 percent of Wave 1; and 10 percent of the time Wave 3 extends more than 261.8 percent of Wave 1.

Corrective Wave 4 statistics: Use Fibonacci retracement tools to determine the price target zone for Wave 4 where 70 percent retrace between 38.2 and 61.8 percent of Wave 3; 15 percent retrace between 23.6 and 38.2 percent of Wave 3; and 15 percent retrace between 61.8 and 76.4 percent of Wave 3.

Impulsive Wave 5 statistics: Use Fibonacci extension drawing tools to determine the price target zone for Wave 5. Using three anchors, anchor the drawing tool at the end of Wave 2, the end of Wave 3 and the end of Wave 4. 70 percent of Wave 3 patterns will extend from 61.8 to 100 percent; 15 percent will extend from 38.2 to 61.8 percent; and 15 % will extend from 100 to 161.8 percent.

If you enter a potential Wave 5 trade at a Wave 4 Fibonacci retracement level (i.e., 38.2 or 50 percent), set your stop around the 61.8 percent retracement level. Be sure to adjust your position size accordingly. Then once you are sure you are in Wave 5, add to your position size using any grounded assessment signal that you can.

Trade only in the direction of Waves 1, 3, and 5 and Wave C of Wave 4 corrections on the primary time frame that you use to base your entries, exits, and risk control.

To confirm or filter your trades, trade only in the direction of Waves 1, 3, and 5 and Wave C of Wave 4 correction on the higher time frame of one Fibonacci degree.

ALTERNATE WAVE COUNTS ARE POSSIBLE

Wave counts can change, and it is possible to have alternate wave counts. For example, you may think you are in a Wave 4 correction until the correction exceeds its maximum retracement level and instead turns into an impulsive Wave 3 in the opposite direction. So you must adhere to your stops to protect your account from excessive losses in the event of a failed wave count.

TIP: At times when counting Elliott waves you may see two possible wave counts if the markets have not yet revealed enough information to give you a clear reading. In times like this, if *both* alternate wave counts put you in a trade pointing in the same market direction (either bullish or bearish), then that is a good enough reason to go ahead and take the trade. Only do this when your entry and exit trading system gives you an entry.

Elliott Wave "Cheat Sheet" Quick Reference

We've included an easy reference table at the back of the book on page 208. It has a concise and easy to use list outlining my Elliott Wave and Fibonacci price retracement and extension statistics for Wave 2, Wave 3, Wave 4 and Wave 5. Below the "Cheat Sheet" table there are also guidelines on how to set-up and anchor your Fibonacci drawing tools properly.

CHAPTER 4

Classic Fibonacci Sequence

Fibonacci's Thirteenth Century Classic Number Sequence is in Harmony with the Wave Principle

Elliott's analysis of the mathematical properties of waves and patterns eventually led him to conclude, "The Fibonacci Summation Series is the basis of The Wave Principle." Numbers from the Fibonacci sequence surface repeatedly in Elliott Wave structures, but Elliott developed his market model before he realized that it reflects the Fibonacci sequence.

CHARLES J. COLLINS INTRODUCED THE FIBONACCI SEQUENCE TO ELLIOTT IN THE 1930S

Elliott stated, "When I discovered the Wave Principle action of market trends, I had never heard of the Fibonacci Series." Elliott observed specific numbers and ratios occurring in the markets before he knew of Fibonacci.

In fact, it was Charles J. Collins who first introduced Elliott to the concept of Fibonacci numbers. Read more about the friendship between Elliott and Collins in Chapter 1 of this book.

Finance professors Roy Batchelor and Richard Ramyar did a study to see if there was any correlation between the stock market and Fibonacci numbers and ratios. The Socionomics Institute reviewed the Batchelor-Ramyar study and said this data shows "Fibonacci ratios do occur more often in the stock market than would be expected in a random environment."

LEONARDO FIBONACCI C. 1170–C. 1250

Leonardo Fibonacci of Pisa, Italy (Figure 4.1) was a thirteenth-century mathematician, and many would say the greatest mathematician of medieval times. He developed the Fibonacci approaches that are used by traders around the world.

FIGURE 4.1 **Leonardo Fibonacci (c. 1170–c. 1250) is known for creating the Fibonacci sequence, which is a series of numbers with a pattern wherein each number is derived by adding the two numbers before it, starting from 0, 1, 1, 2, 3, 5, 8, 13, 21, 34, 55, 89, 144, and out to infinity.**

Fibonacci and Elliott Wave theory are commonly used together. The Elliott Wave has time and time again proven to be remarkably effective in forecasting the market, and Fibonacci levels play an important role in its accuracy.

THE FIBONACCI NUMBER SEQUENCE

The Fibonacci number sequence is based on a series of numbers with a pattern wherein each number is derived by adding the two numbers before it, starting from 0, 1, 1, 2, 3, 5, 8, 13, 21, 34, 55, 89, 144, and out to infinity. The Fibonacci number sequence is a fascinating pattern of numbers found naturally occurring throughout nature, geometry, and architecture.

How Traders Use the Fibonacci Sequence

Fibonacci studies help determine where price corrections will end, price extensions will end (price target zones), and when. Use them alone or in conjunction with the Elliott Wave Principle. Most charting software comes with instructions on how to use them.

Fibonacci price retracements and price extensions use *horizontal* lines to indicate areas of high-probability price support and price resistance levels.

Fibonacci time extensions use *vertical* lines to answer the question of when prices will reach a significant price level.

These studies are not intended to provide the primary indications for timing trade entries and exits. You will need to use your own trading system for determining exact entries and exits. With that said, Fibonacci studies can be used as a trade confirmation tool indicating price levels of significance. These studies are often used with Elliott waves to predict the extent of wave retracements and extensions.

Finding Fibonacci Drawing Tools on Your Charting Platform

At the back of this book in the Resources appendix, you will find a list of charting platforms that offer Fibonacci drawing tools. You may already subscribe to one of the platforms listed.

Virtually every charting platform on the planet has these tools included, and they are easy to use once you learn how. When getting started using Fibonacci tools, if you need assistance just contact your charting platform support team.

Three Different Fibonacci Studies

There are three main Fibonacci studies that are used when working with Elliott Wave analysis. Each study gives us different information that will aid in our trading decisions.

1. **Fibonacci Price Retracements:** The common retracements used in trading are 0.382, 0.50, 0.618, and 0.764. These are used to show how far prices may retrace from the previous wave.
2. **Fibonacci Price Extensions:** Project how far a market might rally as it resumes the trend. Common extensions used in trading are 0.618, 1.000, 1.382, 1.500, and 1.618.
3. **Fibonacci Time Extensions:** Look for clusters of time zones where several time periods overlap within a day or so. Your probabilities of success increase greatly when prices run into a cluster of Fibonacci price levels at the same time it hits a cluster of Fibonacci time ratios. You should look for a market to reverse its previous direction as it hits these levels.

How to Use Fibonacci Levels in Trading and Investing

Fibonacci price levels on a chart do not guarantee that prices will ever reach them. The levels have significant meaning that is used to estimate price target zones.

When prices do get to a Fibonacci level, you want to look for a possible change in price. If prices exceed that Fibonacci price level, look for prices to continue to the next level.

Fibonacci Wave Statistics for All Five Waves

These statistics were outlined in the previous chapter but are included here again for your convenience.

Impulsive Wave 1 statistics: Wave 1 will begin after Wave 5 of the preceding trend ends. Wave 1 will usually be steep and short. Depending on market conditions, Wave 1 may break out of a narrowing channel.

Corrective Wave 2 statistics: (Figure 4.2) Only 15 percent retrace between 23.6 and 38.2 percent of Wave 1; 70 percent retrace from 38.2 percent to 61.8 percent; and 15 percent retrace between 61.8 to 100percent. Wave 2 never retraces more than 100 percent of Wave 1.

FIGURE 4.2 **Using Fibonacci retracement levels. Wave 2 will retrace between 38.2% and 100% of the start of Wave 1 without ever going beyond the start of Wave 1.**

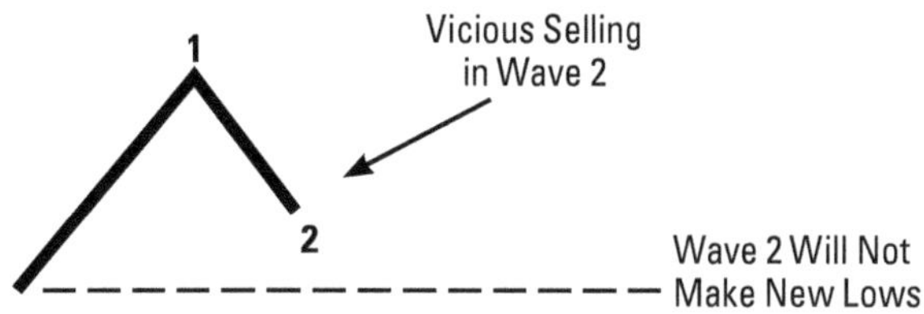

Impulsive Wave 3 statistics: 45 percent of the time Wave 3 extends from 161.8 to 175 percent of Wave 1; 30 percent of the time Wave 3 extends 175 to 261.8 percent of Wave 1; 15 percent of the time it extends from 100 to 161.8 percent of Wave 1; and 10 percent of the time it extends more than 261.8 percent of Wave 1.

Corrective Wave 4 statistics: 70 percent retrace from 38.2 to 61.8 percent of Wave 3; 15 percent retrace from 23.6 to 38.2 percent of Wave 3; and 15 percent retrace from 61.8 to 76.4 percent of Wave 3. Most traders get whipsawed and lose money in Wave 4. Don't assume Wave 4 is over until you can clearly see an ABC wave pattern with the correction ending 38.2 to 61.8 percent between Wave 2 to Wave 3. Wave B is usually 50 percent of Wave A and should not exceed 76.4 percent of Wave A. Wave C is 1 times Wave A or 1.618 times Wave A or 2.618 times Wave A. Wave 4 never retraces more than 100 percent of Wave 3. The higher (deeper) the Wave 4 retracement, the shallower Wave 5 will be.

Impulsive Wave 5 statistics: Use Fibonacci extension tools to determine the price target zone for Wave 5. Using three anchors, anchor the drawing tool at the end of Wave 2, the end of Wave 3 and the end of Wave 4. 70 percent of Wave 3 patterns will extend from 61.8 to 100 percent; 15 percent will extend from 38.2 to 61.8 percent; and 15 % will extend from 100 to 161.8 percent. My studies show that many Wave 5s end between 0.618 to 1.00 when we use the end of Wave 2 and the end of Wave 3 and the end of Wave 4 to determine the calculation.

Failed Wave 5s do occur. You can detect a failed Wave 5 because prices in Wave 5 will not exceed the top of Wave 3. It will appear as a prolonged and complex Wave 4.

> TIP: If you enter a potential Wave 5 trade at a Wave 4 Fibonacci retracement level (38.2 percent or 50 percent), set your stop beyond the 61.8 percent retracement level because the normal maximum Wave 4 retracement level is 61.8 percent. Be sure to adjust your position size accordingly to accommodate the additional risk. Because your stop loss is further away from your entry, you will be taking on more risk and will need to lower your position size.

How to Draw Price Retracements for Wave 4

Here are my instructions on how to draw Fibonacci retracement Wave 4 price levels (Figure 4.3) for a bullish trend. First locate your Fibonacci tools on the charting platform you use and choose the Fibonacci Retracement Line tool.

The key to drawing a Fibonacci retracement wave for price levels is to locate the end of Wave 2. On an uptrend Wave 2 will represent a correction to the downside; on a downtrend Wave 2 will represent a correction to the upside. On Figure 4.3 I will refer to the bullish trend, and for bearish trends just do the opposite.

Using the Fibonacci retracement tool, locate the end of Wave 2 and put your mouse cursor there and move it to the end of Wave 3. You will then see horizontal lines drawn with numbers associated with them. These numbers are the Fibonacci

FIGURE 4.3 **Wave 4 Fibonacci high probability price retracement levels have a target zone between 38.2% and 61.8% of the distance between Wave 2 and Wave 3.**

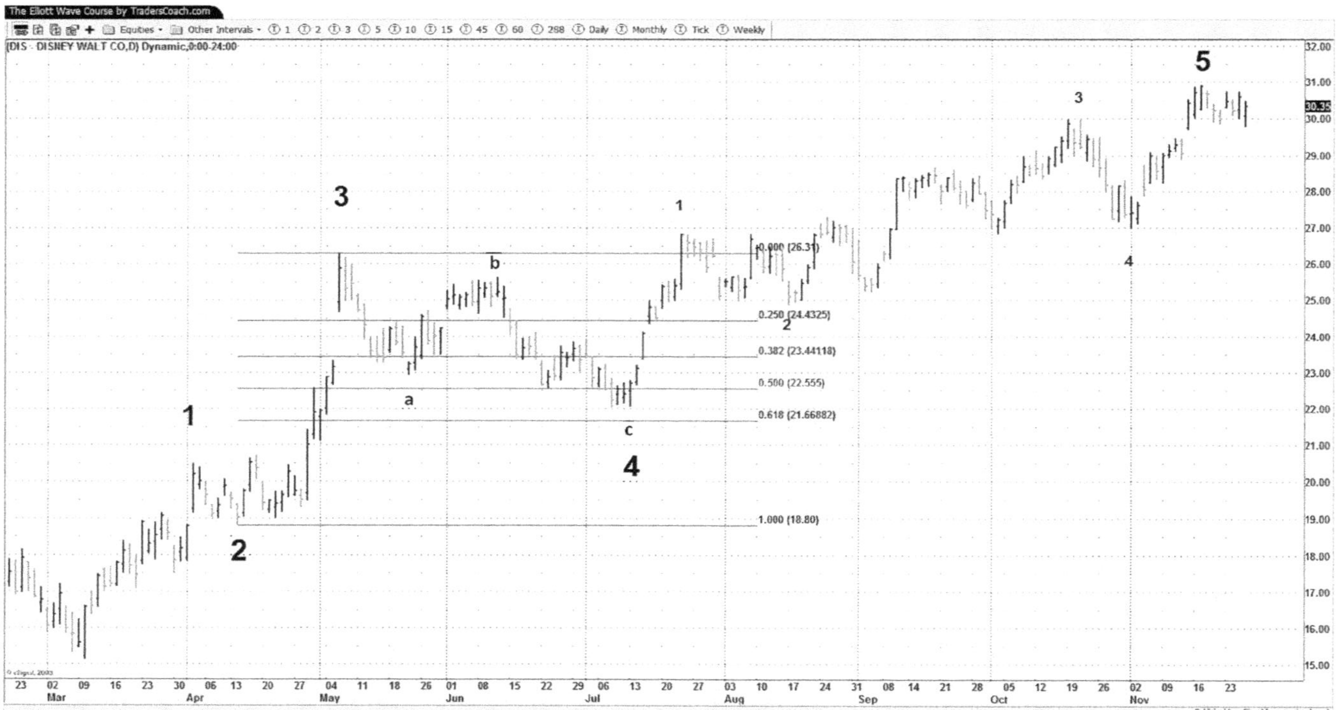

numbers that we pay attention to. We refer to these as *retracement levels.*

A normal Wave 4 correction is between 38.2 and 61.8 percent of Wave 3. So we expect a Wave 4 correction to end between those two levels. On Figure 4.3 it did just that.

There are exceptions where Wave 4 retracements are shallow, and approximately 15 percent of the time they will not make it to the most common Fibonacci level of 38.2 percent. Likewise there are exceptions 15 percent of the time when a Wave 4 will retrace between 61.8 and 76.4 percent of Wave 3 (or up to 100 percent if it turns into a Wave 2) and requires a reevaluation of the wave count. A retracement beyond 76.4 percent usually indicates a Wave 2 rather than a Wave 4.

When a Wave 4 does turn into a Wave 2, you will have a new trading opportunity for the upcoming Wave 3 trade. The example we looked at in Figure 4.3 is for a bullish trend. Note, the same theory and approach applies for drawing Fibonacci retracements on bearish trends except the trend direction is opposite.

How to Draw Price Extensions for Wave 5

Here are my instructions on how to draw Fibonacci extension Wave 5 price levels (Figure 4.4) for a bullish trend. First locate your Fibonacci tools on the charting platform you use and choose the Fibonacci Extension Line tool. Common Fibonacci extensions used in trading are .6180, 1.000, and 1.618.

The key to drawing Fibonacci extensions is to locate the end of Wave 2, the end of Wave 3, and the end of Wave 4. Start at Wave 2 and anchor the first point of the Fibonacci extension by clicking on the Wave 2 price marking the end of Wave 2. Next, move your mouse cursor to the end of Wave 3 and click to anchor to Wave 3. Finally, move your cursor to Wave 4 and click to anchor the extension to Wave 4.

Now you will see the Fibonacci extension lines appear. Wave 5 should end at these Fibonacci numbers with the highest

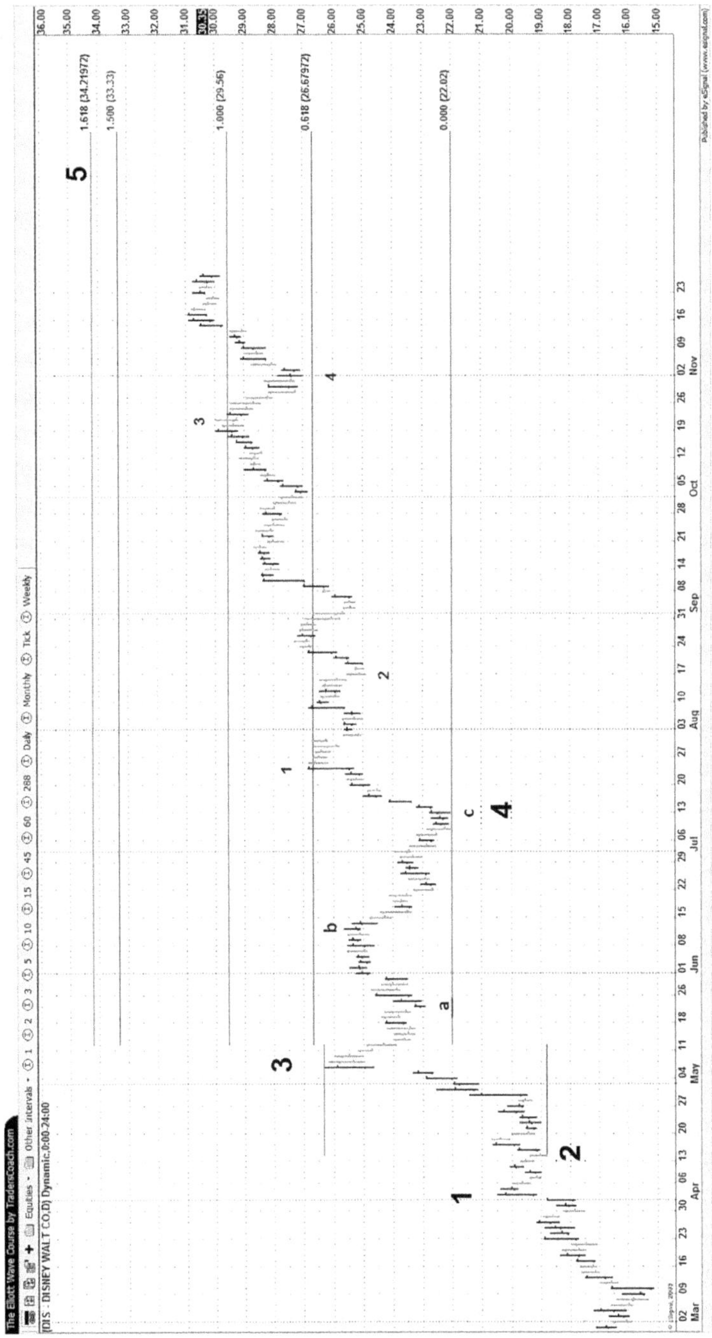

FIGURE 4.4 Wave 5 Fibonacci high probability price extension levels have a target zone between 61.8% and 100%.

probability ending between 0.618 and 1.000. The example we looked at in Figure 4.4 is for a bullish trend. Note, the same theory and approach applies for drawing Fibonacci extensions on bearish trends except the trend direction is opposite.

How to Draw Time Extensions for Wave 5

Here are my instructions on how to draw Fibonacci time extensions Wave 5 price levels (Figure 4.5). First locate your Fibonacci tools on the charting platform you use and choose the Fibonacci Time Extension Line tool.

Unlike the other Fibonacci price methods, time extensions are a series of *vertical* lines. They are composed by dividing a chart into segments with vertical lines spaced apart in increments that conform to the Fibonacci sequence of numbers. These lines indicate areas of time in which major price movement can be expected.

The key to drawing Fibonacci time extensions is to look at the price pivot points on a chart and use the Fibonacci drawing tool to match as many vertical Fibonacci lines as possible to these price pivot points.

Your probabilities of success increase greatly when you combine the use of Fibonacci price retracements or Fibonacci price extensions along with Fibonacci time extensions. When prices run into a cluster of Fibonacci price levels (retracements and extensions) at the same time it hits a cluster of Fibonacci time ratios, you should look for a market to reverse its previous direction as it hits these levels.

Price and Time Extensions for Wave 5

In Figure 4.6, Fibonacci Wave 5 price and time extensions are used together with the price extensions illustrated by horizontal lines and the time extensions illustrated by vertical lines.

FIGURE 4.5 Wave 5 Fibonacci time extensions appear as vertical lines on the chart.

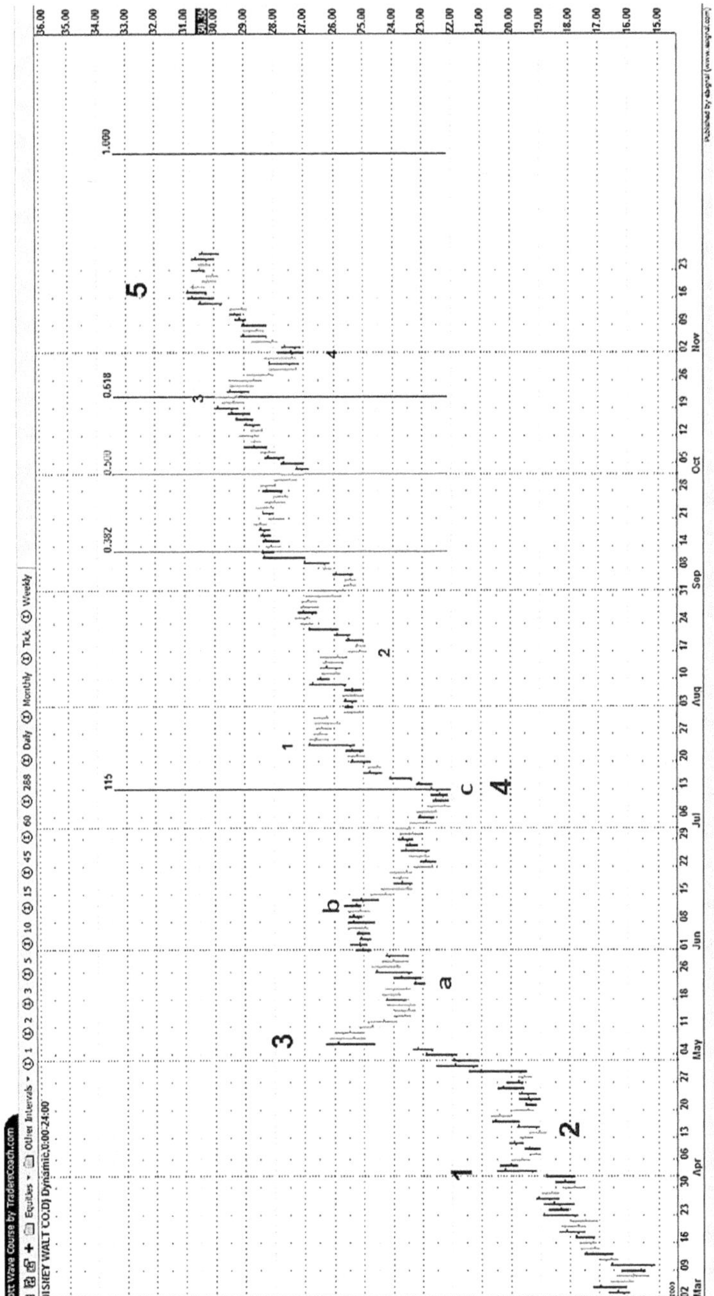

FIGURE 4.6 Fibonacci Wave 5 price and time extensions are used together with the price extensions illustrated by horizontal lines and with the time extensions illustrated by vertical lines.

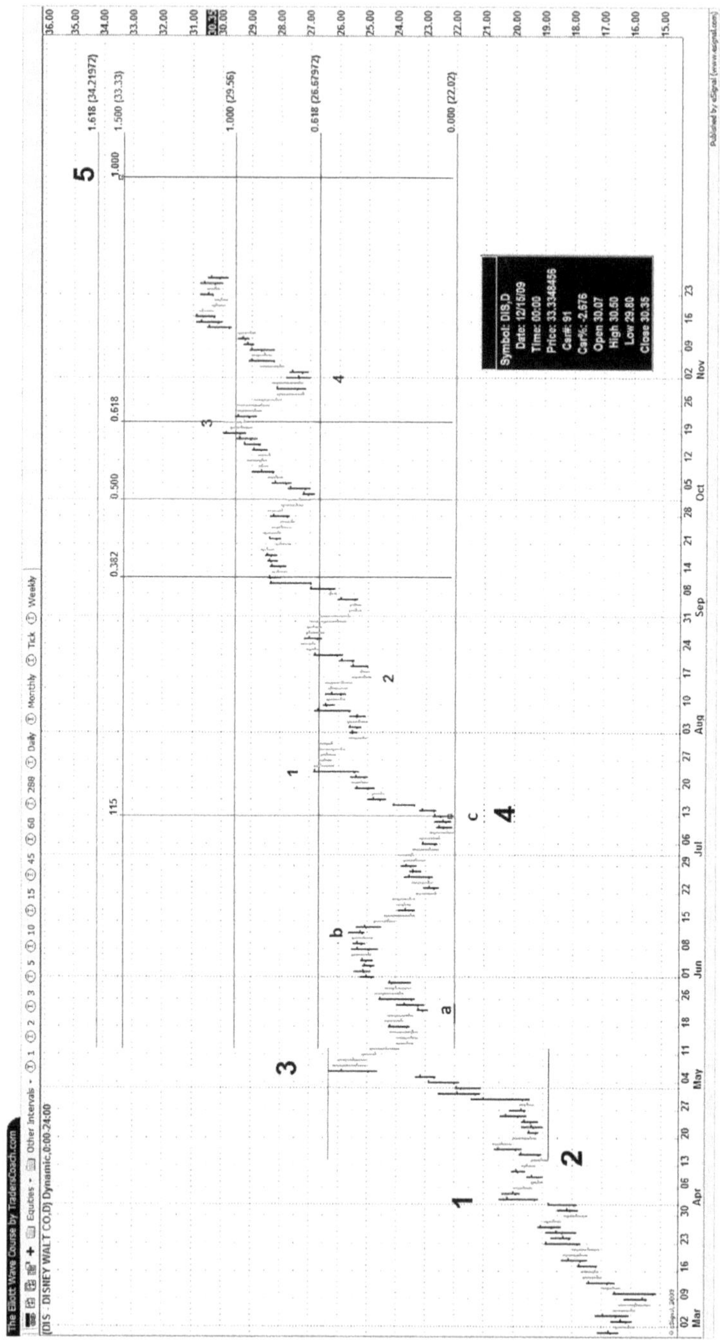

TIP: A correct Elliott Wave "count" must observe three rules:

1. Wave 2 always retraces less than 100 percent of Wave 1.
2. Wave 3 cannot be the shortest of the three impulse waves, namely Waves 1, 3, and 5. Wave 3 does not have to be longest wave, but it can never be the shortest.
3. Wave 4 does not overlap with the price territory of Wave 1, except in the rare case of a diagonal triangle. That means that the bottom of Wave 4 will not breach the top price of Wave 1.

A common guideline observes that in a five-wave pattern, Waves 2 and 4 will often take alternate forms; a sharp move in Wave 2, for example, will suggest a mild move in Wave 4. Corrective wave patterns unfold in forms known as zigzags, flats, or triangles. In turn these corrective patterns can come together to form more complex corrections.

VOLUME ANALYSIS

Volume analysis, like Fibonacci levels, is also considered part of the classic approach to Elliott Wave analysis. The main thing you need to know about volume is that during Wave 3, volume is at its highest of all the waves in the trend.

The reason for this is that as Wave 3 unfolds, prices are moving dramatically in the direction of the overall trend. Market participants see this, and this move is usually accompanied by supporting news in the direction of the trend. This accounts for the high volume on Wave 3.

A great example of this occurred during the 1990s in the Dow Jones Industrial Average as stocks moved hyperbolically upward in a bullish Wave 3, and the volume peaked at that time to the highest we had seen to date.

During this time you couldn't go to a cocktail party without hearing about how great the stock market was doing and how everybody was trading the markets. Trading during the mid to late 1990s was the "in" thing to do, and this type of enthusiasm is often seen during a Wave 3 on a major index like the Dow Jones Industrial Average.

After Waves 3 and 4, Wave 5 emerges in the direction of the trend and prices reach higher new levels in a bullish trend and lower new levels in a bearish trend.

However, the volume on Wave 5 will not be as high as it was during Wave 3. We expect this since there is less enthusiasm (for either the bullish trend or the bearish trend) during Wave 5 than there was during Wave 3, meaning less trading.

This is because the previous Wave 4, which is a nasty corrective wave pattern, usually creates havoc and decays the enthusiastic sentiment that occurred during Wave 3.

So even though Wave 5 exceeds Wave 3 in price, it lacks the enthusiasm and emotional sentiment that was present during Wave 3. You can locate Wave 3 using a volume indicator as it will display the highest volume.

We saw this in the Dow Jones Industrial Average after Wave 3 ended with the dot-com bubble popping in the year 2000. This caused some market participants to become disillusioned, and the number of market participants declined greatly as trading and investing was not as popular as it once was during the mid to late 1990s when the Dow Jones Industrial Average was in Wave 3.

The Dow Jones Industrial Average is just one example, but there are countless examples in stocks, futures, forex, bonds, and all markets of volume decreasing during Wave 5 as compared to Wave 3.

Volume and the Elliott Wave

Understanding the role that volume plays in each of the five waves will help you identify the Elliott Wave pattern more effectively. This section will give you guidelines on what to look for in each wave with regard to volume. These guidelines apply to both bullish and bearish trends.

VOLUME IN THE FIVE-WAVE TREND

Wave 1: Volume might increase a bit as prices rise, but not always enough to alert many technical analysts.

Wave 2: Volume is usually lower during Wave 2 than during Wave 1.

Wave 3: Highest volume occurs in Wave 3. You will see some peak volume spikes.

Wave 4: Volume is usually below that of Wave 3.

Wave 5: Volume is lower in Wave 5 than in Wave 3.

On the chart in Figure 4.7 we see the highest volume as expected during Wave 3. Note the increase in volume as prices begin to trend and volume peaks during Wave 3.

VOLUME IN CORRECTIVE WAVES A, B, AND C

Wave A: Volume remains stable in relation to Wave 3. The fundamental news is usually still positive. Most analysts see the drop as a correction in a still-active bull market.

Wave B: Volume during Wave B should be lower than in Wave A.

Wave C: Volume picks up, and by the third leg of Wave C, almost everyone realizes that a bear market is firmly entrenched.

WHAT FIBONACCI PATTERNS LOOK LIKE IN NATURE

Fibonacci patterns are all around us in nature, we just might not know it because we don't know what to look for. Figure 4.8 helps you see how the Fibonacci number sequence fans out into a spiral.

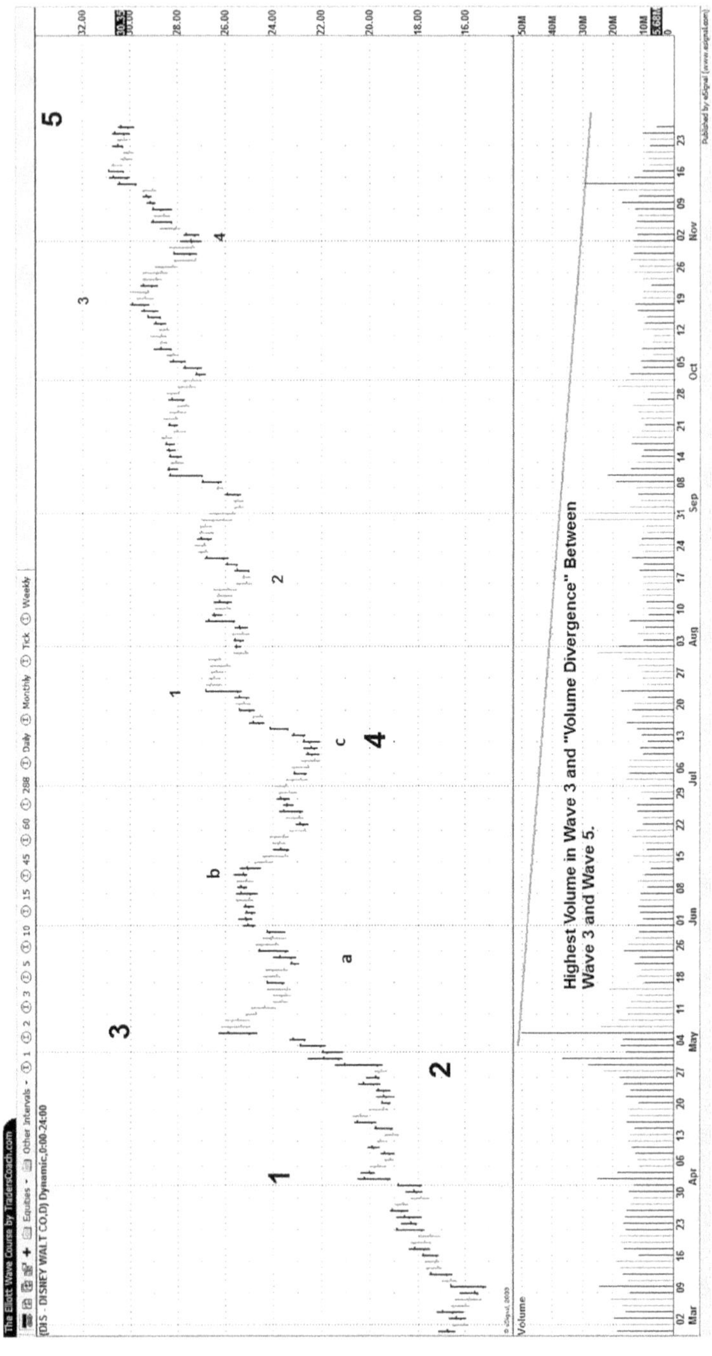

FIGURE 4.7 **Volume is always highest during Wave 3 of the Elliott Wave pattern.**

If you look at Figure 4.9, that same "Fibonacci golden spiral" is clearly evident in this nautilus shell. Although the Fibonacci numerical sequence is very precise and specific, in nature as in the financial markets it takes on its own shape.

Meaning, the beauty of the pattern is that in nature it doesn't always match up "exactly" and yet, visually once you start looking you can spot it everywhere.

FIGURE 4.8 The classic "Fibonacci golden spiral" illustrates the Fibonacci number sequence as it appears in nature all around us.

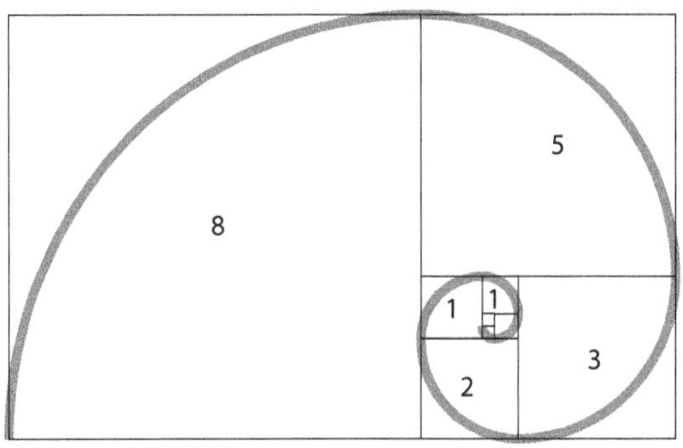

FIGURE 4.9 Look at how a nautilus shell found in nature embodies the "Fibonacci golden spiral" perfectly.

THE GOLDEN RATIO 1.618 AND FIBONACCI

The Golden Ratio, 1.618, is related to the Fibonacci number series in that if you look closely, you will find the Golden Ratio within the Fibonacci number series. The Golden Ratio is also known as "Phi", Golden Mean or Divine Proportion. The companion to Phi is 0.618 and is called "phi."

We know the Fibonacci number series progresses with: 0, 1, 1, 2, 3, 5, 8, 13, 21, 34, 55, 89, 144, 233, 377, 610, 987 and so on as each number is the sum of the previous two numbers. For example 55 plus 89 equals 144.

When you multiply a number in this Fibonacci series by Phi the Golden Ratio of 1.618, the result approximates the following number in the series. For example if you take 233 times 1.618 it equals 376.99. And of course the number in the series after 233 is 377 (very close to 376.99). The ratio becomes more precise as the numbers increase.

When you divide any Fibonacci number by its larger neighbor it approximates 0.618, or phi. For example if you take 55 and divide it by 89 it equals 0.6179 (very close to 0.618).

Fibonacci ratios can be added, subtracted, multiplied, or divided and the result will be another Fibonacci ratio. For example 1 minus 0.618 equals 0.382. Or, 1 plus 0.618 equals 1.618. And, 0.382 times 0.618 equals 0.236. Lastly, 0.382 divided by 0.50 equals 0.764.

Here are some of the most common Fibonacci ratios: 0.146, 0.236, 0.382, 0.50, 0.618, 0.764, 1.00, 1.272, 1.382, 1.618, 2.00 and 2.618.

When these ratios are referred to as percentages, they look like this: 14.6 percent, 23.6 percent, 38.2 percent, 50 percent, 61.8 percent, 76.4 percent, 100 percent, 127.2 percent, 138.2 percent, 161.8 percent, 200 percent and 261.8 percent.

CHAPTER 5

Modern Elliott Wave

Using Computers and Indicators to Confirm Wave Counts

The modern approach adds a unique dimension to Elliott Wave analysis. With the dawning of the age of the computer, the modern approach to Elliott Wave analysis has begun.

Through the use of powerful computers, we are able to add different types of calculations onto the chart. These are displayed in the form of indicators. These indicators measure characteristics of momentum and price movement to confirm the classic approach of the Elliott Wave principle based on price structure alone.

We don't need to abandon the classic approach to Elliott Wave analysis based on price and retracement statistics alone. The addition of the modern approach adds clarity needed in successful trading where consistency requires an edge. This extra layer of analysis is what eliminates the subjectivity so many had experienced when trying to count Elliott Waves using price structure alone.

The modern approach, while adding certain indicators, also relies on your ability to properly interpret these indicators to produce results. After many years of applying the classic and modern Elliott Wave approaches, I've come up with a unique methodology that combines these two techniques to obtain the highest probability Elliott Wave count. This will save you many long hours of sorting out what indicators are best to use in Elliott Wave analysis.

In order to successfully integrate this methodology, a correlation had to be established between indicators, price action, Fibonacci price levels, multiple time frame analysis, and volume in order to make it reliable and reproducible. This is the purpose of the McDowell Probability Matrix™.

This Matrix assigns a numerical weighted value to each element analyzed in deriving the Elliott Wave count. The outcome is a probability percentage that takes into account each indicator in the modern approach and assigns a value along with price structure from the classic approach. It is a form of "connecting the dots." This gives you the advantage of applying a value or probability to the number of dots that you can connect.

This helps to eliminate the subjectivity (and the guessing that goes along with it) that has plagued so many traders in the past. You now have at your disposal the highest probability Elliott Wave count amongst the numerous possible alternate wave counts. It is this Matrix that will give you the "edge" you have been seeking. You will find complete details on how to use the McDowell Probability Matrix later in this book.

Three Modern Tools Help in Counting Elliott Waves

Let's take a look at the major components of the modern approach to Elliott Wave analysis. It is important to realize that these components are all that are needed for the modern part of your analysis.

Master the modern approach using these three tools:

1. Price oscillator histogram using McDowell's secret settings (OWL)
2. Relative strength index (RSI) using McDowell's secret settings (PTF)
3. Multiple time frame analysis

PRICE OSCILLATOR HISTOGRAM OR OWL SOFTWARE

Oscillators are derivatives of price and volume, and while they take you further away from the truths of the market (actual price and volume meanings), they still can be used as filters and provide an additional edge.

One oscillator stands out from the rest and provides key information in confirming Elliott Wave counts. The *price oscillator histogram* is our edge when counting Elliott waves. This histogram plots the difference between two price moving averages represented in a histogram format. As with all indicators, the price oscillator histogram always lags price since it first needs price for its calculations. We therefore refer to this type of indicator as a *lagging indicator.*

Following are the settings and methods as well as guidelines in using the price oscillator histogram to confirm the Elliott Wave counts.

KEY POINT! MCDOWELL'S SECRET PRICE OSCILLATOR SETTINGS

Locate the price oscillator indicator on your charting platform. Once you find it, load it on your chart and change the setting to:

- Short length to 5
- Long length to 35
- Source to low
- Histogram

Some charting platforms use the reverse of these settings. In other words the short length would be set to 35 and the long length would be set to 5. To know which setting to use, use the settings that produce a positive price oscillator histogram (above the zero line) on bullish trends and a negative price oscillator histogram (below the zero line) on bearish trends.

TIP: I've programmed the above settings in an easy to use piece of software called the "Optimum Wave Locator" also known as the OWL. This software is available for purchase at **www.TradersCoach.com**. You can certainly use the above settings to get a similar result to the OWL software, but you may also be interested in using the OWL which is a handy tool to have.

MCDOWELL'S HISTOGRAM METHODS

Look for the highest peak of the price oscillator histogram to spot a Wave 3 of some degree on the chart.

Also look for divergence at the end of Wave 5 or to identify the end of Wave 5 of Wave 3. What I mean by divergence is not just the direction of the indicator increasing or decreasing. For divergence to occur, prices must move in the opposite direction of the indicator as well. Bearish divergence will exhibit rising prices and, at the same time, falling values on the price oscillator histogram. With bullish divergence one would see falling prices while the indicator values are rising. When you see divergence, it means that the current trend is headed toward exhaustion and a new change in trend is not far off.

PRICE OSCILLATOR HISTOGRAM IN RELATION TO ELLIOTT WAVES

Here are guidelines for what the histogram is likely to do in each of the five Elliott Waves.

Wave 1: Price Oscillator Histogram begins to move in the direction of the impulsive Elliott Wave, meaning positive for bullish or negative for bearish.

Wave 2: Price Oscillator Histogram begins to move in the direction of the corrective Elliott Wave, meaning positive for bullish or negative for bearish. Wave 2 histogram does not always go negative but pulls back close to the zero line.

Wave 3: Has the steepest and largest Price Oscillator Histogram value—either positive or negative depending on bullish or bearish impulsive Elliott Wave. Find either the highest or deepest histogram within the last 144 price bars, and you have found the most recent Wave 3 on the chart.

Wave 4: Price Oscillator Histogram begins to move in the direction of the corrective Elliott Wave 4, meaning positive for bullish or negative for bearish. A bullish Wave 4 must exhibit a bullish price oscillator histogram and a bearish Wave 4 must exhibit a bearish price oscillator histogram.

Wave 5: Price Oscillator Histogram begins to move in the direction of the impulsive Elliott Wave 5, meaning positive for bullish or negative for bearish, but the histogram level is not as high or low as in Wave 3. This is known as divergence.

144 PRICE BARS IDENTIFIES THE CURRENT TREND

The most recent 144 price bars (which is a Fibonacci number) usually identify the current dominant trend. You should be able to identify the Elliott Wave in the most recent 144 price bars. Look for Wave 3 since it is easy to identify as the steepest, most dramatic wave. If you do not see Wave 3 in the recent 144 price bars, and the market appears to be channeling or chaotic for the entire 144 recent price bars, then that means the current cycle is most likely a complex correction of major proportions.

Here is an example of how 144 price bars can represent a different amount of time depending on the time frame of the chart you are using:

- Two-minute chart: 4.8 hours
- Daily chart: 4.8 months
- Weekly chart: 2.7 years
- Monthly chart: 12 years

PRICE COMPRESSION, CHANNELS, AND PENNANTS DURING CORRECTIVE ELLIOTT WAVE PATTERNS

The chart in Figure 5.1 was created in October 2008. Note the pennant just before the big 1,000-point drop into Elliott Wave 5. I was on the radio this week doing an interview with Gabe Wisdom and warned the listeners that a 1,000-point drop was coming and likely to occur the following week.

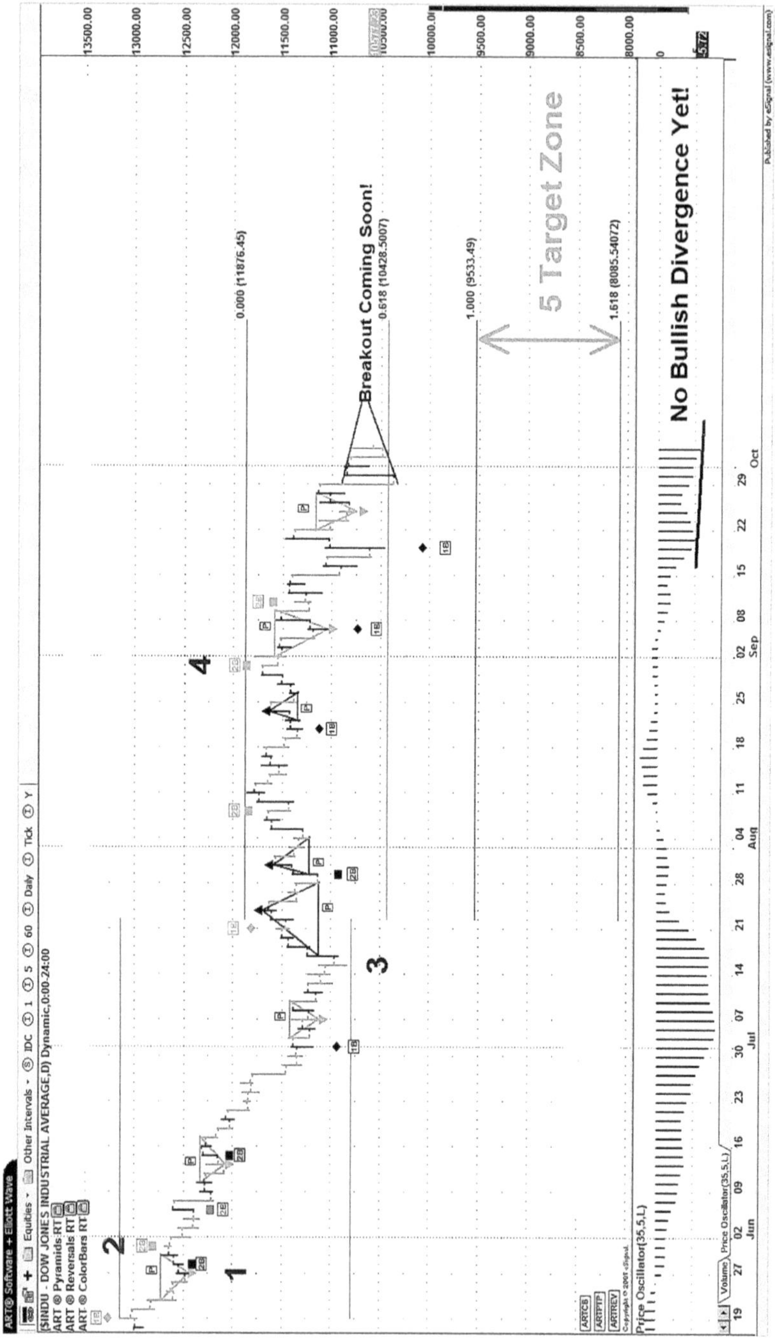

FIGURE 5.1 October 2008 chart with pennant accurately predicting the big 1,000-point drop into Elliott Wave 3.

We had a flood of phone calls to the office before the actual crash with listeners to the radio show saying my prediction was outrageous. Of course after the drop in the market came to pass, everyone wanted to learn how I used Elliott Wave to see these predictable patterns in the market.

This chart is a perfect example of how to combine the classic and the modern techniques to get accurate forecasts. Here by using the price oscillator histogram in addition to the classic Elliott Wave techniques, the pattern was very clear.

Wave 3 must have the lowest price oscillator histogram value on a bearish trend. In Figure 5.1, notice Wave 3's price oscillator histogram does have a lower level then when the price oscillator histogram is moving toward the Wave 5 target zone. Normally this is classic bearish divergence that occurs between Wave 3 and Wave 5. Also, notice the bullish price oscillator histogram confirming Wave 4 that occurred between the Wave 3 price oscillator histogram and the Wave 5 price oscillator histogram.

But see what happens on the next chart of the same market.

FIGURE 5.2 This chart was created after the 1,000-point drop occurred in October 2008 and confirms the Elliott Wave prediction illustrated in Figure 5.1.

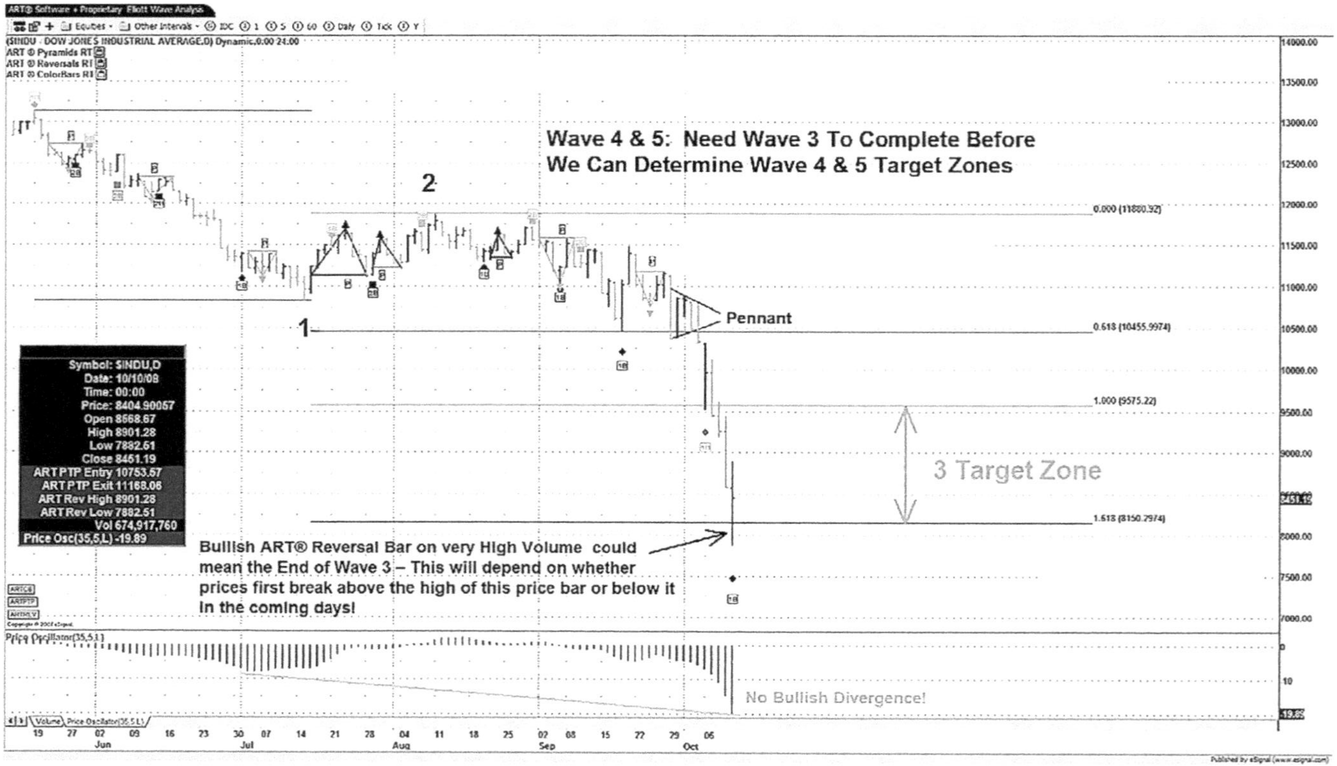

AFTER THE DECLINE OCCURS: HOW TRENDS CAN BECOME EXTENDED

Figure 5.2 was created just after prices broke below the pennant in October 2008. Notice that now the price oscillator histogram on the current downward move has the lowest level, so this *changes the Elliott Wave count*! Prices are currently in a bearish Wave 3, and thus the trend has much further to go than previously anticipated—this is how trends get extended. Thanks to the price oscillator histogram, we know this!

COUNTING WAVES USING THE MODERN APPROACH

Count the Elliott waves in the market in Figure 5.3 using the price oscillator modern approach.

> **Question:** In the chart shown in Figure 5.3, can you count the Elliott Waves using the modern price oscillator histogram approach?
>
> **Answer:** The Elliott Waves in this market using the price oscillator histogram modern approach are shown in Figure 5.4. Note how the histogram counts confirm the analysis on price wave counts.

FIGURE 5.3 **QUESTION: In the chart shown here, can you count the Elliott Waves using the modern price oscillator histogram approach? When counting, be sure to use the March low as the beginning of the trend.**

FIGURE 5.4 **ANSWER: Here are Elliott Waves correctly counted using the modern price oscillator histogram approach.**

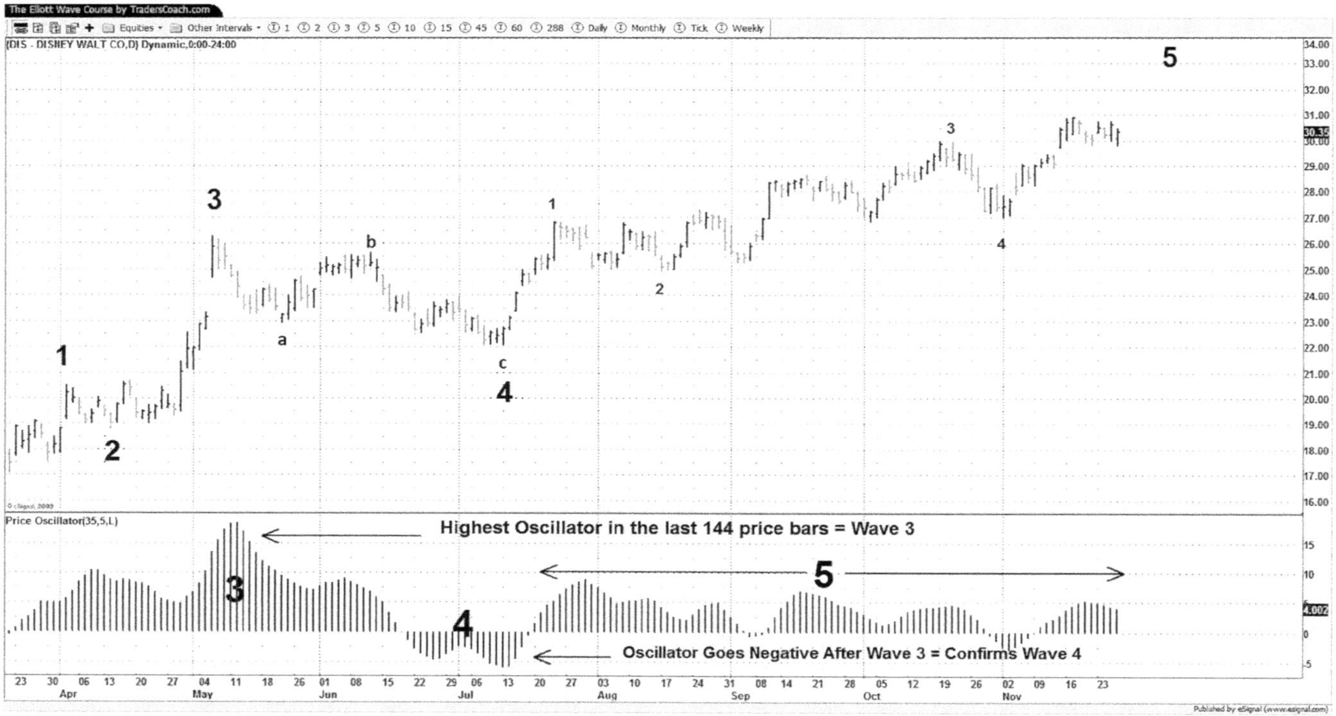

In Figure 5.5, notice how there is bearish divergence between Wave 3 and Wave 5, which is what we expect. This is how we confirm which trend is Wave 3 and which is Wave 5.

Question: Can you count the Elliott waves in the market in Figure 5.6 using the price oscillator histogram modern approach?

Answer: The Elliott Waves in this market using the price oscillator modern approach are shown in Figure 5.7. The histogram is not labeled on this chart, but the prices are. The histogram confirms the price structure count.

TIP: On your charting platform, find how to program the price oscillator as a histogram using our settings. If you can, save those settings as your default or template so you can easily use them again. Or you can use the OWL software to achieve the same result.

Once you have the price oscillator histogram set, or once you are using the OWL software, go ahead and look at different markets and locate the steepest oscillator to find Wave 3. Then look for Wave 4, etc. Once you find Wave 3, you should be able to count all the waves in that impulsive wave. Practice this on many charts until you are comfortable doing it.

RELATIVE STRENGTH INDEX (RSI) OR PTF SOFTWARE

The relative strength index is the second indicator we use in the modern approach for Elliott Wave analysis. We use this indicator in a different way than it was originally designed to be used. J. Welles Wilder Jr. developed the RSI, and he had a specific way to use it.

Wilder considered a security overbought if it reached the 70 level, meaning that the speculator should consider selling. Or conversely oversold at the 30 level. The principle is that when

FIGURE 5.5 In this bull trend bearish divergence occurs in the modern price oscillator histogram between Wave 3 and Wave 5 with prices rising as the price oscillator histogram falls. Note that the reverse will be true in a bear trend.

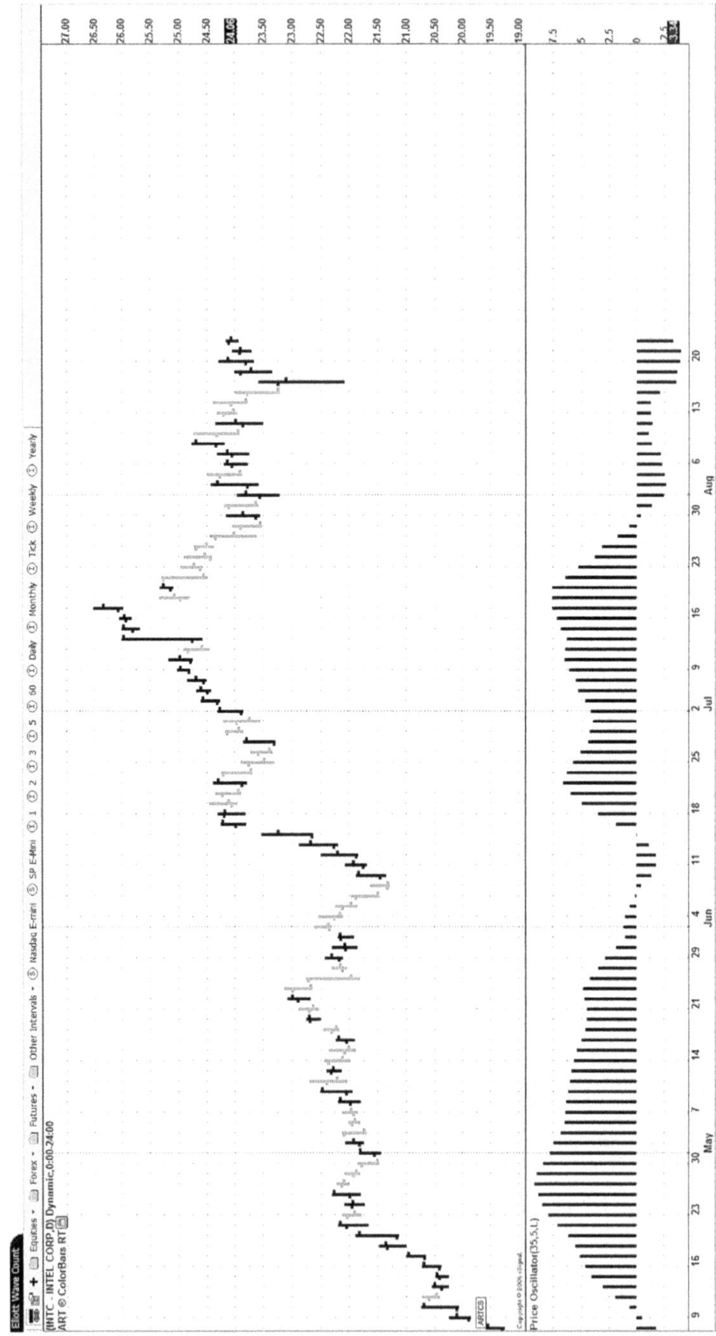

FIGURE 5.6 **QUESTION: In the chart shown here, can you count the Elliott Waves using the modern price oscillator histogram approach?**

FIGURE 5.7 **ANSWER: Here are Elliott Waves correctly counted using the modern price oscillator histogram approach.**

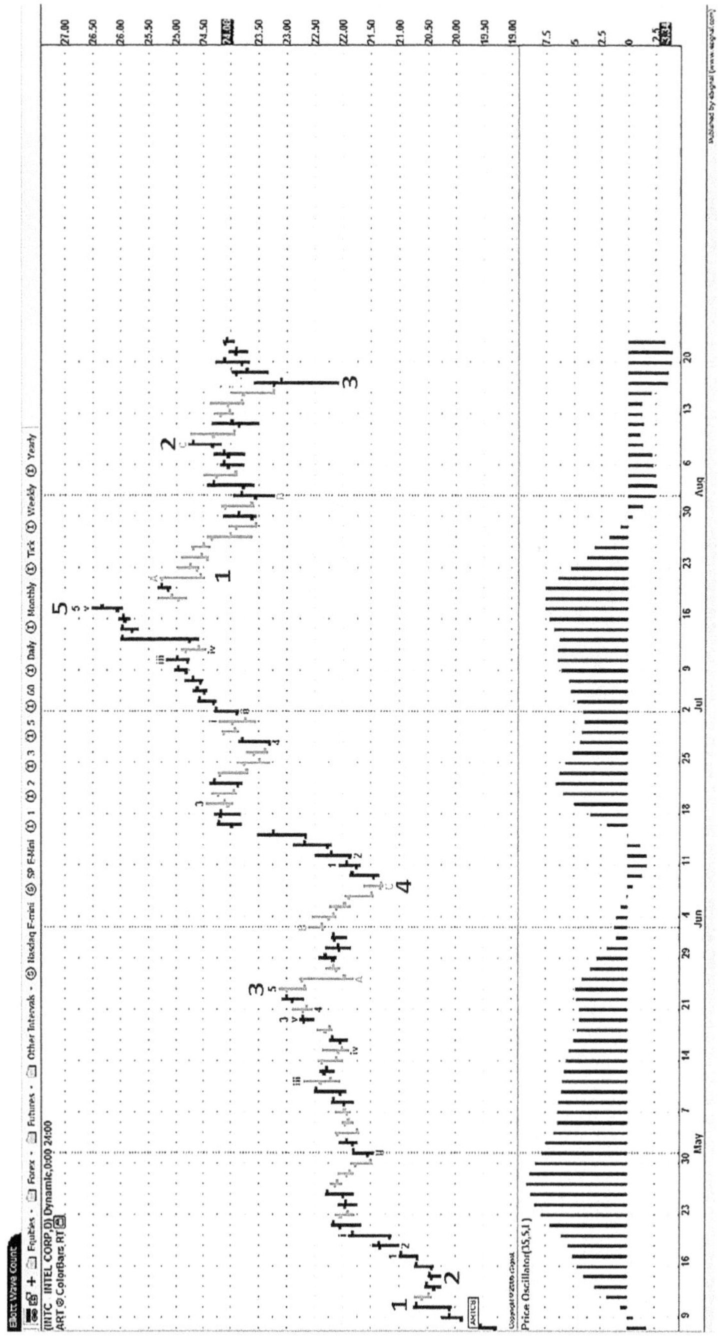

there's a high proportion of price movement in one direction it suggests an extreme, and prices are likely to reverse. Levels 80 and 20 are also used, or may be varied according to market conditions (e.g., a bull market may have an upward bias).

The RSI is popular because it is relatively easy to interpret. J. Welles Wilder published it in *Commodities* magazine (now called *Futures* magazine) in June 1978 and in his book *New Concepts in Technical Trading Systems* the same year. Note that the term *relative strength* also refers to the strength of a security in relation to the overall market or to its sector.

WE USE RSI IN A DIFFERENT AND UNIQUE WAY!

Instead of relying on the RSI to indicate overbought and oversold conditions, I found it to be extremely valuable in Elliott Wave analysis to determine if the trend has ended or not. In adjusting the settings of the RSI, I was able to formulate a use where it is approximately 75 percent accurate. This can be valuable information to confirm a Wave 3 versus a Wave 5 and also to help determine when a correction is over.

But in order to use the RSI in this fashion, you must use McDowell's secret RSI settings.

KEY POINT! MCDOWELL'S SECRET RSI SETTINGS

Locate the RSI indicator on your charting platform. Once you find it, load it on your chart and change the setting to:

- RSI length set to 9 on the close
- Upper band set to 80 percent
- Lower band set to 20 percent

TIP: I've programmed the above settings in an easy-to-use piece of software called the "Precision Trend Filter" also known as the PTF. This software is available for purchase at **www.TradersCoach.com.** You can certainly use the above settings to get a similar result to the PTF software, but you may also be interested in using the PTF, which is a handy tool to have.

TIP: Look for periods when the RSI penetrates above the 80 percent band or below the 20 percent band.

RSI penetrates above the 80 percent band: The market is usually making a new significant high and will most likely return, even after a temporary sell-off, to take out the market high.

RSI penetrates below the 20 percent band: The market is usually making a new significant low and will most likely return, even after a temporary rally, to take out the market low.

You can use this RSI technique to see if the market has made a high probability significant bottom or top.

RSI AND HIGHER HIGHS

Note where the RSI first goes above the upper band in the chart in Figure 5.8. When this occurs there is approximately a 75 percent chance that higher highs will eventually occur. We see this a lot on bullish Wave 3 tops or bearish Wave 3 bottoms. This makes sense, since Wave 3 usually has the most momentum to create this kind of reading on the RSI. Note that during Wave 5, the RSI has not peaked above the upper band. This is also quite typical of Wave 5s since there is less momentum in Wave 5 as compared to Wave 3.

RSI AND LOWER LOWS

On the chart in Figure 5.9, we see a bearish downtrend with the RSI penetrating the lower band, and each time it does it indicates there is approximately a 75 percent chance that lower lows are coming. Notice on the right-hand side of the chart as prices make a final low, the RSI does not penetrate the lower band anymore. We see this frequently at the end of a Wave 5, which signals the end of the trend. In this case it's the end of a bearish trend.

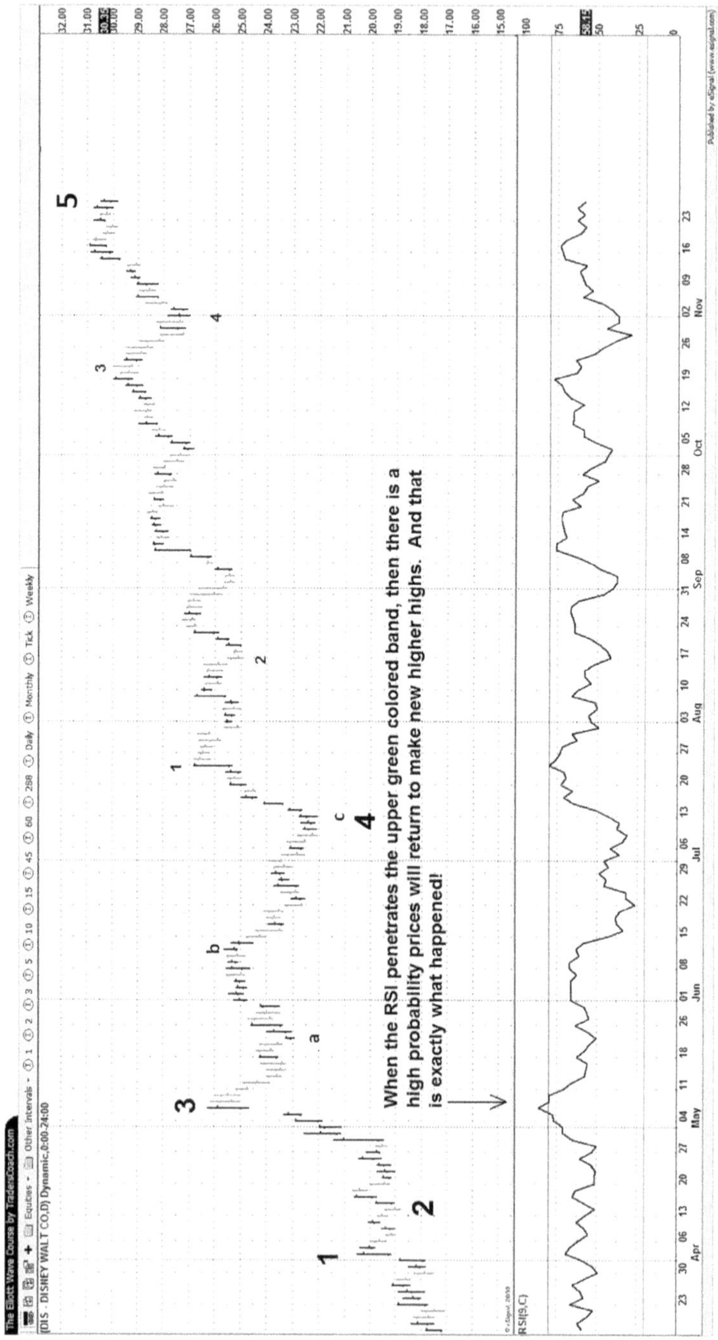

FIGURE 5.8 In a bullish trend, when RSI penetrates the upper band, there is a 75% probability that prices will return to make new higher highs, which is what happened during Wave 5 on this chart.

FIGURE 5.9 Notice that on the right-hand side of this bearish chart as prices make a final low, the RSI did not penetrate the lower band. This occurs frequently at the end of a Wave 5, which signals the end of a trend—in this case the end of a bearish trend.

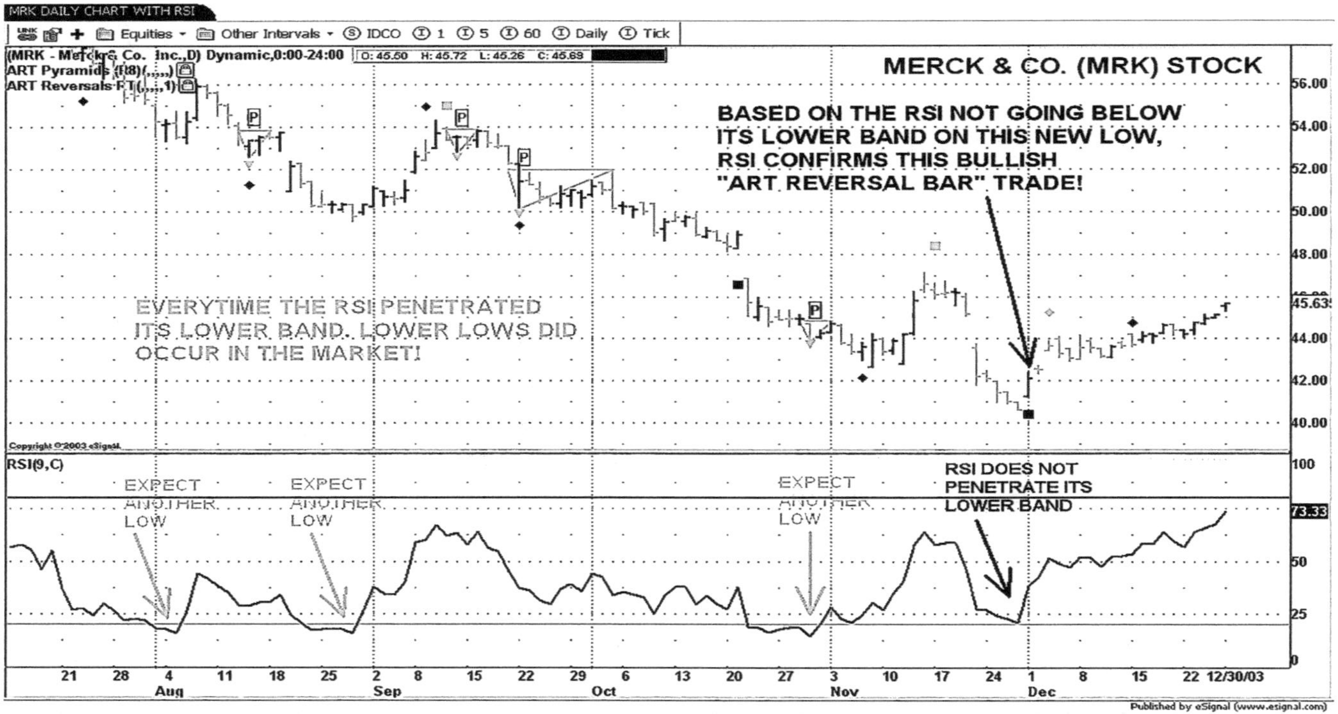

RSI AND DIVERGENCE

The chart in Figure 5.10 illustrates divergences in the RSI as well as band penetration. Starting at the left side of the chart, we see the RSI penetrating the lower band followed by lower lows in price. However, we also notice bullish divergence in the RSI oscillator line and then the price moves upward.

Then we see the RSI penetrating the upper band in the middle of the chart. However, this time we do not see higher highs in prices; instead the market sells off and the RSI now penetrates the lower band. When this occurs, the upper band penetration failed to produce the desired result of higher highs, so this is one of the 25 percent of times it fails.

Once the RSI penetrated the lower band, that replaces the higher high forecast from the previous upper band penetration. Then notice that the lower band penetration was followed by lower lows in price.

MULTIPLE TIME FRAME ANALYSIS

Multiple time frame analysis is another critical component in deriving accurate Elliott Wave counts. It's based on fractal symmetry, meaning there are waves (parent and child waves) inside waves in Elliott Wave counts.

Therefore there should be confirmation between the different time frames that substantiate the Elliott Wave count on any given time frame or interval.

If you look at a chart and cannot make sense of the Elliott Wave count, go up to a higher time frame until the count becomes clear. The reason it was unclear on the current time frame you were looking at more than likely has to do with the fact that it was in a complex correction on that time frame and you had trouble recognizing anything. A good rule is that if, for whatever reason, you cannot get a clear read on what the count is, don't trade it. The odds are not in your favor.

FIGURE 5.10 When the RSI fails, which happens 25% of the time—see on this chart how in June the RSI penetrates the upper band, which is a signal to expect more higher highs, but instead the market sold off indicating a failed RSI.

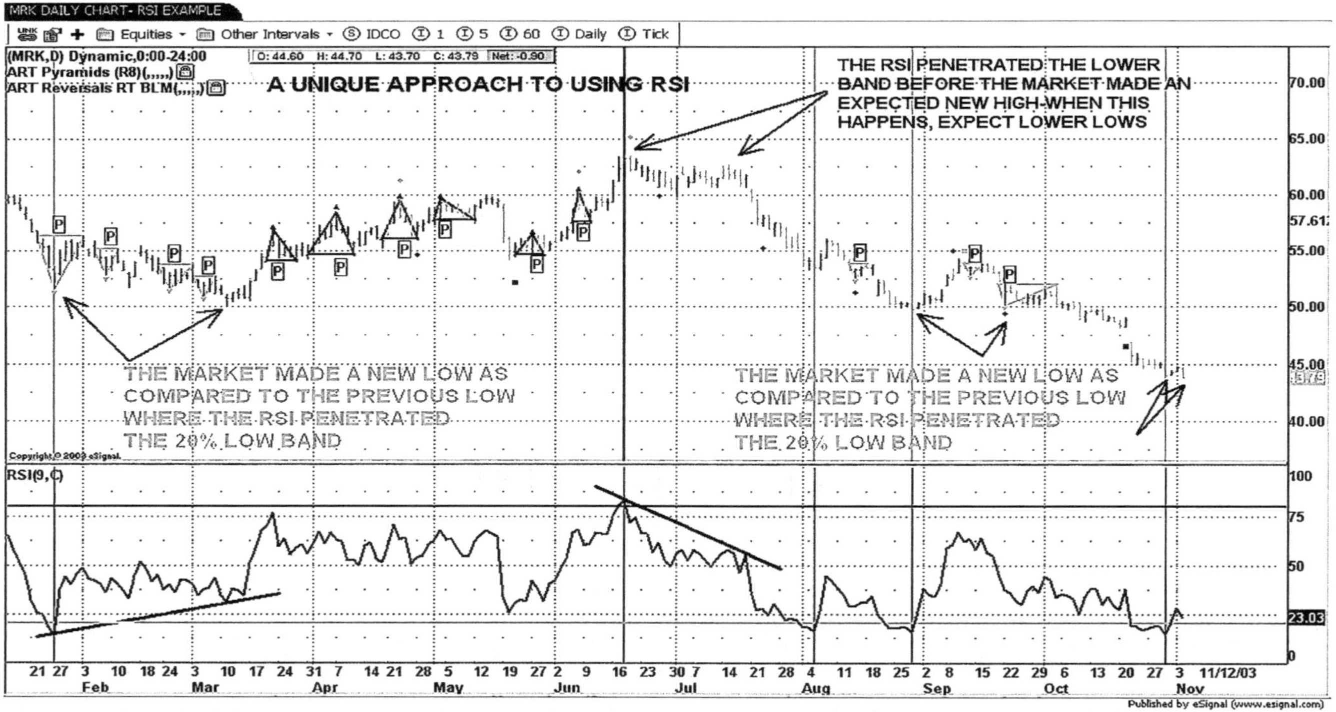

Complex corrections are messy and hard to trade. It is best to stand aside until clarity returns with the next impulsive trend. By analyzing the higher time frames you will get clarity on where the next trend should begin based on Elliott Wave tools that you are learning in this book.

No matter what time frame you are trading, this technique can be used. If you're a day trader, swing trader, or investor, you can use this trading technique. Significant trends involve traders and investors from many time frames trading in the same market direction at the same time.

FRACTAL SYMMETRY—WAVES WITHIN WAVES

The following list of time frames will help you in determining how to use multiple time frame analysis.

- 1-minute chart: Recommended higher time frame to use is the 5-minute chart
- 2-minute chart: Recommended higher time frame to use is the 10-minute chart
- 5-minute chart: Recommended higher time frame to use is the 15- or 25-minute chart
- 10-minute chart: Recommended higher time frame to use is the 40- or 50-minute chart
- 15-minute chart: Recommended higher time frame to use is the 45- or 75-minute chart
- 20-minute chart: Recommended higher time frame to use is the 60- or 100-minute chart
- 25-minute chart: Recommended higher time frame to use is the 75- or 125-minute chart
- 30-minute chart: Recommended higher time frame to use is the 90- or 150-minute chart
- 35-minute chart: Recommended higher time frame to use is the 105- or 175-minute chart
- 40-minute chart: Recommended higher time frame to use is the 120- or 200-minute chart

- 60-minute chart: Recommended higher time frame to use is the 180-minute or daily chart
- Daily chart: Recommended higher time frame to use is the weekly chart
- Weekly chart: Recommended higher time frame to use is the monthly chart
- Monthly chart: Recommended higher time frame to use is the quarterly chart
- Quarterly chart: Recommended higher time frame to use is the yearly chart

Choose time frames at least three to five intervals apart until you can see a clear Elliott Wave pattern.

For position traders using the daily charts to calculate entries and risk control, use both the weekly and monthly charts to see the fractal symmetry between time frames.

Fractal symmetry is the relationship of waves within waves. For example a Wave 4 (ABC) correction on a weekly chart should be represented on a daily chart as impulsive five-wave sequences for Waves A and C. That represents fractal symmetry.

FRACTAL SYMMETRY IN DAILY, WEEKLY, AND MONTHLY TIME FRAMES

Following are two examples of the fractal symmetry between time frames. The purpose of these charts is to illustrate how the Elliott Wave makes sense among the different time frames. These examples uses daily, weekly, and monthly charts to show that while trend cycle severities may be different, they are all in sync and make sense of the fractal symmetry between time frames.

FIGURE 5.11 The TSLA daily chart here is in sync with the TSLA weekly chart in Figure 5.12 and the TSLA monthly chart in Figure 5.13, which confirms the accuracy of the wave count on all three charts, showing how using the "multiple time frame" method can be effective in confirming higher probability wave counts and weeding out lower probability wave counts.

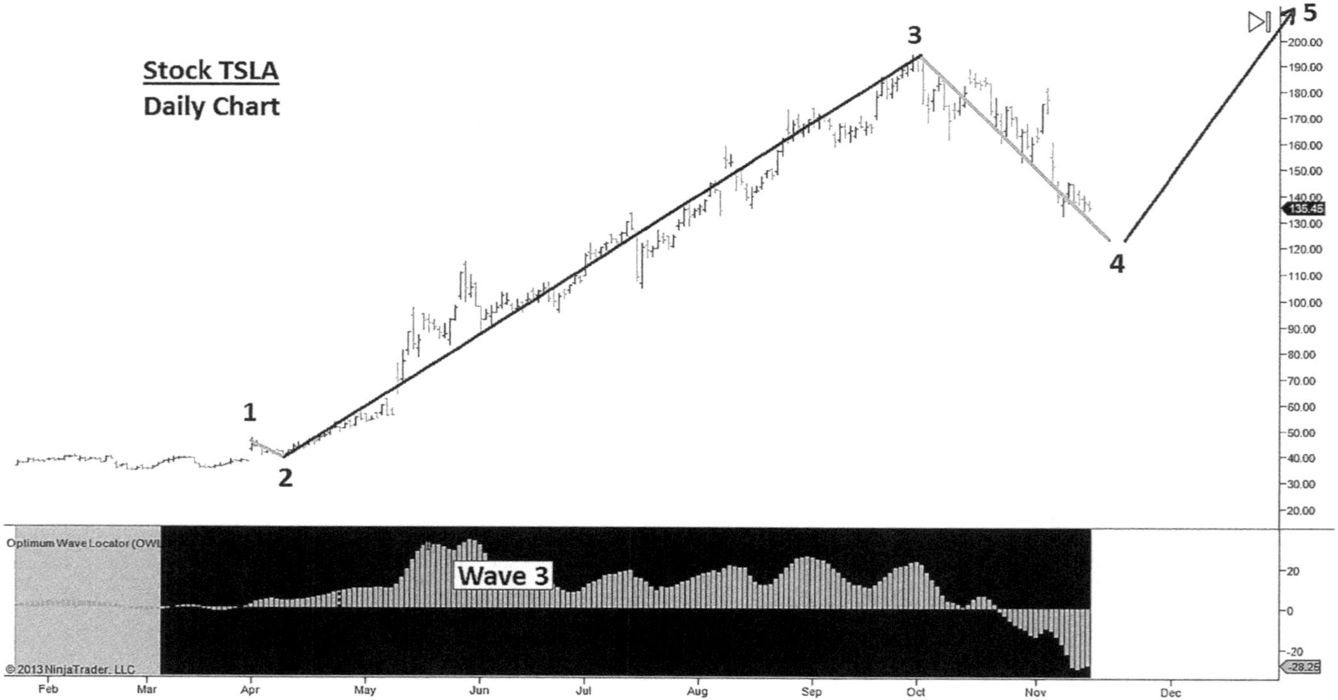

TSLA: In Figure 5.11, a daily chart of TSLA, note that the price oscillator is currently negative (on the right side of the chart), indicating that a mature Wave 4 correction is under way.

Next is the TSLA weekly chart (Figure 5.12). Note that the price oscillator is not negative like on the daily chart. Instead on this weekly chart the price oscillator (OWL histogram) is still bullish, meaning we are still in a weekly Wave 3. So Wave 4 on this weekly chart is called a *minor Wave 4* since it is inside a major Wave 3. Wave 3 on this weekly chart will end when Wave 5 ends on the daily chart.

And finally the TSLA monthly chart (Figure 5.13). Note that like the weekly chart, the monthly chart is still in Wave 3.

AAPL: For a second example, let's look at Apple, stock symbol AAPL (Figures 5.14 through 5.16).

Apple (AAPL) is perfectly in sync among all three time frames shown. Based on multiple time frame analysis, Apple's bullish Elliott Wave impulsive trend cycle will result in new all-time highs.

On the monthly chart, Apple has finished Wave 4 and the price oscillator histogram is now bullish indicating the emergence of Wave 5.

On the weekly chart we see the ABC simple zigzag corrective pattern in Wave 4. We also see the current bullish Wave 5 price oscillator histogram as prices climb again. This is in perfect sync with the monthly chart.

On the daily chart we see the bullish Wave 5 pattern of Wave 3 that occurred on the weekly and monthly charts. And then bearish Wave 5 of Wave C of Wave 4 that was on the monthly chart. The child waves of the bullish Wave 5 occurring on the weekly and monthly chart are visible on this daily chart.

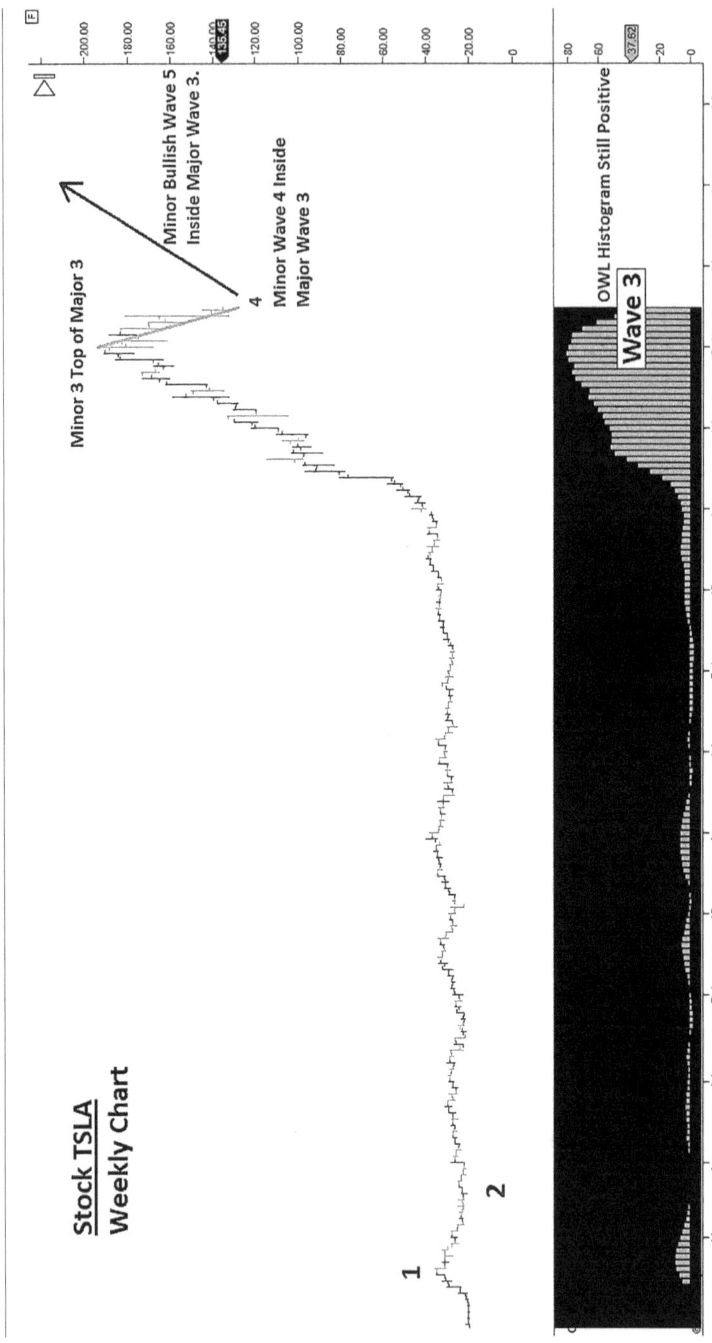

FIGURE 5.12 TSLA weekly chart illustrates the "multiple time frame" method when compared to Figure 5.11 and Figure 5.13.

FIGURE 5.13 TSLA monthly chart illustrates the "multiple time frame" method when compared to Figure 5.11 and Figure 5.12.

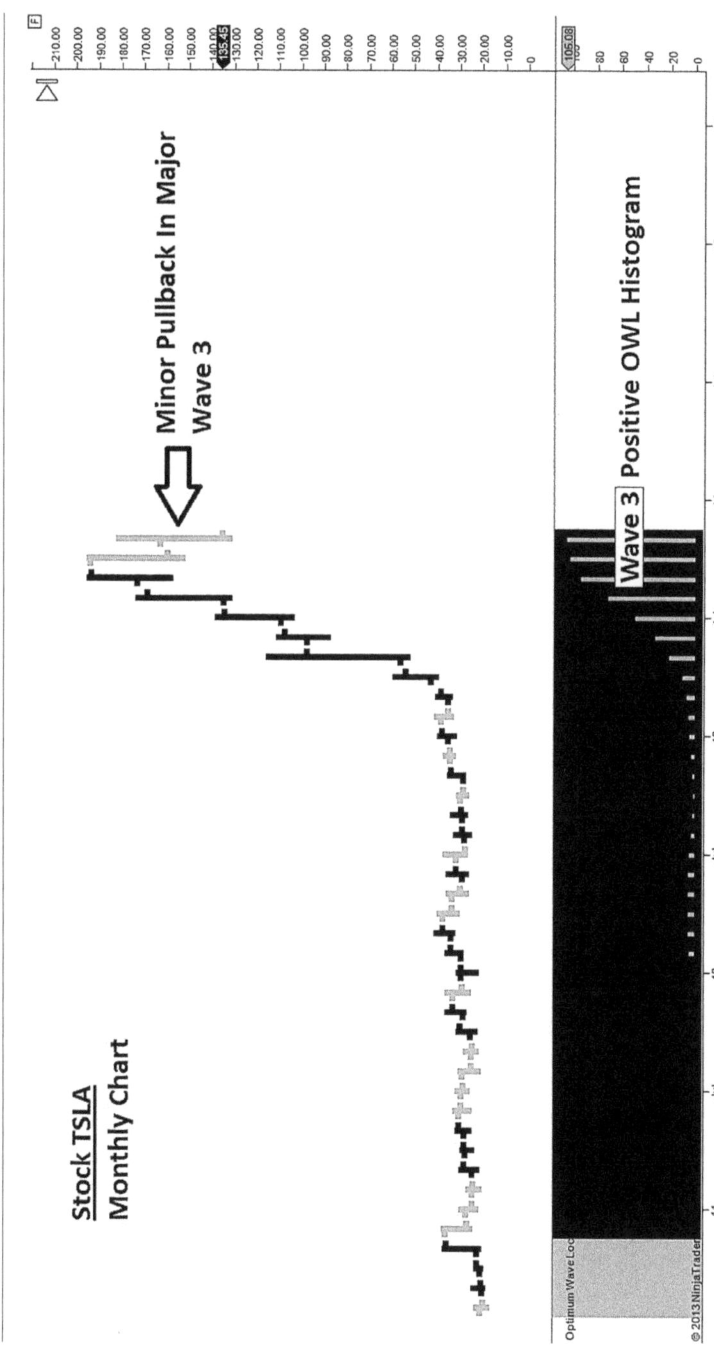

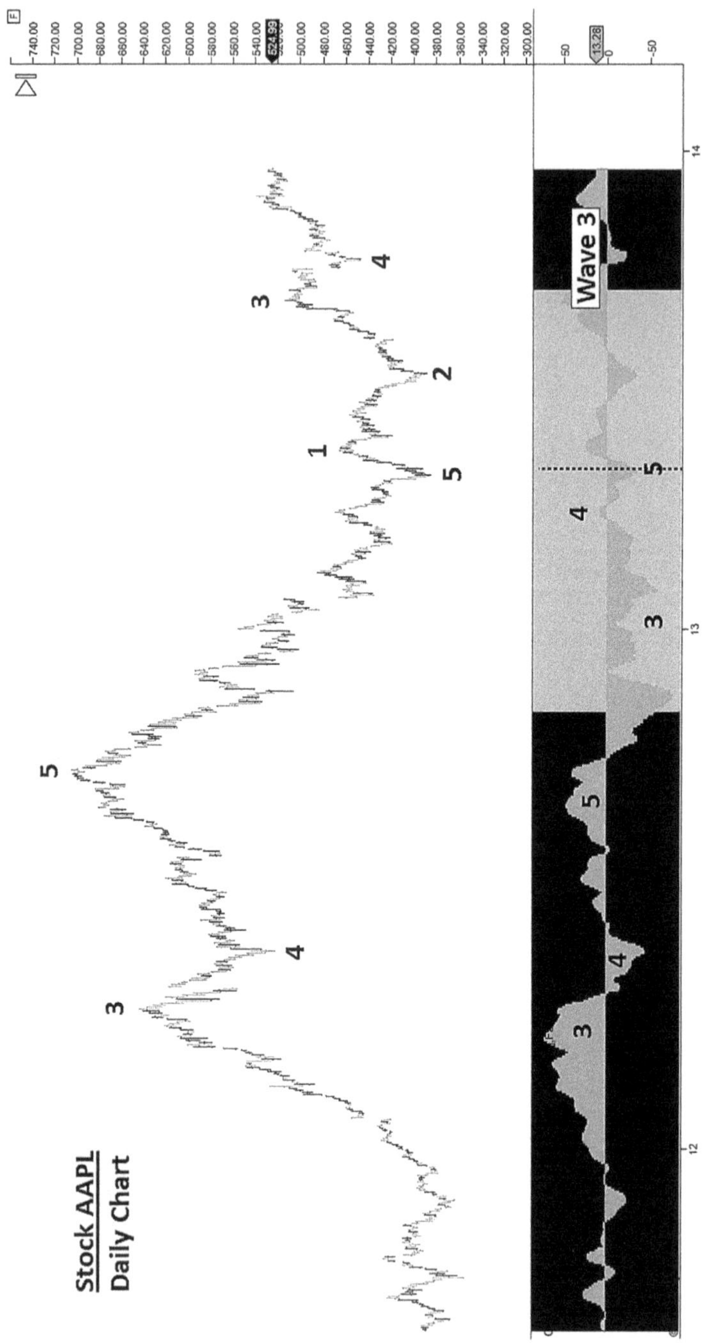

FIGURE 5.14 The AAPL daily chart here is in sync with the AAPL weekly chart in Figure 5.15 and the AAPL monthly chart in Figure 5.16, which confirms the accuracy of the wave count on all three charts, illustrating how using the "multiple time frame" method can be effective in confirming higher probability wave counts and weeding out lower probability wave counts.

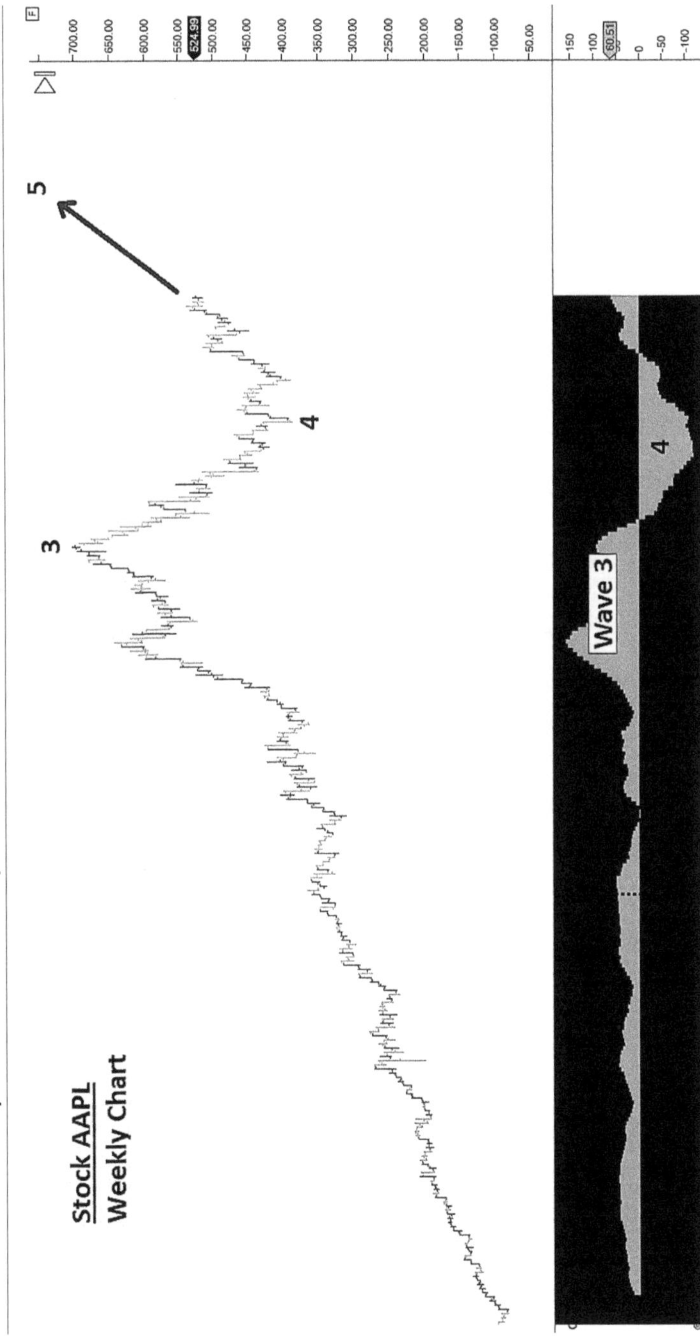

FIGURE 5.15 AAPL weekly chart illustrates the "multiple time frame" method when compared to Figure 5.14 and Figure 5.16.

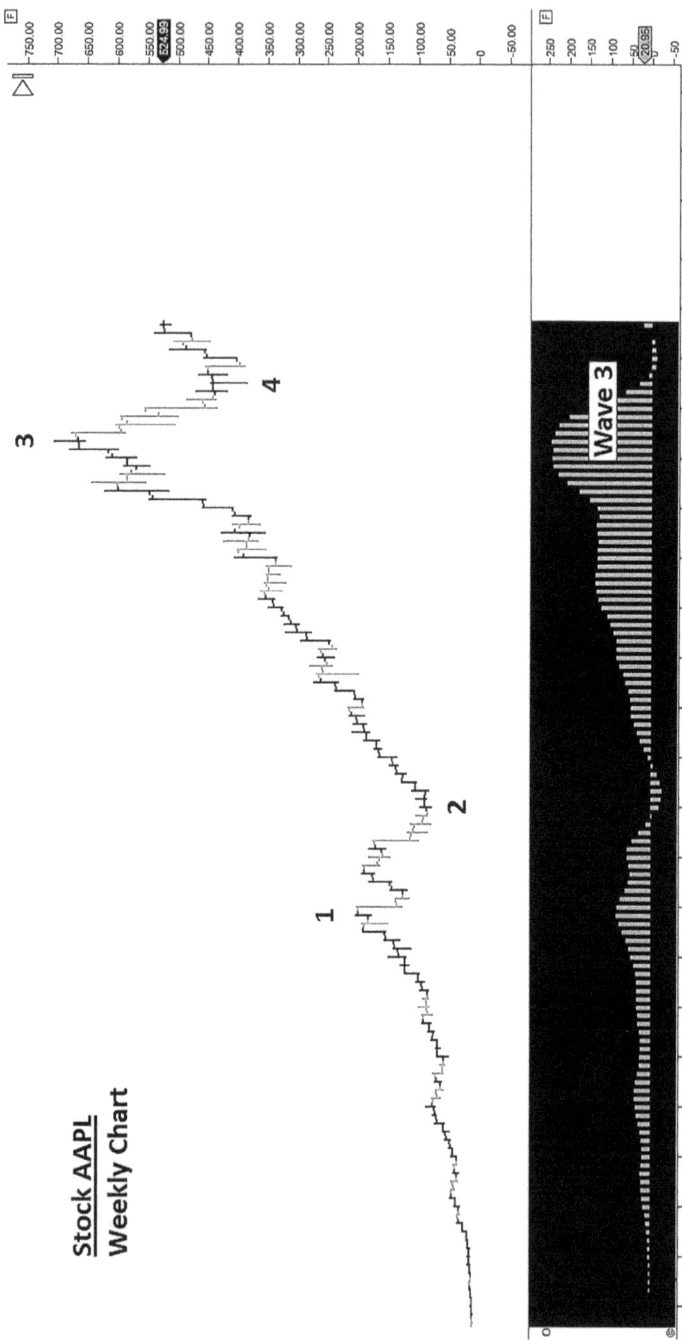

FIGURE 5.16 AAPL monthly chart illustrates the "multiple time frame" method when compared to Figure 5.14 and Figure 5.15.

TIP: While the price oscillator histogram and RSI oscillator are sufficient, there are two comprehensive software tools you may be interested in purchasing that you can use in place of the price oscillator and the RSI oscillator. The Optimum Wave Oscillator (OWL) indicator has more bells and whistles then the price oscillator. And the Precision Trend Filter (PTF) oscillator can replace the RSI oscillator. These are available at **www.TradersCoach.com®**.

CHAPTER 6

Combining Classic and Modern Techniques for a Better Result

The Best of Both Worlds

This chapter is all about "connecting the dots." What you're going to learn is how to combine the modern Elliott Wave approach with the classic Elliott Wave approach. This will allow you to arrive at high probability Elliott Wave forecasts quickly and efficiently and in a cookie-cutter fashion. You then will be able to apply this approach with confidence to any market and any time frame, and have reproducible positive results.

There are times when using the Elliott Wave approach that you will have a primary wave count and an alternate wave count. This usually occurs during corrections that turned into new impulsive waves due to exceptions in the Elliott Wave analysis such as failed Wave 5s, shallow Wave 4s, and other times when an exception occurs.

As you learn how to combine classic and modern Elliott Wave analysis, you will have this problem less frequently than others relying on just the classic approach. Using the McDowell Probability Matrix, you will learn how to assign a probability percentage to each alternate wave count when they occur. This will greatly help you in choosing the wave count with the highest probability of success.

Alternate Wave Counts in the Same Direction

There are times when two alternate wave counts have forecasts that point in the same direction. Obviously this setup has a high probability of success because the alternate counts agree with each other regarding the ultimate direction the market will move in. If you should enter the market, either trade will be profitable if the wave count does not fail—it is just a matter of how profitable. As the trade matures, the true wave count will reveal itself.

While the Elliott Wave is a great tool we use to forecast the direction of trends in the market, we still need to know how to enter and exit the market at certain price levels that complement the direction of the Elliott Wave count we've determined to be the highest probability of where prices are going. It is important to understand that any form of forecasting is basically a theory or fantasy of where prices are going to go. Like a weather forecast, I like to think of our forecast in terms of chances that are the most likely to occur over time.

Using a forecast based on high probabilities gives us a dependable direction of price movement, but when used in conjunction with price action analysis that provides exact price entries, exits, and risk control you get a complete trading system.

Using Both Grounded and Ungrounded Assessments While Trading

Current price is reality, the forecast price is not. Therefore I use a trading system that tells me exact price levels to enter and exit a market. I call this making *grounded assessments* since entries and exits are based on the realities of price.

The idea is that your trading system of entries and stop-loss levels used for exiting the market always supersedes the "forecast" model or theory used to forecast price direction. Thus use your forecast to determine trend direction and only take trades in the direction of the forecast.

This concept of using a trading system in conjunction with a forecasting method is what I call *grounded* and *ungrounded* assessment trading as follows.

Using grounded versus ungrounded assessments requires understanding the difference between a forecast and a structured trading approach used for entries, exits, and risk control:

> **Grounded assessments:** Decisions based on current market realities like trade entries, stop-loss exits, and risk control. Grounded assessments are your rules to enter and exit the market along with risk control. Ungrounded assessments never supersede grounded assessments.
>
> **Ungrounded assessments:** Decisions based on forecasting methods, theories, and fantasy of where price is going like calculating target zone retracements, etc.—*Elliott Wave forecasting!* Ungrounded assessments may filter which entries you want to take so that you are trading only in the direction of the forecast, but they usually do not tell you when to get into or exit the markets.

Six Areas to Analyze When Creating an Elliott Wave Forecast

There are six areas to analyze to obtain high probability Elliott Wave forecasts. The idea here is to connect the dots of all six areas to create a thorough Elliott Wave analysis. These areas consist of three classic and three modern Elliott Wave techniques to achieve a high probability count.

1. **Clear price structure** (classic rule): Can I easily count the waves based on price structure? Or is this a messy and unclear market?

2. **Clear price oscillator histogram/OWL** (modern rule): Can I find Wave 3, and does it make sense based on the price oscillator histogram/OWL levels?
3. **Volume analysis** (classic rule): Is volume what it is supposed to be according to the Elliott Wave volume guidelines?
4. **Fibonacci levels** (classic rule): Is price hitting the Fibonacci high probability price target zones? Is the chart holding up to the Fibonacci price guidelines?
5. **(RSI) Relative strength index/PTF** (modern rule): Is this indicator aligned and in agreement with the forecast?"
6. **Multiple time frame alignment in sync** (classic rule): Are the higher time frames in sync and alignment with the lower time frames for the Elliott Wave pattern you are looking at? Do the higher time frames agree with the lower time frames in terms of what direction the market is going? Is there fractal symmetry on all time frames?

Once you have mastered the six areas, you will be able to analyze a chart very quickly and in a very structured procedural form of analysis. In Chapter 7 we apply percentages to each of these areas, thus forming an Elliott Wave probability matrix called the McDowell Probability Matrix.

Previously in Chapters 3 and 4 you learned about the classic Elliott Wave rules, and in Chapter 5 you learned about the modern Elliott Wave rules. So now it's time to combine the classic Elliott Wave rules with the modern Elliott Wave rules to produce high probability Elliott Wave counts.

1. CLEAR PRICE STRUCTURE (CLASSIC)

Count the waves based on price structure. You must be able to "see" the waves on the chart you are analyzing. The waves must be clear enough to make a sensible Elliott Wave count. Locate Wave 3 on the chart you are analyzing. Does it make sense based on price levels and Wave 3 Elliott Wave classic rules? Note: The entire long-term trend may be decades long. To trade the current trend, focus on the trend in the recent 144 price bars.

Figures 6.1 and 6.2 capture this current bullish trend that ended and a new bearish one that is forming. Figure 6.1 illustrates the overall dominant wave count of the daily Apple chart. You can easily see each of the five waves in the pattern, which is an example of very clear price structure.

Figure 6.2 illustrates waves within waves known as *child waves*. This is the fractal symmetry that exists in the markets.

2. CLEAR PRICE OSCILLATOR HISTOGRAM/OWL (MODERN)

Locate Wave 3 on the chart you are analyzing (Figure 6.3). Does it make sense based on both of the price oscillator histogram levels and the rules associated with using the histogram?

3. VOLUME ANALYSIS (CLASSIC)

Is volume what it is supposed to be according to the volume analysis guidelines? Wave 3 *always* has the highest volume of all the five waves (Figure 6.4).

FIGURE 6.1 **AAPL daily chart clearly identifies each of the five waves in the Elliott Wave pattern using price structure alone, which is the classic approach.**

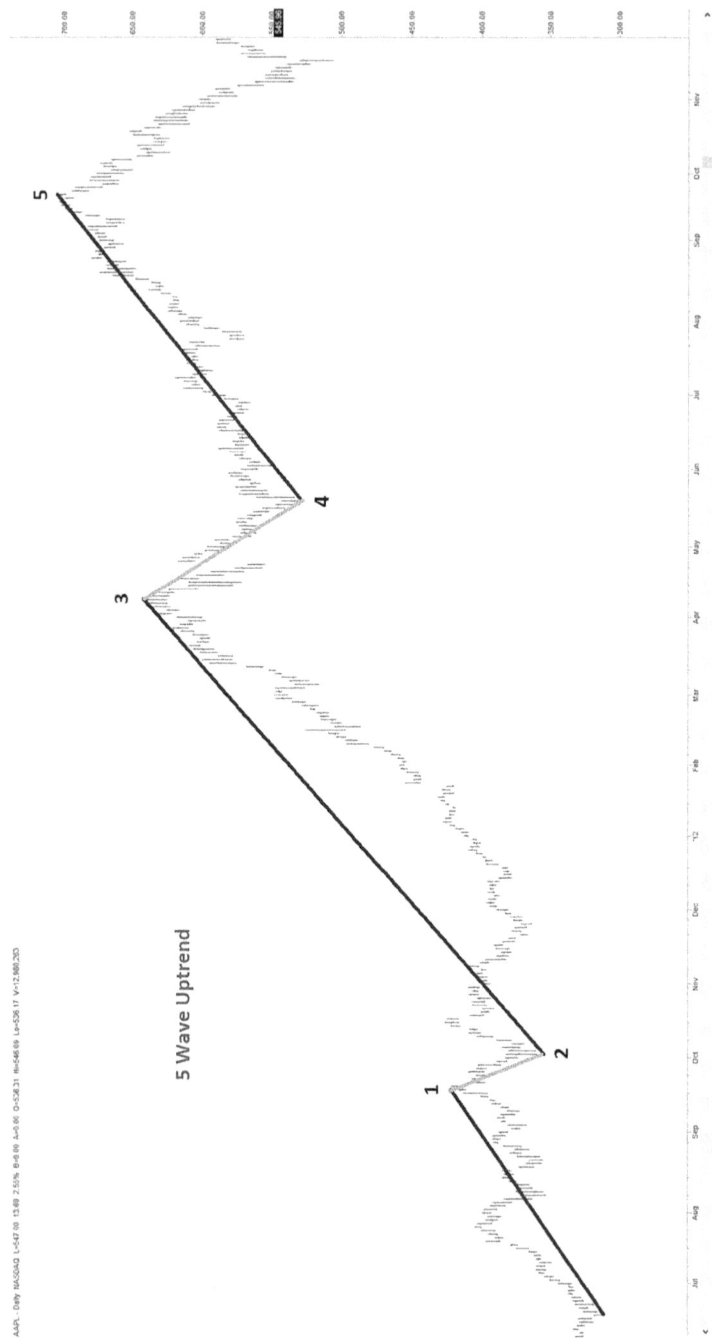

FIGURE 6.2 **AAPL daily charts showing "child" waves within "parent" waves that represent the underlying substructure of the overall wave count.**

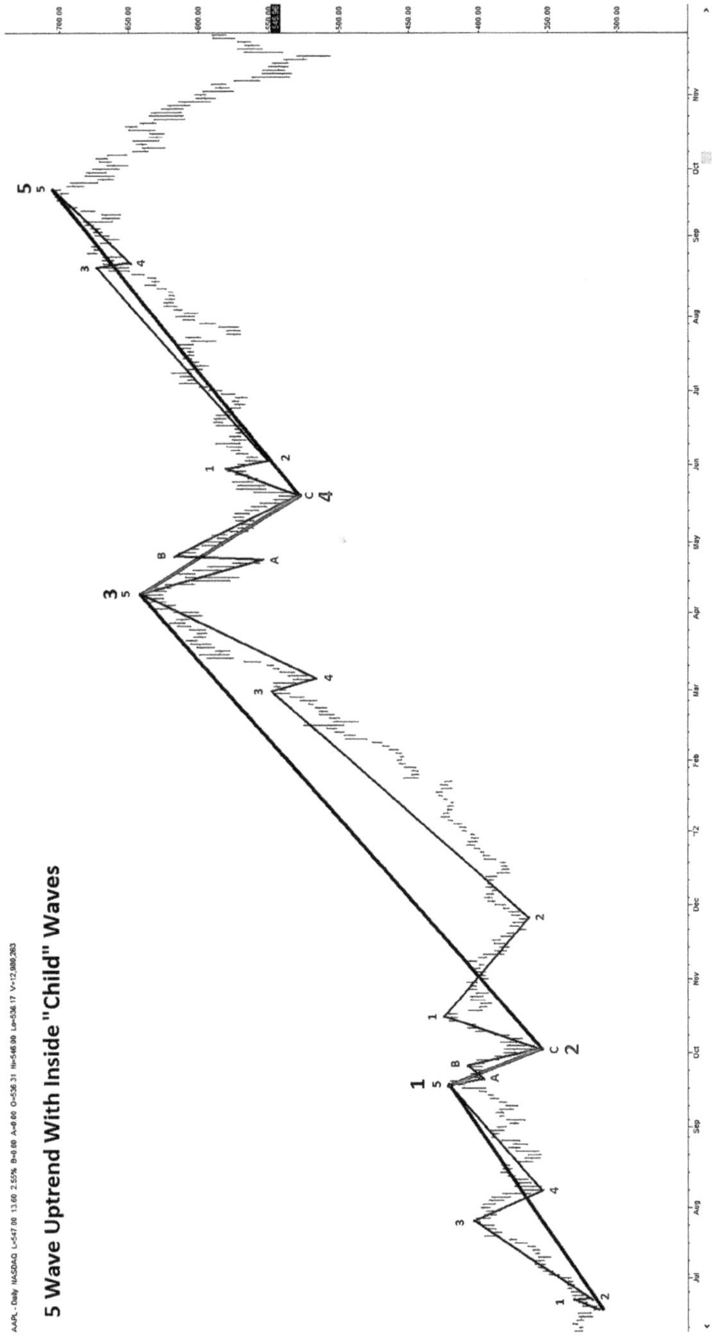

FIGURE 6.3 **AAPL daily chart shows bearish divergence between bullish Wave 3 and bullish Wave 5 in the "price oscillator," which is an example of using the modern approach.**

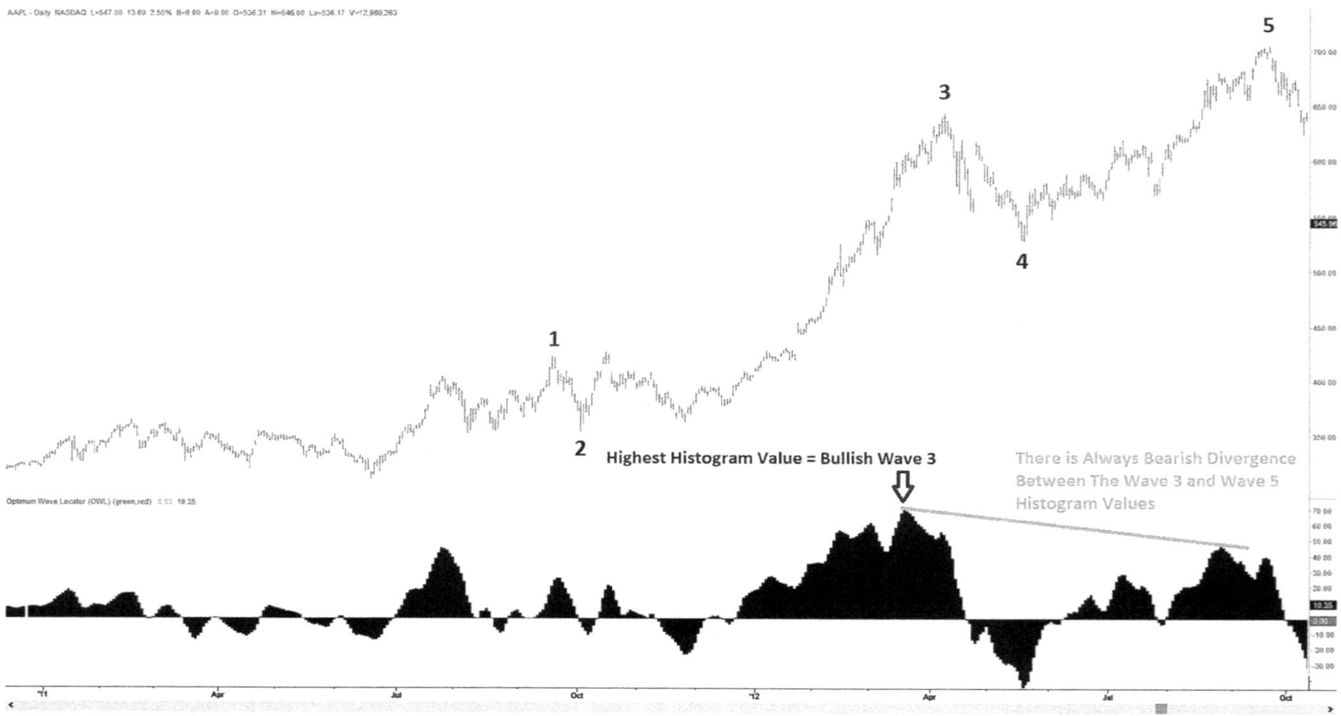

FIGURE 6.4 Volume increases and peaks during Wave 3, where the highest volume always occurs.

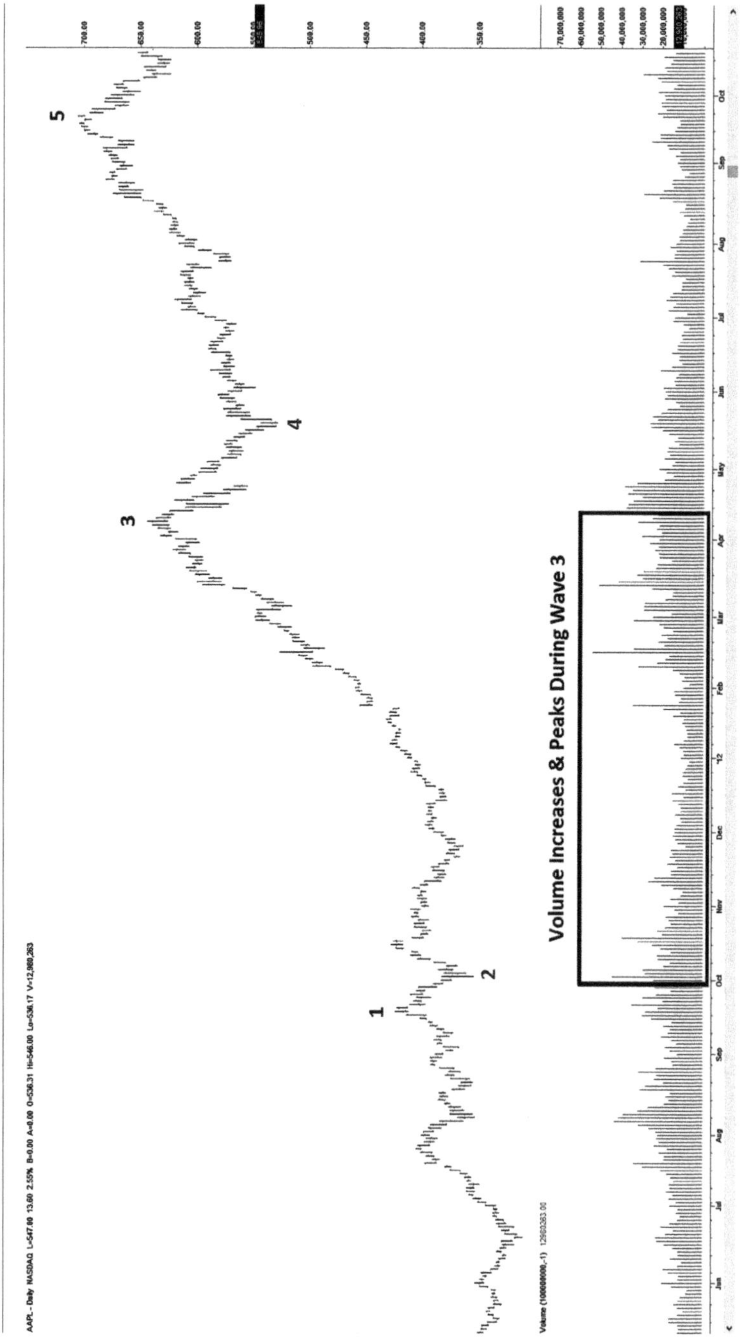

4. FIBONACCI LEVELS (CLASSIC)

Do Waves 2 and 4 adhere to Fibonacci price level retracements? And does the previous Wave 5 end at the correct Fibonacci Extension price level? Be sure to check all the Fibonacci rules for each of the waves to confirm that the wave count is correct.

Fibonacci price retracement levels (Figure 6.5) are used to identify Wave 4 price target zones. You can also add Wave 2 retracement levels, but Wave 2 can retrace up to 100 percent of Wave 1, so target zones are primarily established for Wave 4 since Wave 4 does not usually retrace more than 61.8 percent.

Fibonacci extension levels (Figure 6.6) are used to identify Wave 5 price target zones.

Fibonacci time extension levels (Figure 6.7) are used to identify when swing highs or lows should occur. By using points A and B on the chart in Figure 6.7, the Fibonacci time extensions predicted when key price pivot points would occur. Note the key swing highs associated with the Fibonacci extension time projections.

5. (RSI) RELATIVE STRENGTH INDEX/PTF (MODERN)

Bullish trends usually drive the RSI oscillator to peak levels above the 80 percent indicator line (Figure 6.8). In a bullish trend, if a wave top has PTF above the 80 percent line, then that is a bullish indication that higher highs are probable and the trend is still going higher. Vice versa for bearish trends. Wave 5 usually ends on a neutral RSI, meaning the RSI oscillator is between the upper and lower indicator bands.

FIGURE 6.5 Fibonacci price retracement levels were met on this chart using this classic Fibonacci price target zone approach.

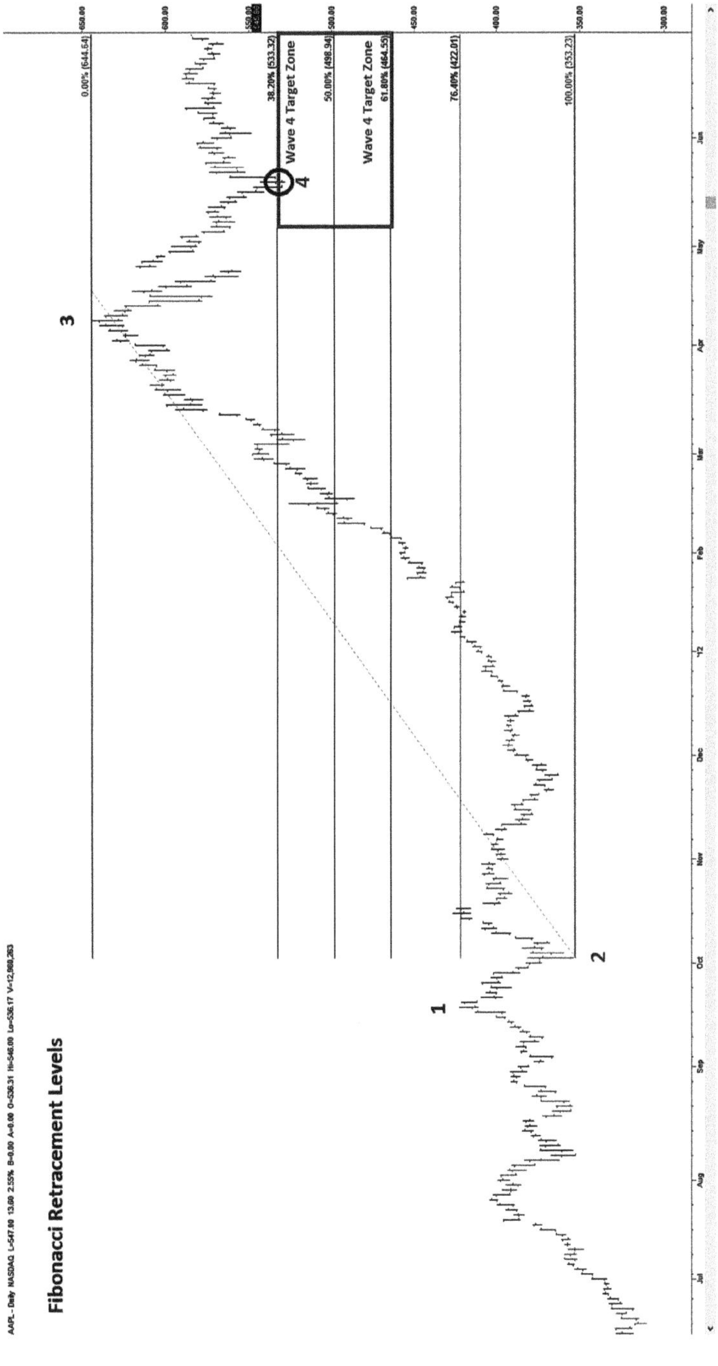

FIGURE 6.6 Fibonacci price extensions identify Wave 5 price target zones.

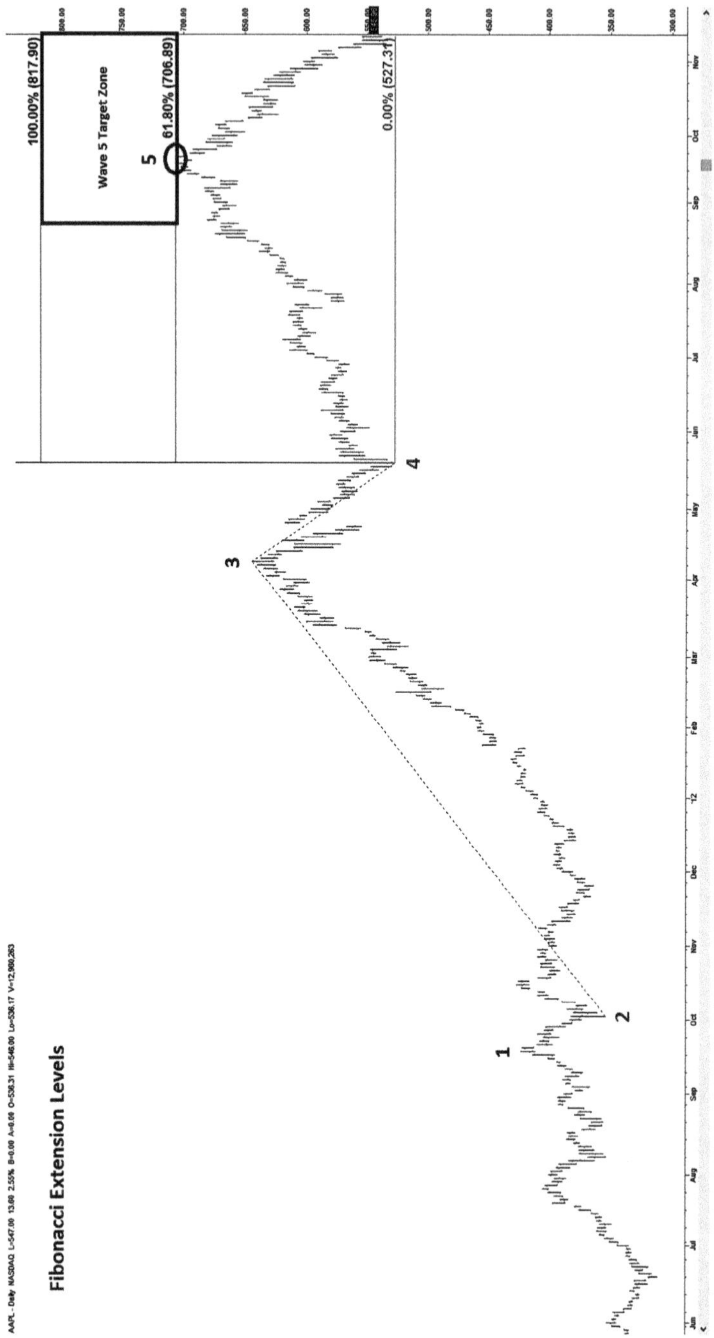

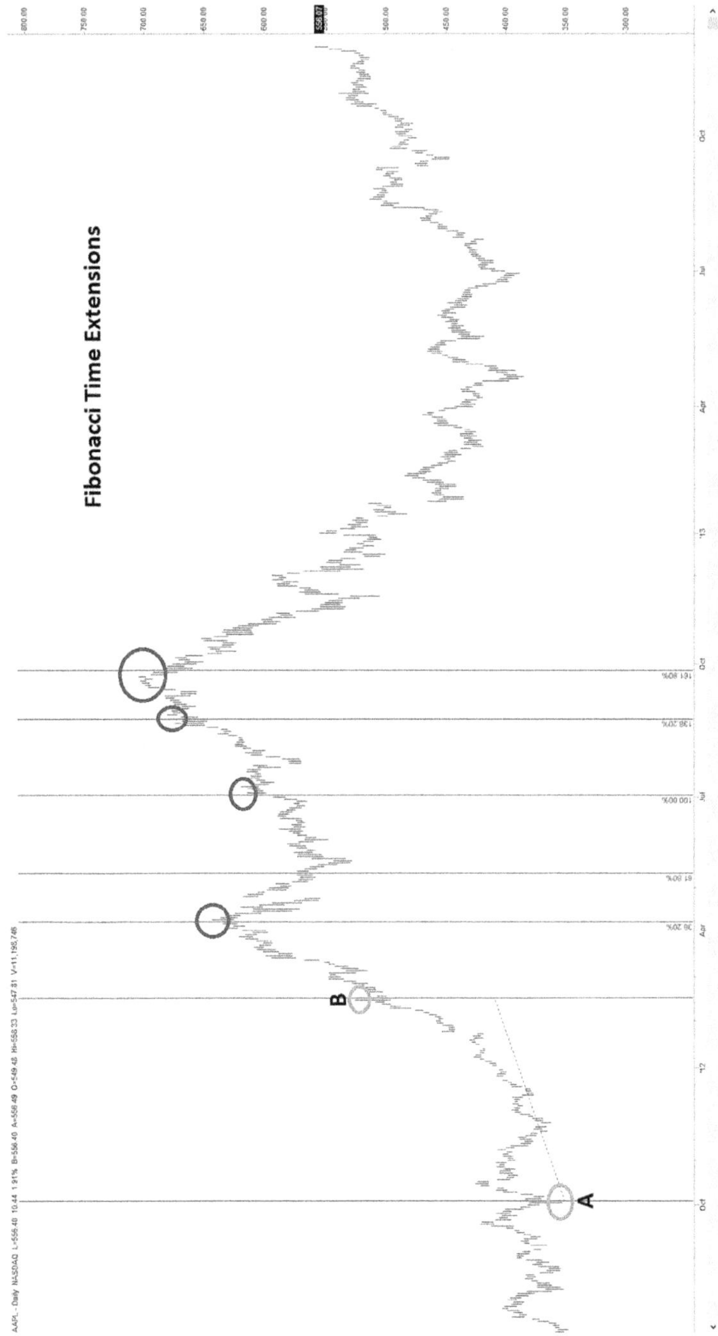

FIGURE 6.7 **Fibonacci time extensions identify *when* highs or lows should occur and can time turning points in the market.**

FIGURE 6.8 RSI peaks during impulsive bullish waves.

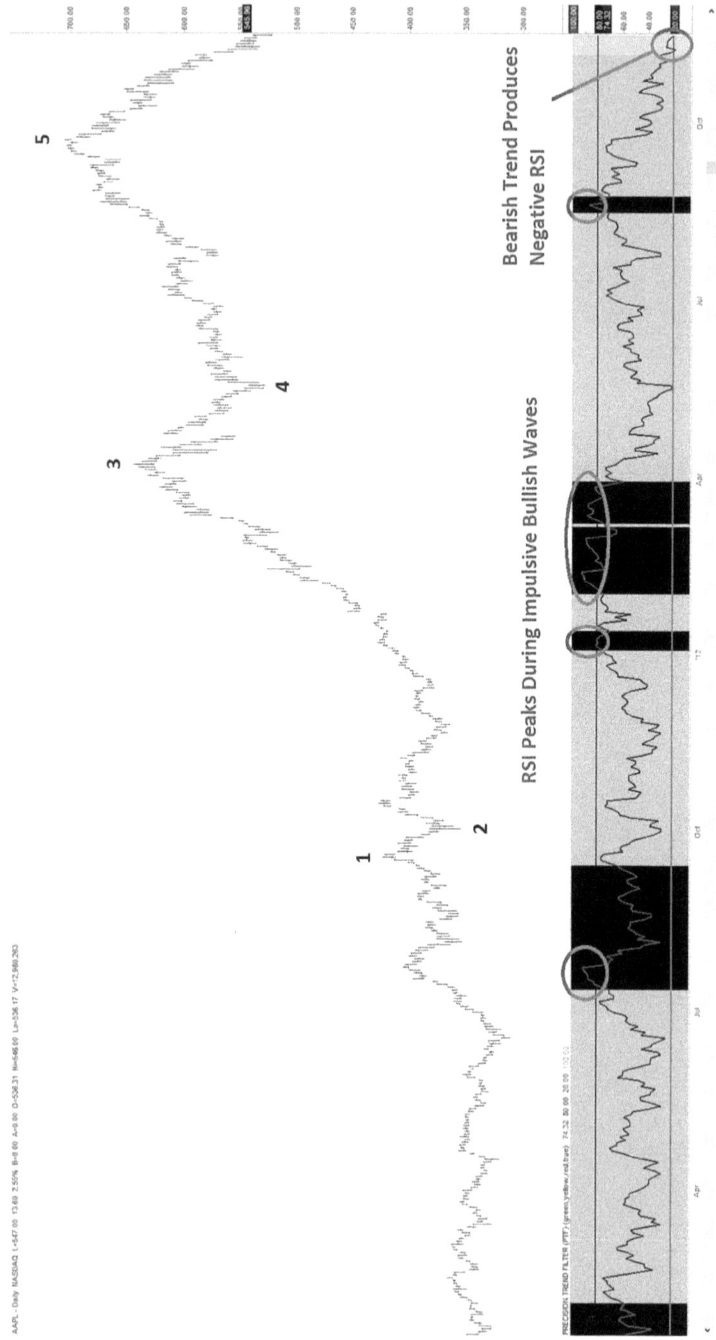

6. MULTIPLE TIME FRAME ALIGNMENT (MODERN)

Are the higher time frames in alignment with the lower time frames? Notice on the chart in Figure 6.9 that we have three time frames, monthly, weekly, and daily. When going from the monthly to the weekly, we are zooming in on the Elliott Wave structure, and we can see more individual waves on the weekly chart than on the monthly. When we go to the daily chart, we zoom in again and see even more waves within waves. Notice how the Wave 5 top on the daily chart is Wave 5 of a major Wave 3 on the weekly chart.

UNCLEAR PRICE PATTERNS CAN RESULT IN ALTERNATE WAVE COUNTS

When price action does not do what it is supposed to do based on our Elliott Wave count, a red warning flag is raised. Usually it will mean that we have an alternate wave count, and should determine if that alternate wave count is in conflict with our original assumption. If that is true, any trade should be scrubbed until the wave count becomes clear. Although they may appear different, if both the alternate and original wave counts have a forecast in the same direction and thus are not in conflict, a trade can be considered.

Think of a street map for a moment—you may have two different routes that take you to the same destination. One route may be a little longer than the other, but both routes go generally in the same direction until they reach the final destination. This is similar to having two alternate wave counts that have forecast prices going in the same direction but take different routes.

TIP: If you have done a complete analysis using both the classic and modern Elliott Wave approaches and the result is unclear, move on to another market or time frame until you find an Elliott Wave count that is clear. Do not spend too much time overanalyzing a chart trying to find an Elliott Wave count that makes sense.

FIGURE 6.9 Multiple time frame analysis showing fractal symmetry in the markets.

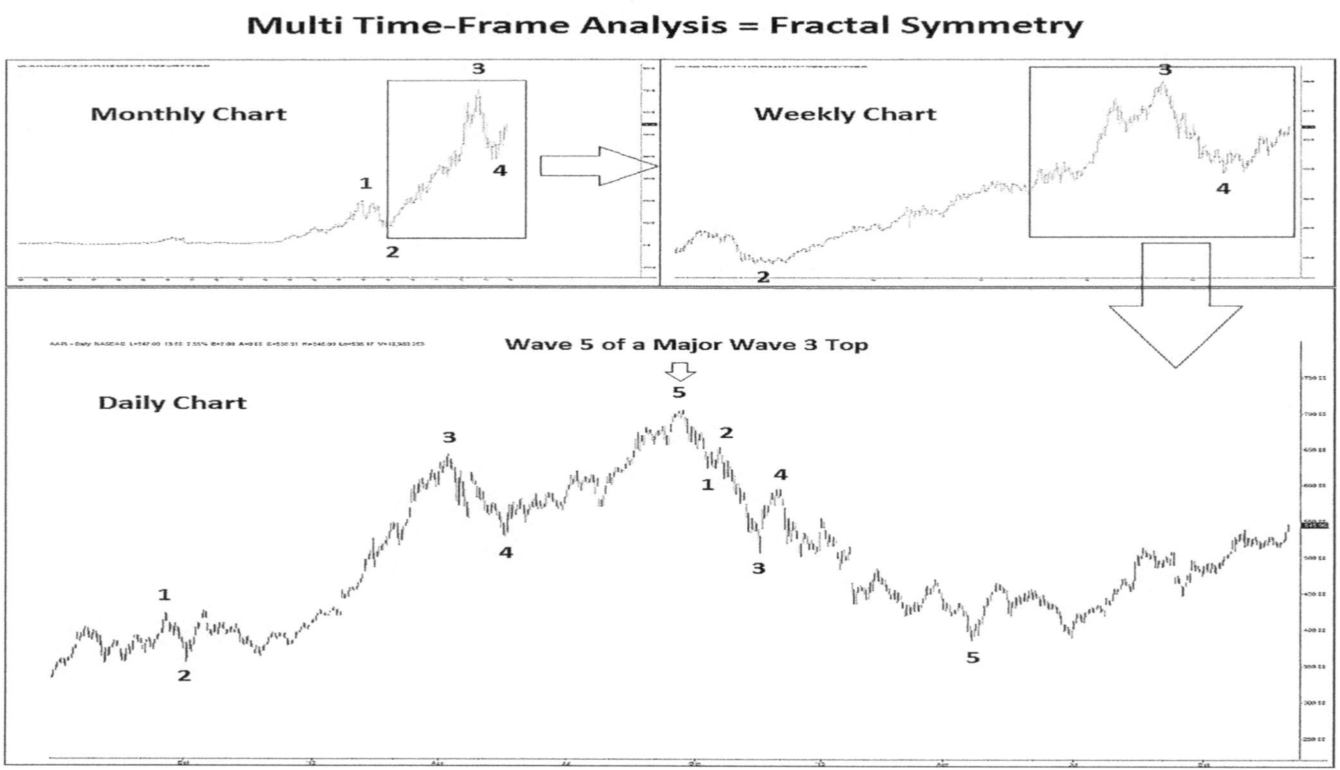

There are enough markets and enough time frames that you can find a wave count that you can see with clarity, and these are the ones you want to trade. Markets move in cycles, so charts that are messy and unclear will eventually become clear again. Usually, when a chart is a mess, it is because it is in a complex corrective wave on multiple time frames.

Use common sense, and if you cannot get a good "read" on a chart, pass on it and find one where you can see the "road map" clearly.

CHAPTER 7

Using the McDowell Probability Matrix to Trust and Verify Signals

Finding the Highest Probability Wave Counts

The McDowell Probability Matrix creates a framework in which we are able to place a numerical value on a wave count that can then be expressed as a percentage of probability. The markets are all about probabilities. Nothing is 100 percent certain when trading and investing in the financial markets. In this chapter you will learn how to connect the dots mathematically by using the McDowell Probability Matrix.

MONEY MANAGEMENT AND RISK CONTROL ARE ESSENTIAL

Knowing that nothing is 100 percent guaranteed in life or trading, it is clear that we must use risk control when trading and investing in the financial markets. While the McDowell Probability Matrix puts the odds in your favor, there will be times that a wave count will have a high probability of success and will still be wrong.

How many times have you seen a weather forecast that predicted sunshine and blue skies and yet it's raining outside? Or a respected market commentator confidently states that a certain stock is going to surge to new heights, and then it plummets to new lows? Probabilities in trading work in the same way, which is why we stress risk control on each and every trade.

In my book *A Trader's Money Management System: How to Ensure Profit and Avoid the Risk of Ruin* (John Wiley & Sons, 2008), I cover money management and risk control for traders and investors. In this book there are a number of very easy-to-use formulas and techniques that help put the odds in your favor regarding risk control.

For one, it is important to carefully select the proper trade size on every trade. Too often traders will get into a trade with such a large trade size (also known as position size) that they are overextended and have taken on far too much risk for their portfolio. In times like this if the trade goes against them, their loss can devastate and possibly ruin their account.

Beyond the desire to avoid the risk of ruin, implementing effective money management can actually make a trader more profitable. By implementing meaningful stop loss exits, ones that are based on actual market dynamics and not just random stops, you will essentially be getting out of the losing trades quicker and staying with the winning trades longer. It is the age-old formula for success and profitability in trading.

And, as I mentioned before, any trading approach, no matter how brilliant, will ultimately fail if one does not manage both money and risk properly.

McDowell Probability Matrix Gives You Six Key Areas to Analyze

The matrix you see in Figure 7.1 outlines six important areas that determine if a wave count has a high probability of accuracy or not. After analyzing the markets and paying close attention to these six areas, you'll have created a probability matrix that will allow you to connect the dots and place a probability percentage on the accuracy of your forecast.

FIGURE 7.1 **The McDowell Probability Matrix™, also known as the MPM Worksheet, will assist you in calculating what the probability is that your wave count is accurate.**

"The McDowell Probability Matrix"—MPM Worksheet

By www.TradersCoach.com®

Description Of Chart: Date Range Of Chart:

	CATEGORY DESCRIPTION	SCORE RANGE	SCORE
1	Elliott Wave Price Structure Is Clear—Classic	0 1 2 3 4 5	
2	Price Oscillator Histogram Is Clear (OWL)—Modern	0 1 2 3 4 5	
3	Volume Is Correct For Each Wave—Classic	0 1 2 3 4 5	
4	Fibonacci Levels Are Holding—Classic	0 1 2 3 4 5	
5	Relative Strength Index (RSI) Is Clear (PTF)—Modern	0 1 2 3 4 5	
6	Multiple Time Frame Alignment In Sync—Modern	0 1 2 3 4 5	
NOTE: Score each of the six categories above with a value from zero to five (five being the HIGHEST probability and zero being the LOWEST probability). Circle the correct value in the "Score Range" column. Then write each of the six scores in the "Score" column. Finally, add up all six of the category scores and write the "Total Score" in the grey box to the right. This "Total Score" value will tell you what the probability is that your wave count is correct. The higher the "Total Score" the higher the probability that your wave count is correct. "Total Score" range will be zero to thirty.		**TOTAL SCORE**	

You will find much greater detail on these six areas in Chapter 6 and throughout this book. But for the purpose of clarity, these areas of importance are listed here:

1. Clear price structure (classic rule)
2. Clear price oscillator histogram/OWL (modern rule)
3. Volume analysis (classic rule)
4. Fibonacci levels (classic rule)
5. (RSI) Relative strength index/PTF (modern rule)
6. Multiple time frame alignment in sync (classic rule)

Again, at times there may be alternate wave counts when performing your analysis using these six areas of importance. Because there is always the possibility of a failed wave count, no matter how high the probabilities are, you must use effective risk control to protect yourself in the event of an unexpected outcome.

Scoring Each of the Six Areas of Importance—My Secret Formula!

When analyzing the six areas of importance that are outlined in the McDowell Probability Matrix (Figure 7.1), you will be assigning numbers to each area ranging from 0 to 5. When using this matrix the number 0 will have the lowest probability and the number 5 will have highest probability.

You can see on the worksheet there is a column for you to place your score for each of the six areas. Once you add up the score of all six numbers and arrive at a total score, you will have the number that tells you how likely it is that your wave count is correct.

Refer to Table 7.1 to see what meaning this total score has. Given that there are six areas of importance and the maximum value that can be assigned to each area is 5, then the maximum total score is going to be 30.

Likewise, if the total score is 00 to 09 there will be a "minimal probability" that your wave count is correct. And, if the total score is 28 to 30 there will be an "outstanding probability" and that your wave count is correct.

TABLE 7.1 **Once your analysis is completed using the McDowell Probability Matrix worksheet, you can take the total score from the worksheet and refer to this table to find out what the probability is that your wave count is correct.**

TOTAL SCORE RANGE	PROBABILITY OF CORRECT WAVE COUNT	CHANCE THAT WAVE COUNT IS CORRECT	CLARITY OF WAVE COUNT
00 to 09	Minimal Probability	00% to 49%	No wave count at all
10 to 13	Poor Probability	50% to 54%	Poor clarity
14 to 18	Moderate Probability	55% to 60%	Moderate clarity
19 to 22	Good Probability	61% to 69%	Good clarity
23 to 27	High Probability	70% to 79%	High clarity
28 to 30	Outstanding Probability	80% to 99%	Outstanding clarity

MASTER YOUR ABILITY TO USE THE MCDOWELL PROBABILITY MATRIX

In order to become proficient in using the MPM, you will need to master your ability to assess each of the six areas of importance: Elliott Wave price pattern, price histogram, volume, Fibonacci levels, RSI, and analysis of multiple time frames.

It is recommended that you focus first on understanding and knowing how to apply the items in the MPM so the MPM yields an accurate reading for you. It will take time to master, but just as in learning how to spot Elliott Waves on your charts, you will see that once you learn it, you'll know it for a lifetime. You will be able to quickly look at a chart and know if there is a clear pattern or not in a matter of seconds. Then, if it is a clear chart, you will easily be able to see each of the five waves and know where they each start and end.

While you are gaining expertise, you want to be on the conservative side on how well you can read these. The score you come up with is only as good as your accuracy in determining what the score is. Then, assuming your score is realistic, you must make a determination: At what score are you going to enter a trade?

I cannot tell you which score to use for your own personal trading. Certainly I do not advise trading a wave count that has a low total score. Depending on your tolerance for risk, you will need to come up with a score that is right for you.

Since the first order of business is to stay in business, you must manage your money and risk and preserve your capital. You will not succeed by relying on luck. You will succeed by learning what you are doing, becoming more proficient with time, and having a rule-based trading approach. Like medicine or law, this is a business that can be learned.

Connecting the Dots

If you have read and studied all the chapters this far, you have learned how to combine several key studies and components to increase your probabilities to accurately count Elliott Waves. While most courses focus on just one or two of these components, you have learned six areas of importance to increase accuracy. This is what has made our Elliott Wave forecasts so accurate over the last 20 years. And, I'm confident that these techniques will improve your accuracy as well if you study and learn them and apply them to your trading.

Real-Life Case Studies

CHAPTER 8

My Favorite Trade Setups

In this chapter you will learn some of my favorite trade setups. These setups can be used on all time frames and all markets, and on both bullish and bearish trend breakouts. Master these and you will be well on your way to success.

FLAT BOTTOM CHANNEL BREAKOUTS

The flat bottom channel breakout is one of my favorites. When the trend emerges it really moves. The purpose of this setup is to get into the trade in time for Wave 3. You don't want to miss Wave 3 because it has the greatest potential for profit.

To scan markets for this type of setup, we have a scanner at TradersCoach.com® called the ART® Scanner that can scan for bracketed and channeled markets and help to uncover these breakouts. Most charting platforms also have scanners built in, and you can use them to find these bracketed markets. You can find information on TradersCoach.com and on charting platforms in the appendixes at the back of this book.

The breakout will be the beginning of a new trend that should unfold as a five-wave impulsive Elliott Wave trend. Flat bottom breakouts can have huge and very profitable gains. Here are a few examples (Figures 8.1 through 8.3).

FIGURE 8.1 AMMRQ daily chart with a flat bottom breakout, which is one of my favorite setups. This shows how profitable a trade can be when it breaks out of a flat bottom channel and begins a major trend.

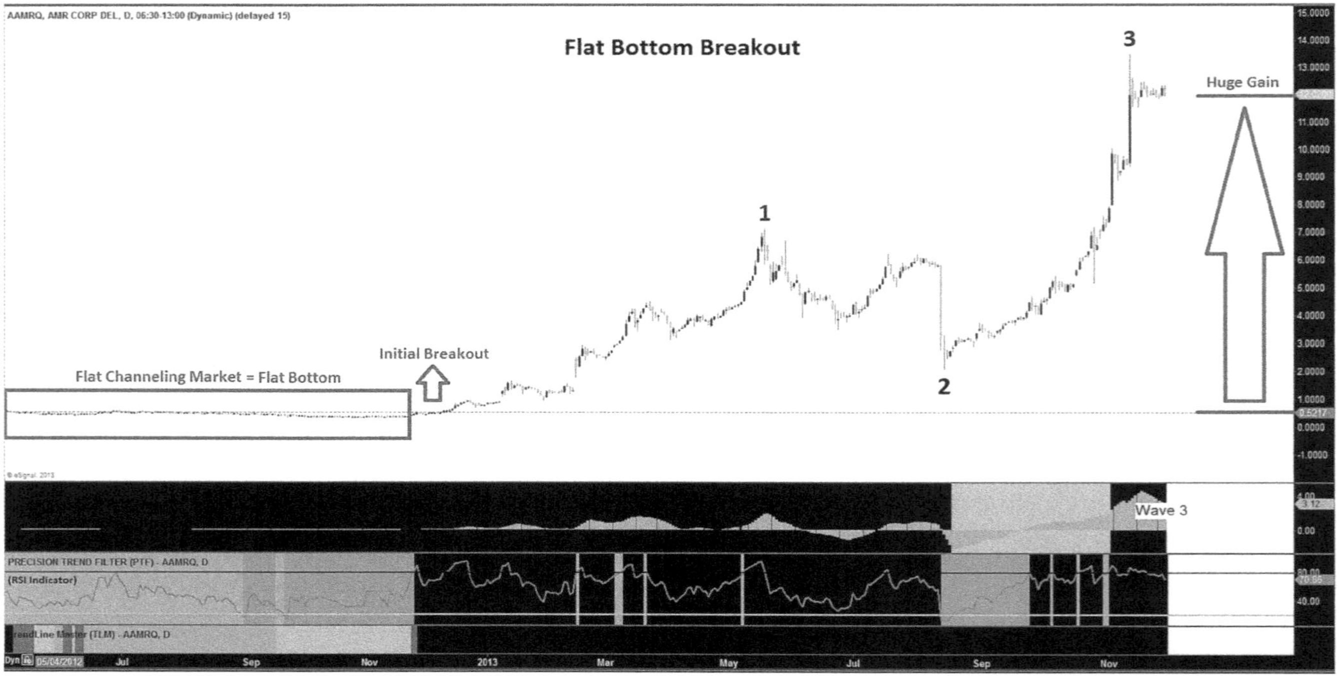

FIGURE 8.2 **SPWR daily chart with a flat bottom breakout**

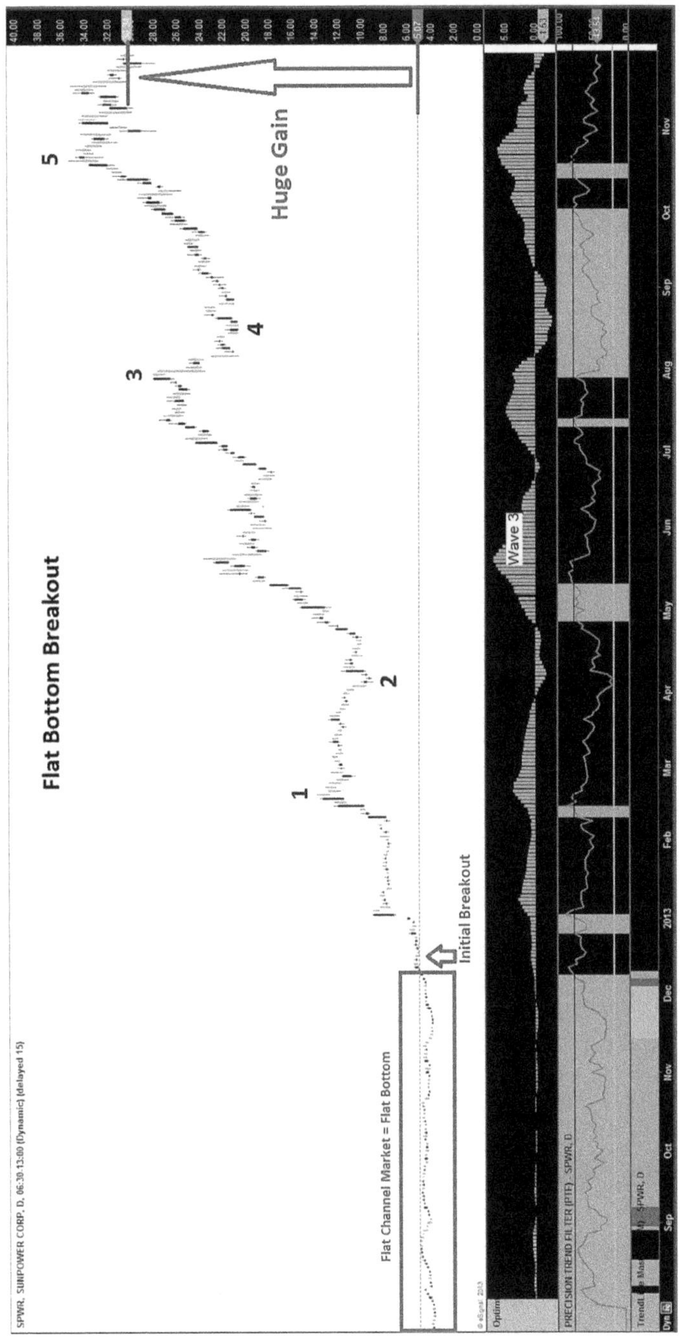

FIGURE 8.3 **LEE daily chart with a flat bottom breakout**

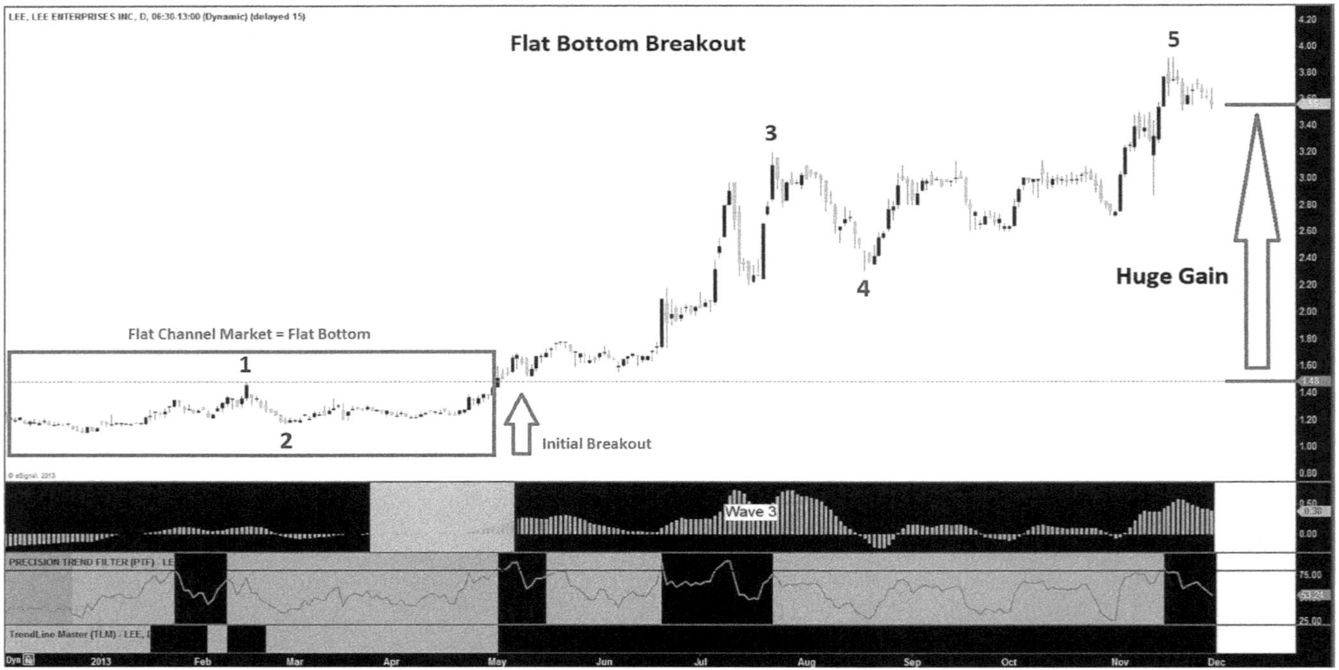

BULLISH FLAT BOTTOM CHANNEL BREAKOUT TRADE RULES

Channel breakouts occur at the beginning of a new trend. The purpose of trading this pattern is to get into the trend early enough so that you catch Wave 3.

Scan to locate opportunities for this setup, and when you do, here are step-by-step instructions on how to enter this trade on a bullish trend.

1. Identify the most recent area after a big trend down where prices are basing and channeling—preferably after the completion of a recent bearish Wave 5 marking the end of that trend.
2. The channel needs to be narrow and at least 20 price bars long. The longer and narrower the channel is, the better. See the bottom left side of the chart in Figure 8.1 for a visual example of what to look for.
3. Draw two horizontal lines, one marking the resistance at the top of the channel and one marking the support at the bottom of the channel. This makes it easier to see the channel and notice visually when prices break out of the channel.
4. Set an alarm in your charting platform to alert you when prices break above the upper line of the channel and break out above the resistance price level.
5. When prices do break above the upper line of the channel, this is called a *channel breakout.*
6. Next, wait for a higher low and then a higher high after the channel breakout before initiating a trade.
7. The trade should be initiated when prices go above the second higher high. (Or if you use the ART Trading Software by TradersCoach.com, wait for a bullish Pyramid Trading Point® entry signal.)
8. The price oscillator histogram (or OWL indicator) needs to also be bullish (with a positive value above the zero line) for a long trade.
9. Initial stop-loss goes below the higher low, if close enough at the low of the channel where support line is.

10. Trail your stops in subsequent higher lows, which will represent new levels of price support on the bullish trend. (Or if you use the ART Trading Software by Traders Coach.com, wait for a Pyramid Trading Point signal.)

BEARISH FLAT BOTTOM CHANNEL BREAKOUT TRADE RULES

Scan to locate opportunities for this setup, and when you do, here are step-by-step instructions on how to enter this trade on a bearish trend.

1. Identify the most recent area after a big trend up where prices are channeling. Preferably after the completion of a recent bullish Wave 5 marking the end of that trend.
2. The channel needs to be narrow and at least 20 price bars long. The longer and narrower the channel is, the better. See the bottom left side of the chart of Figure 8.1 for a visual example of what to look for. (Figure 8.1 is a bullish example, bearish will be the same except it breaks out in the opposite direction.)
3. Draw two horizontal lines, one marking the resistance at the top of the channel and one marking the support at the bottom of the channel. This makes it easier to see the channel and notice visually when prices break out.
4. Set an alarm in your charting platform to alert you when prices break below the lower line of the channel and break out below the support price level.
5. When prices do break below the lower line of the channel, this is also called a *channel breakout.*
6. Next, wait for a lower high and then lower low after the channel breakout before initiating a trade.
7. The trade should be initiated when prices go above the second lower low. (Or if you use the ART Trading Software by TradersCoach.com, wait for a bearish Pyramid Trading Point signal.)
8. The price oscillator histogram (or OWL Indicator) needs to also be bearish (with a negative value below the zero line) for a short trade.

9. Put your initial stop-loss below the lower high or if close enough at the high of the channel where the upper resistance line is.
10. Trail your stops in subsequent lower highs, which will represent new levels of price support on the bearish trend. (Or if you use the ART Trading Software by Traders Coach.com, wait for a Pyramid Trading Point signal.

CATCHING BULLISH AND BEARISH WAVE 5 BREAKOUTS

Using Fibonacci retracement price levels, we can time the end of Wave 4 and look for Wave 5 to emerge. The key is to use Fibonacci retracement price target zones and then look for momentum to come back and take out a key level of resistance, take the trade, and place your stop-loss exit one tick on the other side of Wave 4.

It is important, when you can justify a Wave 5 entry, to be sure you're getting in early enough so that there is enough profit potential based on the Fibonacci price extension target zone. I suggest at least a 2:1 reward-to-risk ratio. If there is not enough, pass on the trade and look for another.

Here are a couple of examples of bullish Wave 5 breakouts (Figures 8.4 and 8.5). You'll notice in Figure 8.4, the Wave 4 price target zone is marked, based on the classic Fibonacci retracement price levels. And in Figure 8.5, the Wave 5 price target zone is marked, based on the classic Fibonacci extension price levels.

FIGURE 8.4 DZZ daily chart showing Fibonacci Wave 4 price target zone and a Wave 5 breakout setup, which is another one of my favorites.

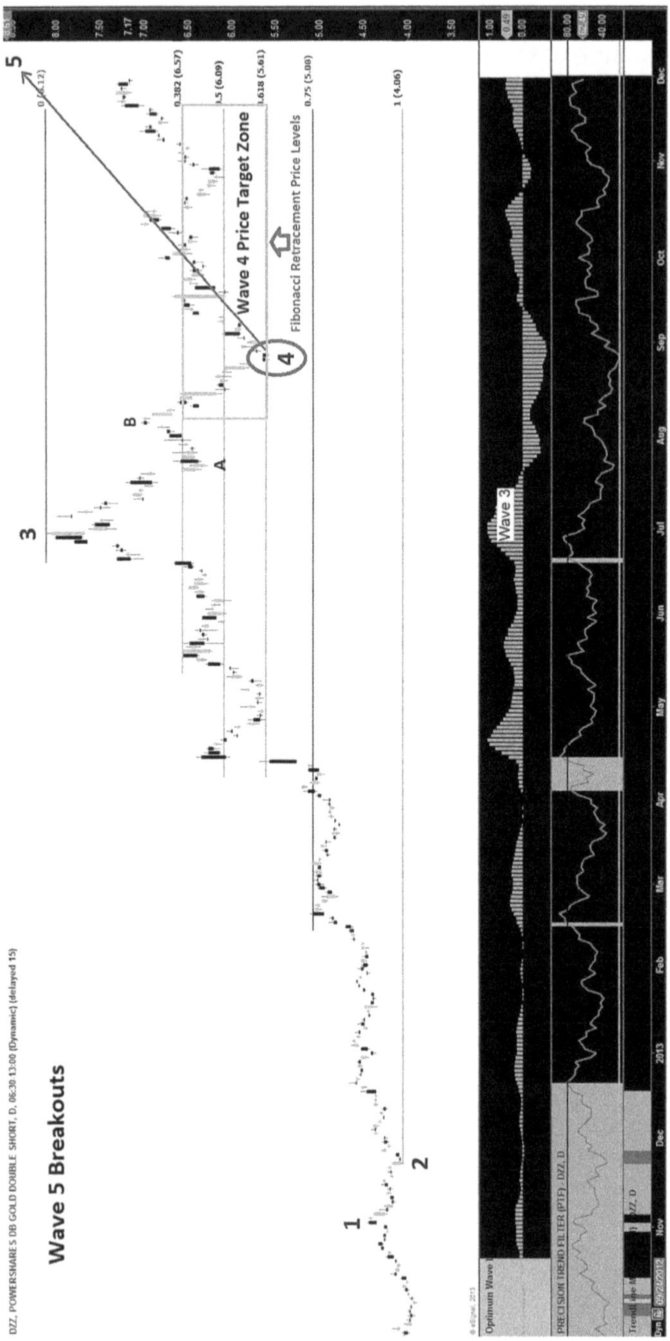

FIGURE 8.5 DZZ daily chart showing Fibonacci price extension levels for a Wave 5 target zone.

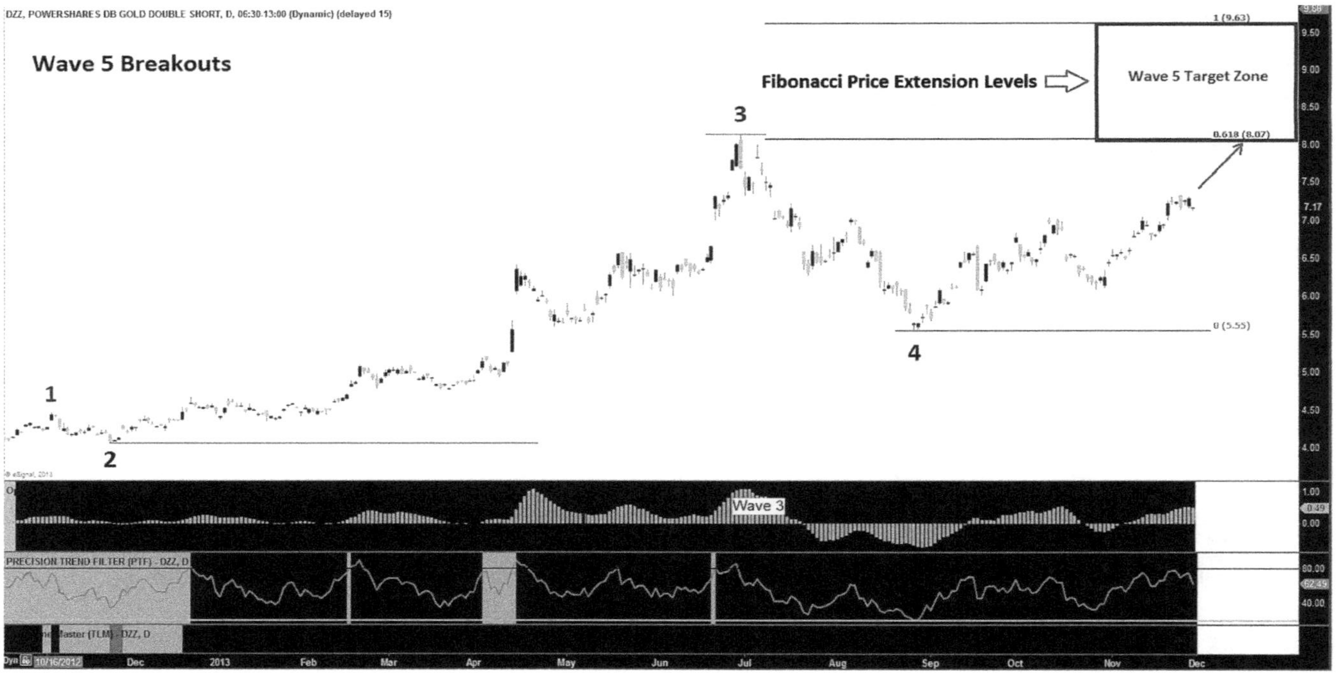

FIGURE 8.6 **TSLA daily chart showing the trend emerging from a flat bottom breakout, and on the far right of the chart, once Wave 4 ends, we look for a Wave 5 breakout.**

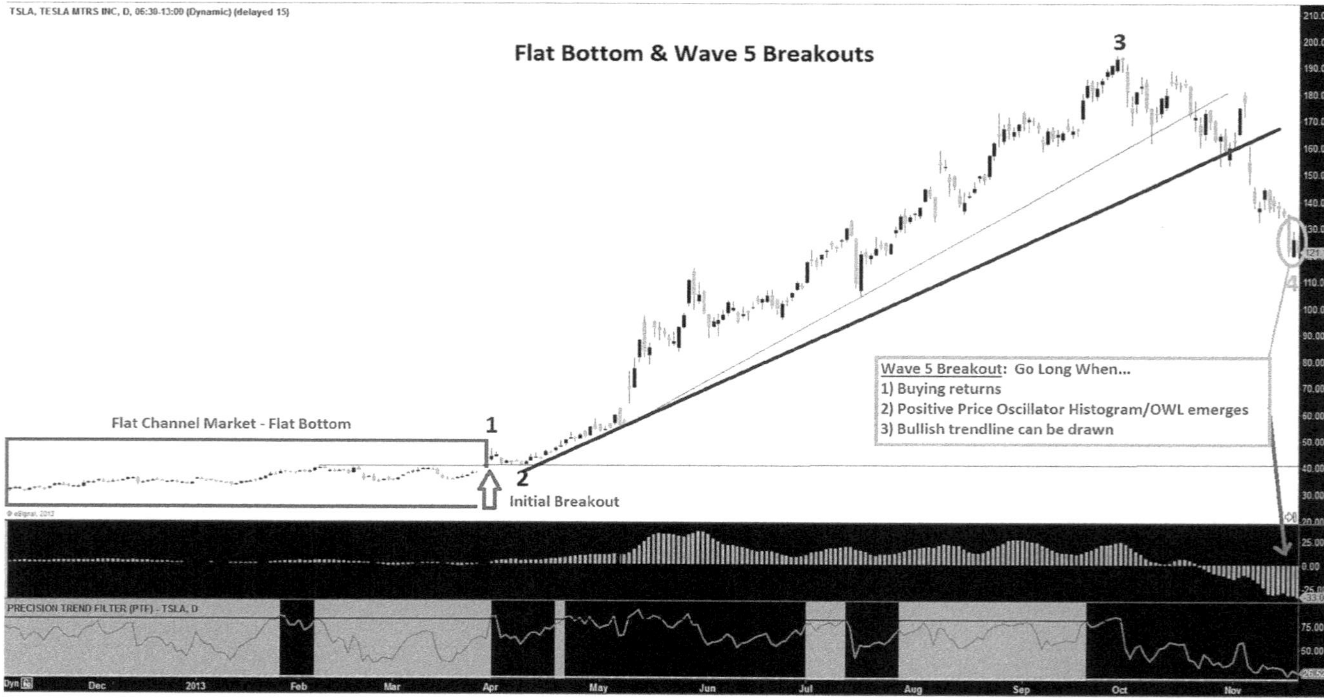

Figure 8.6 shows a chart with *both* flat bottom and Wave 5 breakouts. This TSLA trade was one that I was able to catch very early because of my Elliott Wave techniques. It was a trade I posted in my stock picking service for my clients, and, as you can imagine, it was one of my favorite trades that year.

BULLISH "CATCHING WAVE 5" TRADE RULES

The purpose of trading this pattern is to get in early enough just after Wave 4 ends to ride the entire run of Wave 5. You must get in early enough so you lock in profit before Wave 5 reaches its target zone, which is when the trend changes direction.

Scan to locate opportunities for this setup, and when you do, here are step-by-step instructions on how to enter this trade on a bullish trend.

1. Identify the most recent bullish Wave 3.
2. Next draw in the Fibonacci Wave 4 high probability target zone using the Fibonacci Retracement line tool. Use Wave 2 and Wave 3 as anchoring points. (See Figure 8.4.)
3. Wait for a bearish correction that retraces into the Fibonacci Wave 4 target zone (38.2 to 61.8 percent).
4. If the retracement does not reach the high probability target zone or exceeds 75 percent, do not trade, and instead move on to another market to trade.
5. Once prices reach the high probability Wave 4 target zone, look for bullishness to return.
6. The price oscillator histogram (or OWL Indicator) needs to also be bullish (with a positive value above the zero line) for a long trade.
7. Next draw in the Fibonacci Wave 5 high probability target zone (61.8 to 100 percent) using the Fibonacci Extension line tool.
8. Next, wait for a higher low and then higher high after the Wave 4 low before initiating a trade.
9. The trade should be initiated when prices go above the second higher high. (Or if you use the ART Trading

Software by TradersCoach.com, wait for a bullish Pyramid Trading Point entry signal).

10. Place your initial stop-loss exit below the bottom of Wave 4 or the most recent key level of support that formed after Wave 4.
11. Trail your stops under key levels of support, especially after Wave B (in Wave 4) has been breached by higher prices associated with Wave 5.
12. When prices enter the Wave 5 target zone, trail your stops aggressively using the three-bar-back stop-loss method (place your stop at the bottom of the third price bar to the left of current prices). Or if you use the ART Trading Software by TradersCoach.com, wait for a Pyramid Trading Point exit signal.
13. Exit 100 percent of the trade if stop trade when prices go below the low of this third price bar, or if using the ART Trading Software by TradersCoach.com, wait for a bullish Pyramid Trading Point exit signal.

BEARISH "CATCHING WAVE 5" TRADE RULES

Scan to locate opportunities for this setup, and when you do, here are step-by-step instructions on how to enter this trade on a bearish trend.

1. Identify the most recent bearish Wave 3.
2. Next draw in the Fibonacci Wave 4 high probability target zone using the Fibonacci Retracement line tool. Use Wave 2 and Wave 3 as anchoring points.
3. Wait for a bullish correction that retraces into the Fibonacci high probability Wave 4 target zone (38.2 to 61.8 percent).
4. If the retracement does not reach the high probability target zone or exceeds 75 percent, do not trade, and instead move on to another market to trade.
5. Once prices reach the high probability Wave 4 target zone, look for bearishness to return.

6. The price oscillator histogram (or OWL Indicator) needs to also be bearish (with a negative value below the zero line) for a short/sell trade.
7. Next draw in the Fibonacci Wave 5 high probability target zone (61.8 to 100 percent) using the Fibonacci Extension line tool.
8. Next, wait for a lower high and then lower low after the Wave 4 low before initiating a trade.
9. The trade should be initiated when prices go below the second lower low. Or if you use the ART Trading Software by TradersCoach.com, wait for a bearish Pyramid Trading Point entry signal.
10. Place initial stop-loss exit above the top of Wave 4 or the most recent key level of support formed after Wave 4.
11. Trail your stops above key levels of support, especially after Wave B (in Wave 4) has been breached by lower prices associated with Wave 5.
12. When prices enter the Wave 5 target zone, trail your stops aggressively using the three-bar-back stop-loss method (place your stop at the top of the third price bar to the left of current prices). Or if you use the ART Trading Software by TradersCoach.com, wait for a bearish Pyramid Trading Point exit signal.
13. Exit 100 percent of the trade if stop trade when prices go above the low of this third price bar, or if using the ART Trading Software by TradersCoach.com, wait for a bearish Pyramid Trading Point exit signal.

PENNANT BREAKOUTS

Pennants usually form during corrections. This means they occur most often in Waves 2 and 4. If you see one in Wave 2, take it, because it will get you in early enough for Wave 3, which is the big moneymaker.

On the chart in Figure 8.7, notice Elliott Wave numbers 1 and 2 and the Wave 3 target zone. You will also see a pennant just before the market sold off. Pennants are important to recognize because of the dramatic price movements that occur when they are breached. As prices become compressed, the market acts like a volcano where pressure is building inside.

As traders wait for new news to enter the market, the pressure mounts and eventually must be released. When new news does enter the market and traders react, it is sudden and abrupt.

You will usually see a hyperbolic move out of the pennant in one direction or the other depending on the traders' reaction to the news. The breakout move usually follows in the direction of the Elliott Wave impulsive trend because the "smart money" has already determined the trend with the initial Wave 1.

To anticipate the direction of the price breakout, look to find Wave 1, and that will tell you the most likely direction of where prices are headed. This is because Wave 1 is usually also the initial breakout from the channel.

Pennants usually form inside Waves 2 or 4, which accounts for the dramatic Wave 3 or Wave 5 that will follow. When you see prices begin to be compressed and a pennant does form, get ready to take the trade if that fits within your trading rules.

Pulling It All Together

Now that you've learned about my approach to using the Elliott Wave, and how I like to combine what I call the classic and the modern techniques to arrive at a more accurate wave count, take a look at these charts in Figures 8.8 and 8.9 to see how we can pull it all together.

FIGURE 8.7 DJIA daily chart with pennant—May 2008 to October 2008 shows how to effectively use these technical analysis tools to bring together the classic and modern Elliott Wave approaches to form an accurate forecast.

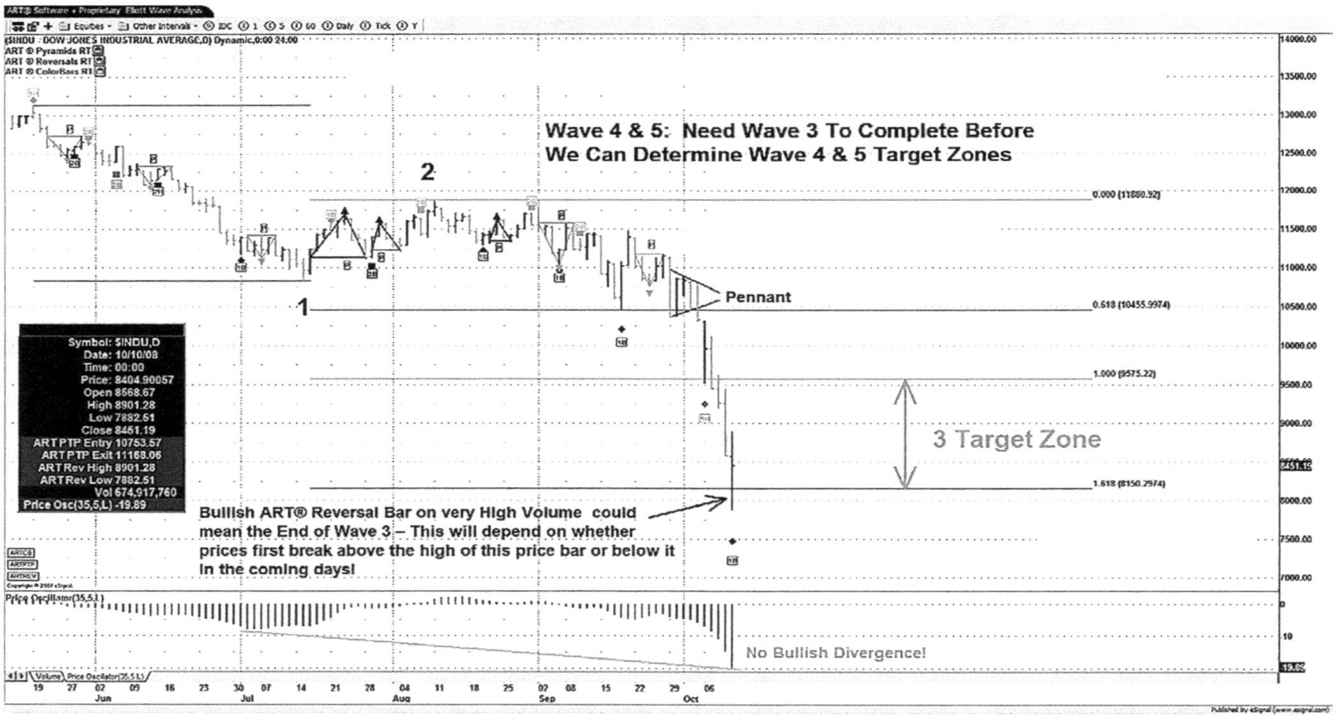

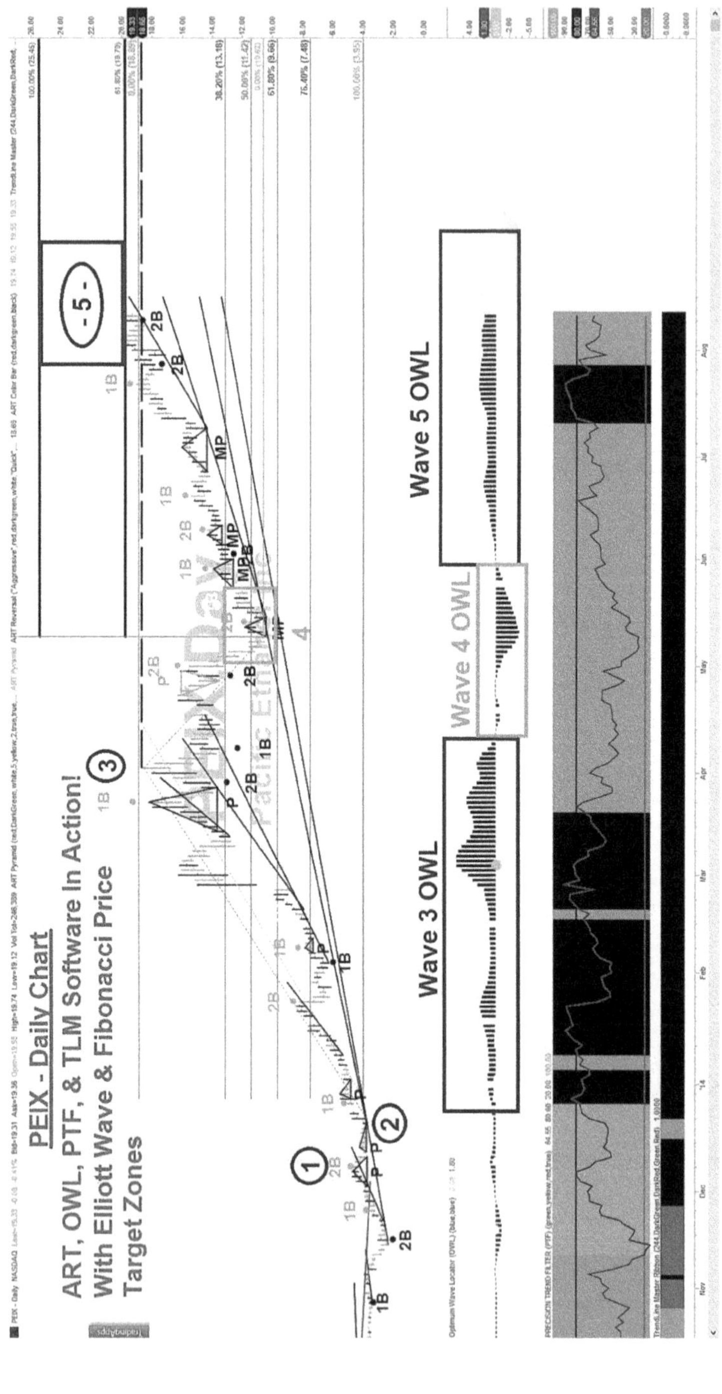

FIGURE 8.8 PEIX daily chart combining the classic and modern Elliott Wave approach to achieve a high probability Elliott Wave forecast.

FIGURE 8.9 AAPL daily chart pulls all the concepts together for a better forecast.

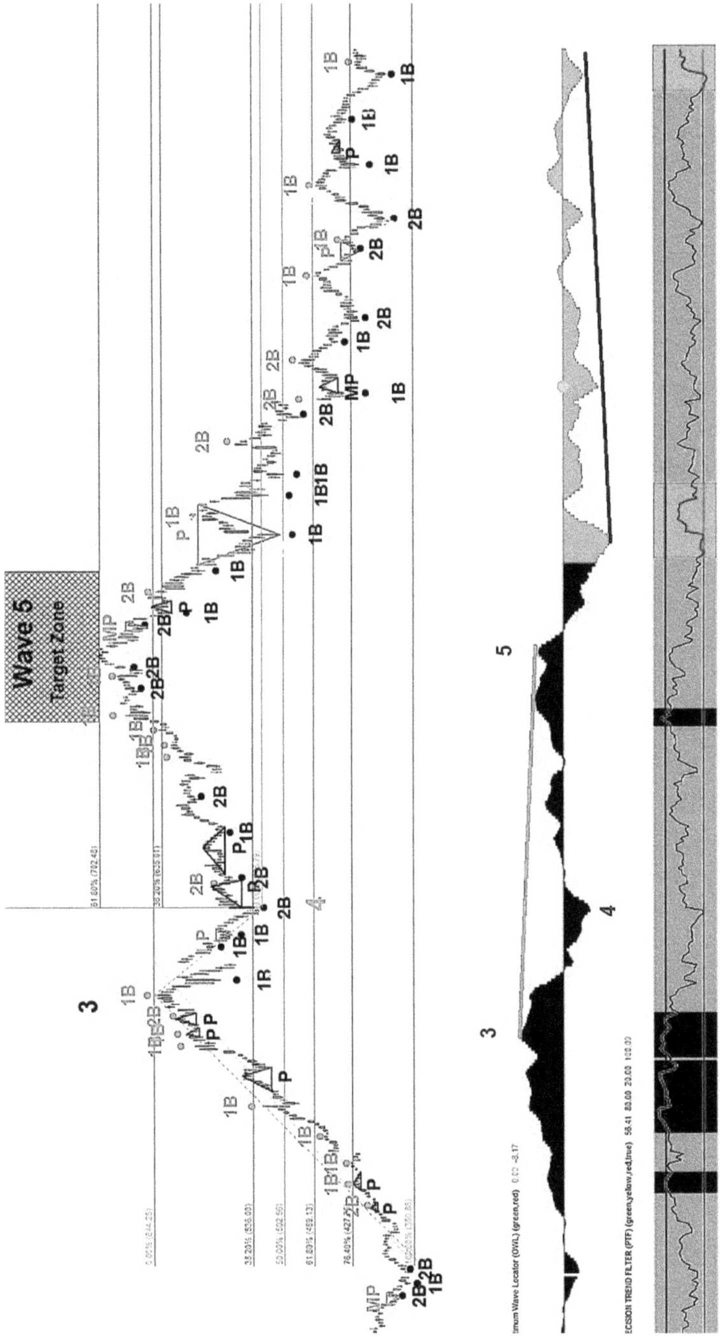

You can see here that knowing what the wave count is can really help us to enter and exit trades at the best times to make the maximum profit. We all know that timing the markets exactly is never possible, but if we can improve our timing even a small amount by using the waves, we can dramatically improve our end-of-year net gains.

My Advice Is to Stay Out of Messy Markets

My students hear me say all the time, "If you don't see a clear wave count, then move on to another chart!" I'm a big fan of avoiding what I call *messy markets* because there is unlimited opportunity in the universe and in the markets, and it is pointless to try and force a wave count on a chart that simply doesn't have one.

Typically messy markets are going to end up becoming complex corrections, and yes, I'm sure there are traders that enjoy trading these markets. For me, though, and especially for newer traders, these markets do not have enough of a reward-to-risk ratio. My time is better spent on the higher probability trades.

You of course can choose to either take my advice or not, you need to find what works for you.

How I Make Money in the Financial Markets

In closing, I want to caution you that 90 percent of traders lose money. These are the amateurs who simply do not know what they are doing. They trade by guessing with their emotions. They view trading as a hobby. Or, they refuse to take the time and effort it takes to learn how to trade successfully and make it a business. And yes, this is a business that can be learned.

Professional traders, on the other hand, *have* taken the time and effort to learn trading as a business. And, since there is a winner and a loser for every trade, *amateurs are necessary* in the marketplace for professionals to profit. Amateurs usually lack a structured approach that can produce consistent profits. And amateurs have not developed the trader's mindset.

In short-term trading, markets are driven by reactions to news and events. Some of these reactions are logical, while others are emotional. Amateur traders usually trade more from an emotional mindset, whereas professional traders use a systematic, objective approach that includes risk control.

However, in order for the professionals to profit, they rely on an *emotional market* as well. They rely on the underlying market emotions that cause market swings which they exploit for a profit. And what better tool for reading emotions in the market than Elliott Wave?

So the way I make money in the financial markets is by having a healthy respect for their power and by learning something new every day. Of course I learned Elliott Wave many years ago, but had I not explored new frontiers like the wave theory my trading would not be what it is right now.

I want you to push the envelope, and continue to learn something new every single day, even after you think you know everything ☺ and I think that is how you too will make money in the markets.

MY CLOSING THOUGHTS AND WISHES FOR YOU

Having studied this book, you will now have the tools you need to exploit and profit from emotional traders in the market. I'm hoping that you will be professional in your trading and that these ideas will arm you with the knowledge you need to profit on a consistent basis. And, I'm hoping that you remember to always use risk control on every trade you take.

May All Your Dreams Come True

And finally, my sincerest wish for you is that all your dreams come true. The best of luck and good fortune to you in your trading and your life. The universe has much to offer you if you are willing to ask for it, so don't be afraid to ask.

You may be pleasantly surprised at the outcome—I know I have been.

CHAPTER 9

A Student's Perspective

By Dean Jenkins of
www.FollowMeTrades.com

My name is Dean Jenkins, and I've been a student of Bennett McDowell's for around three years. By telling you my story, my hope is that you will see the value of Elliott Wave techniques and will be encouraged to implement them into your trading and investing if you haven't already done so.

Intel Corporation Trade from 2000

It was September 21, 2000, and I was sitting in a lecture hall at the UW Foster School of Business. I was in my final year of the Executive MBA program. I should've been listening to the professor's lecture, whatever it was—in retrospect, listening to the lecture would have been much more profitable. Instead, I was online and reading the earnings report from my employer, Intel Corp., and watching the after-hours trading. The earnings report was negative, and INTC dropped from $61.48 to about $45. At this point I had worked for Intel for seven years and had watched the stock double and split every two years like clockwork.

I was heavily invested in INTC through stock option grants and the employee stock purchase program. I had done really well with INTC and other tech stocks through the latter part of the nineties. Who hadn't? The market went straight up!

When the stock dropped on earnings, I thought "buy on the dip, great opportunity!" After all, I was a great stock picker and had made good money. I bought heavily at $45—and about a year later closed the position at $14.

You can see the chart of this trade in Figure 9.1. In Figure 9.2 you can see the same trade, except on this chart I marked where the Elliott Waves were. If I had only known then what I know now!

Let me say that this particular trade is quite memorable, because after 14 years I still get to claim $3,000 per year of the loss on my taxes, and I will continue to have this honor for several years to come. A $90,000 loss divided by $3,000 equals a lot of years of deductions.

Now, as I look back at the INTC chart for that time period (Figure 9.2), using Elliott Wave techniques and the analysis tools I have now, the picture couldn't be clearer that it was time to *short* this stock, well ahead of the earnings announcement.

There were two major problems with my trade: (1) I was basing it purely on what I thought the market *should* do, not the *realities* of the price action, and (2) I had no risk control in place, whatsoever. Not only did I not define how much I was willing to lose, I really wasn't willing to lose any money. I fully expected large gains and was not prepared, at all, for what happened.

After the INTC trade and a few others like it, I lost my appetite for trading. It wasn't fun anymore. In the early 2000s I just put my money in index funds and let it sit. Eventually I wasn't even comfortable with that and moved it to money funds and was happy that it earned a few percentage points and didn't go down in value. It was pure luck that I made this move in mid-2008 and avoided the big decline of 2008–2009.

FIGURE 9.1 Intel Corporation, INTC, trade from September 2000 to October 2001, where I lost $90,000. This trade was made before I knew how to use Elliott Wave Analysis and risk control.

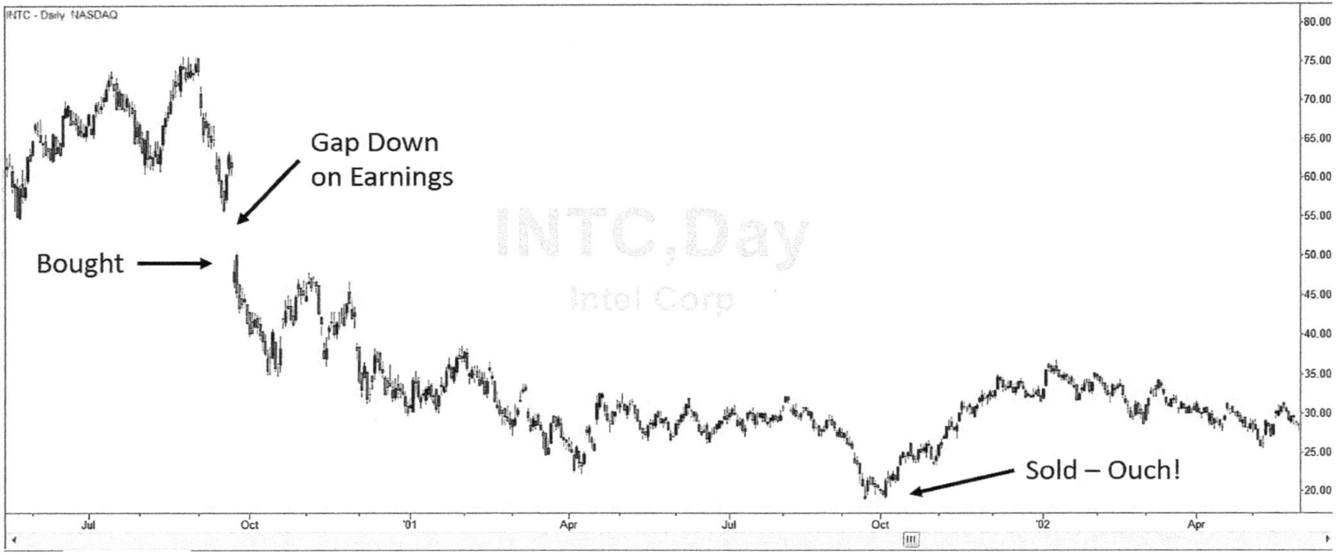

FIGURE 9.2 This is the same trade as Figure 9.1, except that this chart shows how the Elliott Wave pattern was so clear. If I had known how to use wave counts, I would have made a short entry instead of a long entry and would have made a nice profit instead of a loss.

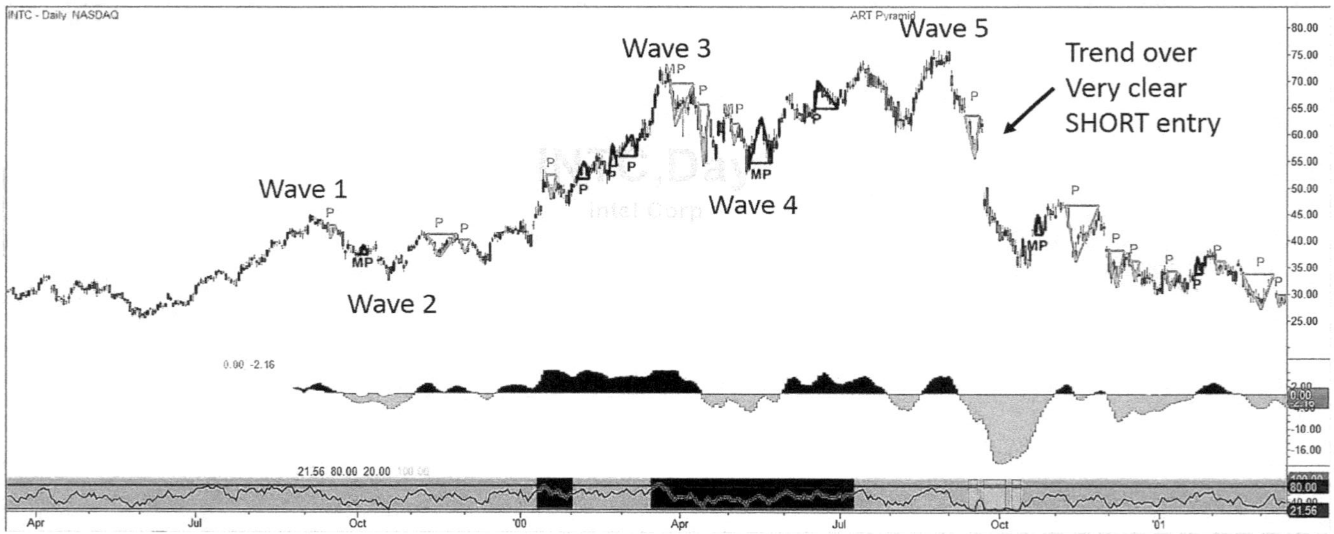

BOA TRADE FROM 2011

Here is a happier story, sort of.

In late 2011 I was ready to try investing and trading again. I say investing and trading because I didn't really have a strategy or a plan. There was no definition for what I was doing. I just wanted my money to gain some value. On December 20, 2011, I decided to buy stock in Bank of America (Figure 9.3).

Basically, I bought into the "too big to fail" narrative that was pervading the news at the time. I noted that BAC had come down from the mid-fifties to about $5. Surely Bank of America wasn't going to go out of business. If anything, the government would bail them out, right? So, I bought shares in BAC at $5.25, a lot of shares. About one-third of my net worth in BAC shares.

I held them until February 21, 2013, and sold at $12.25, a 233 percent gain.

Who could argue with a result like that?

Well, there were a few problems with this trade as well. Three problems, to be exact: (1) I was stressed out for over a year! I had too much money in this trade and could not afford to have it fail. Every day I checked the stock price and agonized over whether to sell it or hold it. (2) Once again, I had no risk control in place, no defined exit point if things didn't work out and the stock went down. I wasn't mentally prepared, or willing, for the trade to be a loss, I could only accept a win. (3) I had no idea of when to get out of the trade and take my profit. Would it keep going up? Would it go down? I had no idea and finally just closed the trade, with profit.

You can see the chart for this trade in Figure 9.3. And then in Figure 9.4 you can see what my strategy would have been using the approach I use today. My current approach puts me in control and limits my risk, so there is far less stress.

Once again, as I look back at the chart for BAC (Figure 9.4), using Elliott Wave and the tools I now have, I see things differently. There are two or three really clear trades in BAC that

FIGURE 9.3 BOA trade from December 2011 to February 2013, where I made a nice profit but was stressed out for a year because I had not used sound risk control.

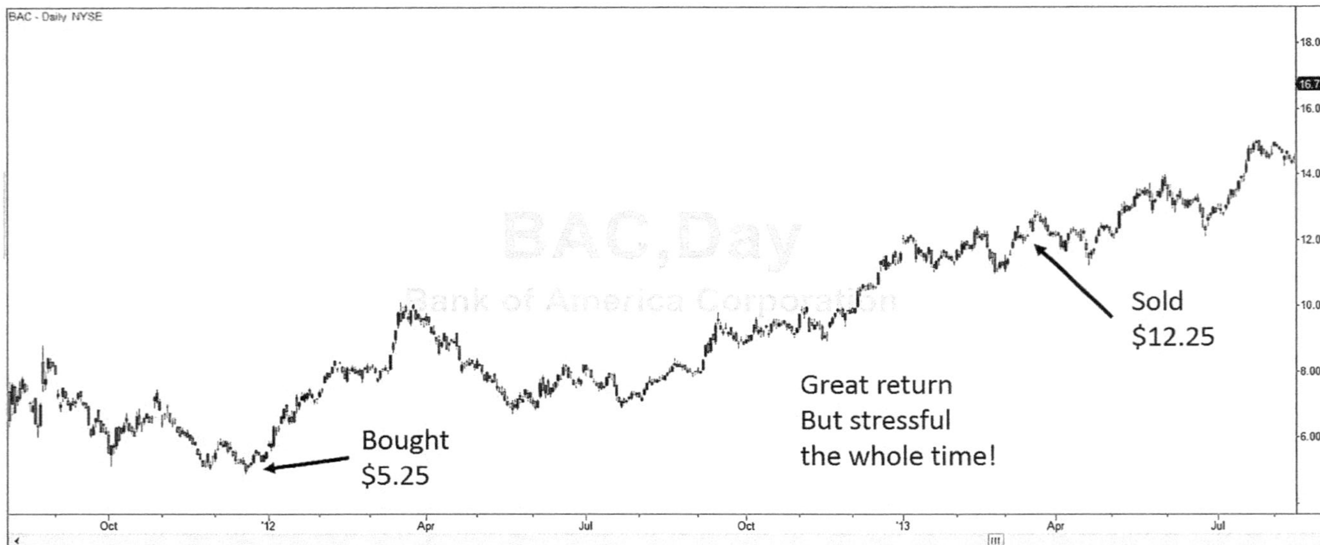

FIGURE 9.4 The same trade as in Figure 9.3, but here I've marked what my strategy would have been had I known then what I know now.

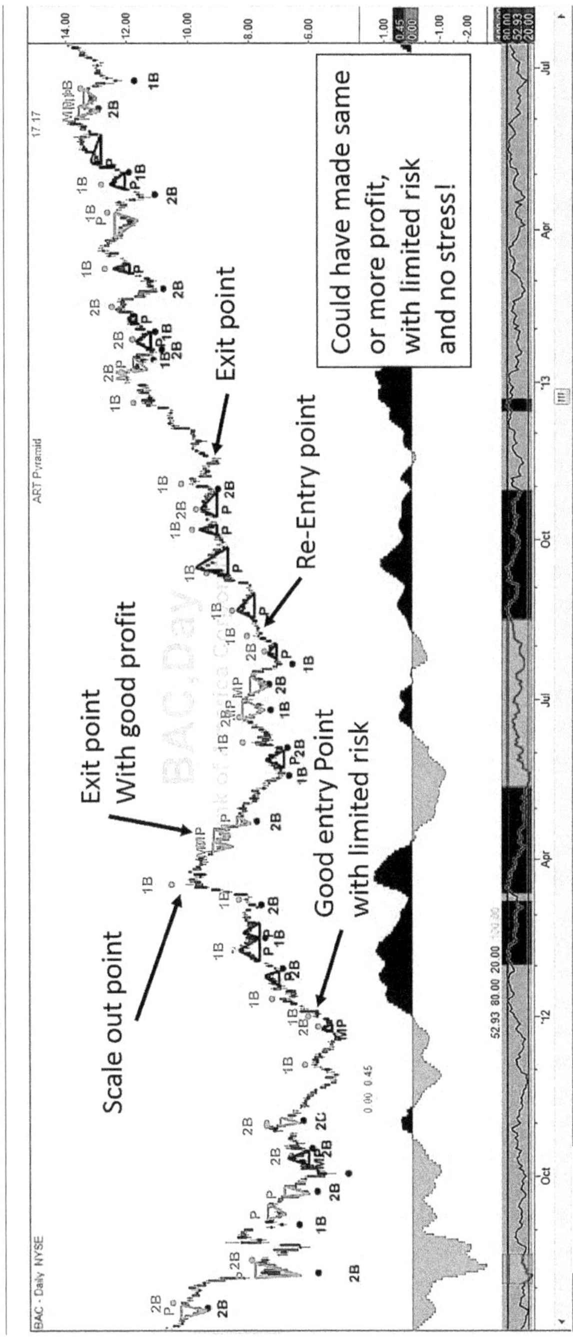

I could have taken, using the reality of price action and Elliott Wave and ART trading that would have been low-risk, low-stress trades and would have netted me even *more* profit in *shorter* time frames than the trade I actually executed.

I had always thought that stocks seemed to move in patterns and that there must be a way to analyze those patterns and be able to predict with some degree of probability what a stock was going to do. I have an MBA and can do all kinds of fundamental analysis for a company. I can read balance sheets and earnings statements. I can calculate ratios, and I understand what EBITA means. I can evaluate a company's products, market position, and management effectiveness.

What frustrated me was that stock price didn't seem to do what I thought it *should* do. Good company, good products, good management, good earnings report. Stock price should go up, right? Why did it go down? I recall from business school the concept of "market efficiency" and "perfect information." The basic idea is that whatever information I have, the rest of the market has too, and is acting on it. In many cases, others may have faster and better information than I do. It seemed that the market was moving more on the *expectation* of information than on the actual information itself.

Here is a great quote from when I was in business school, from Benjamin Graham (considered to be the grandfather of investing): "In the short term, the stock market behaves like a voting machine, but in the long term it acts like a weighing machine (i.e., its true value will in the long run be reflected in its stock price)."[1] If the market is efficient and has perfect information and is "voting," acting on emotion more than on fundamentals, how could I have a chance? How could I consistently get gains? Was it possible? I saw patterns, but could they be predicted, ahead of time, for gain?

These questions started me on the journey of learning that led me to Elliott Wave analysis and the Applied Reality Trading (ART) system. I have learned that the market often does move in predictable patterns and that it is possible to identify high probability trades and to capitalize on them.

The Importance of Money Management

Even more important, I think, than price action patterns, I learned about risk management and how to define and minimize my risk and exposure on each and every trade. I was amazed to learn that even with a mediocre trading system, one that only wins 50 percent of the time, it is possible to be profitable if you have really good risk control in place and if your wins are bigger than your losses. And if you have a really good trading system, with good risk control—it is possible to do really, really well.

My Personal Performance Results

I'm extremely satisfied with my own personal results. After going through Bennett's ART system training, his Elliott Wave course, and one-on-one coaching, I can report that I've placed trades of stocks and exchange-traded funds (ETFs) that I've found on my own, based on my own ART and Elliott Wave analysis. Seventy-seven percent of those trades have been profitable, and I have a payout ratio of 2.6, meaning that the amount I've won is 2.6 times the amount I've lost. You can see my results from calendar year January to December 2014 in Figure 9.5. The year 2015 has not closed out yet, but my success rate has been consistent and similar to 2014.

Those are solid performance numbers by any measure. Not only am I pleased with those results, but more important, I was never exposed, on any given trade, to more than a 2 percent loss of my trading account. Because of that limited risk, I was never uncomfortable or stressed out.

I share these numbers not to boast, but as an illustration.

FIGURE 9.5 Printout of my performance results for 2014 using TradeStation as my broker and my trading platform

TradeStation Performance Summary Page 1 of 1

Dean Jenkins: Equities and Options Account
1/1/2014 - 12/31/2014

TradeStation TradeManager Performance Report

TradeStation Performance Summary

	All Trades	Long Trades	Short Trades
Total Net Profit	$37,365.80	$37,445.80	($80.00)
Gross Profit	$74,153.41	$73,778.41	$375.00
Gross Loss	($36,787.62)	($36,332.62)	($455.00)
Profit Factor	2.02	2.03	0.82
Total Number of Trades	136	133	3
Percent Profitable	70.59%	71.43%	33.33%
Winning Trades	96	95	1
Losing Trades	40	38	2
Even Trades	0	0	0
Avg. Trade Net Profit	$274.75	$281.55	($26.67)
Avg. Winning Trade	$772.43	$776.61	$375.00
Avg. Losing Trade	($919.69)	($956.12)	($227.50)
Ratio Avg. Win:Avg. Loss	0.84	0.81	1.65
Largest Winning Trade	$6,456.00	$6,456.00	$375.00
Largest Losing Trade	($1,691.54)	($1,691.54)	($285.00)
Max. Consecutive Winning Trades	15	15	1
Max. Consecutive Losing Trades	4	4	2
Max. Shares/Contracts Held	n/a	n/a	n/a
Total Shares/Contracts Held	91,523	91,503	20
Account Size Required	n/a	n/a	n/a
Return on Initial Capital	37.37%		
Annual Rate of Return	34.42%		
Return Retracement Ratio	20.52		
RINA Index	n/a		
Trading Period	11 Months, 1 day, 20 hours, 50 Minutes		
Percent of Time in the Market	87.27%		
Max. Equity Run-up(Daily)	$40,370.05		
Max. Drawdown(Daily)			
Value	($11,038.33)	($10,583.33)	($455.00)
Net Profit as % of Drawdown	338.51%	353.82%	-17.58%
Max. Drawdown(Trade Close)			
Value	($10,031.60)	($9,576.60)	($455.00)
Net Profit as % of Drawdown	372.48%	391.01%	-17.58%
Max. Trade Drawdown	($1,669.90)	($1,669.90)	($280.00)

It's not like I have any special qualities or a monster IQ that makes these results possible. I'm convinced that anyone who is willing to invest the time to learn what Bennett is teaching, anyone who has the patience and discipline to study and practice the principles, can succeed. It is not easy, and it does take time and hard work. It takes discipline to define and then follow your own trading rules, based on the principles that Bennett teaches. But if you want to be a professional trader, to enjoy the freedom and fruits that a trading career offers, then it is worth the effort.

PERFECT PRACTICE MAKES PERFECT

Everyone has heard the saying "practice makes perfect." But it is not really true. Vince Lombardi said, "Practice does not make perfect. Perfect practice makes perfect." This makes a lot more sense. Practicing unhealthy habits or incorrect techniques doesn't make someone better at anything, and trading is no different.

What is needed is to learn the basics of a trading system and then to practice using them correctly, over and over again, in a variety of market conditions. This is where coaching comes in. I'm sure it is possible to have a high-quality book like this one and to read it and practice the concepts on your own. The methods are relatively simple and repeatable. But, there is always some subjectivity involved and questions come up, and the charts that you look at and try to analyze will never match the examples perfectly.

When I was first learning Elliott Wave, I would have bookmarks in my training material and printouts of wave patterns taped to my desk. I referred to the material and wave patterns constantly. With every chart I looked at, I asked myself, "Is there a Wave 3? A Wave 1 and 2? Where do I put the retracement lines and the extension lines?" In most cases, I was trying to analyze charts that didn't have any pattern at all.

During my first couple of coaching sessions with Bennett, I would bring up a chart and start trying to analyze it, and Bennett would say, "There is no pattern here, it's a mess, move on!" That was valuable. We would then find a chart with a promising pattern and work on it. He would have me analyze it and then give me feedback on my work, make corrections, and use the chart in front of us to point things out. I typically scan about 100 stock charts per week, and it doesn't take me that long. I can look at a chart and within a few seconds know whether it is a pattern that is worth spending time analyzing or not.

I never look at any reference material anymore. I can recognize patterns really quickly and have the key parameters for wave counts memorized, really deeply ingrained. Out of 100 charts, I probably only really spend time looking at and analyzing 5 to 10 of them. The reason I can do this is that, early on in my training, I got help learning how to do this correctly. I learned how to "practice perfectly" and not waste time or get frustrated. I can't emphasize coaching enough in helping to develop both technique and confidence.

STRENGTHEN YOUR TRADING PSYCHOLOGY

In addition to helping to learn the fundamentals of Elliott Wave, coaching helps with something that is probably even more important—psychology. You can have perfect technical skills and still fail at trading because of psychology.

When I first heard the term *psychology* applied to trading, it sounded kind of weird. What did that mean? Was I going to lie on a couch and talk about my childhood? What did that have to do with trading? I just wanted to pick winning trades and make money.

What I learned was that psychology, as it relates to trading, is about preconceived notions, attitude, expectations, and most important, stress. Psychology helps you to choose the right account size to trade with. If you are trading more money than you can afford to lose, it is going to create stress, and that stress is going to affect how well you trade. That stress will keep you from taking a good trade and make you get out of good trades too early.

A good coach can also help you set realistic expectations for your trading. It is possible to be profitable trading, to make really good money at it. I know this because it has been true for me. But it is tempting to have unrealistic expectations, to think that you will get very wealthy from trading in a short amount of time and that it will be easy. A good coach can help you set realistic expectations and learn to deal with losses.

Losing trades are inevitable and are a part of life for traders. It is essential to learn to take losing trades in stride—to expect them and not to let them shake your confidence or cause you to start fiddling with your trading system. Going through your trades, both winners and losers, with a coach is a great way to build confidence and to develop the trader's mindset that is more concerned with whether you are following your trading rules than with whether a particular trade was a winner or loser.

I really wanted to learn to trade successfully. I thought that it was possible and would fit with my personality and with my life. It would give me the income and flexibility to spend time on things that were really important to me, but that did not generate income. I had spent over 20 years working for high-tech companies, making a really good salary, but increasingly being asked to spend more time and to invest more emotional energy into something that no longer interested me or gave me a sense of purpose and satisfaction.

Trading seemed to be a really good answer. But there was a problem. The term *day trader* had negative connotations for me. I didn't like the picture that came to my mind when I heard it, and I was not comfortable telling people that that was what I did for a living. Having this negative view of the profession was an obstacle that I had to overcome before I could really be successful at trading and have it be something that I was comfortable with, both for myself and my perception of what other people would think of it.

Coaching helped me work through this successfully. I now am quite happy to be a trader and to talk to other people about it. It often starts some pretty interesting conversations. Some people do have a negative view of trading, a lot of misconceptions and so on. But I am comfortable with it, I know who I am and what I am doing, and that makes a big difference.

When I Started . . .

What I really wanted was a "black box" system. I wanted an automated trading system that I could turn on and it would determine trades and place them and manage them, basically a system that ran by itself and printed money. If you find one that does this, please let me know! I say that a bit tongue-in-cheek because I'm convinced that it doesn't exist. Sure there are automated systems, the "high-frequency" systems that are talked about in the news quite a bit, in use at large institutions, but these are not money printing machines.

They have teams of PhD "quants" who continuously revise the trading algorithms as market conditions change. They also have mainframe computers that reside at or close to the exchanges and have connections that allow order execution to take place in microseconds, and they have relationships that enable their fills to happen much quicker than those of retail traders. None of us have access to these kinds of resources. But we can have trading systems, based on Elliott Wave and a few other simple indicators like the ART system, that can make us consistently profitable.

It's hard to remember all of the trading systems that I have evaluated. There have been so many that looked promising. Lots of really impressive graphics and colors and, of course, some examples of trades that the system identified, with large profits.

What I found, the hard way, in evaluating these systems was that they did not adjust to changing market conditions. Just about any system can be optimized for a particular market and period in time and be shown to be profitable.

In TradeStation EasyLanguage I could write a simple moving average strategy in about 30 minutes. This strategy could trigger trades based on moving average crossovers. I could optimize the settings so that it would be very profitable for yesterday's two-minute chart on the S&P 500 e-mini futures market.

But it would lose money on the day before that, and today. Bummer! As I said, I've spent a lot of time on this, and I'm convinced that a consistently profitable "black box" just doesn't exist. It is possible to be consistently profitable, but it is an "art," and it takes some work. It takes learning Elliott Wave, practicing and proving a trading strategy, developing a mature trader's mindset, and then putting in time analyzing charts and trading according to your rules. Just like other areas of life, there is no free lunch in trading.

As I said, I've looked at a lot of trading systems. Not just "black box" automatic systems but other methods that included indicators and chart analysis. I've looked at systems that used the standard indicators that come with all trading platforms, at systems that used proprietary indicators and systems that used pure price action, no indicators at all.

What I found was that no system could produce consistent, repeatable results, for me, the way that Bennett's approach to Elliott Wave does. I'm sure there are other systems out there that are successfully used by traders. But the system has to work for the individual using it. It has to make sense to the individual and fit with the person's personality, thought process, and psychology.

Bennett's approach to Elliott Wave does that for me, and I think it would be the same for a lot of people. Elliott Wave itself can be pretty complicated. There are lots of books available on Elliott Wave and lots of websites with information.

Bennett simplifies the theory to Elliott Wave patterns so that they can be recognized very quickly, and he offers simple guidelines for wave count that anyone can learn, and I like that. He also uses contemporary software tools to help in the wave analysis.

My analysis and trading is based on Bennett's Elliott Wave guidelines and on his ART software to help me identify good, high-probability trades and then define risk management parameters and establish stop-loss points and profit targets and exit points. I've not seen another system that does all of this.

THEY CAN'T AGREE ON WAVE COUNTS

One of the interesting or frustrating things with Elliott Wave theory is that most Elliotticians cannot seem to agree on wave counts. Material on several websites dedicated to Elliott Wave has contradictory information or discusses completely different approaches. When I read through some of this material, I start feeling pretty overwhelmed.

There is so much detail and there are so many exceptions and so many different patterns that I don't think I could apply that information to a chart, to use it in consistent, repeatable analysis.

Bennett's approach simplifies the theory significantly without losing the basic principles that Elliott Wave was founded on. His method helps the trader to focus on a few patterns, on simple tools and techniques to analyze those patterns, and then how to trade them. Again, I think this is a method that most people can learn and use with some study, practice, and a bit of hard work.

TAKING STRESS OUT OF THE EQUATION

Trading should not be stressful. If you are experiencing stress while trading, something is wrong. Something is wrong with either your system or your psychology. I remember being stressed about trades. I think one of the worst feelings, in trading, is not knowing what to do, and that causes stress.

Whether your trade is up for a profit or is underwater with a loss, not having a basis for making decisions about what to do next—whether to close the trade, to scale out or get out completely—is paralyzing and can't help but create stress. Of course it is worse to be in a losing trade and not know what to do.

I've experienced this. I've taken a position only to have it go down and be a loss. And then it keeps going down. I've experienced the feeling of near desperation thinking, "I can't get out now—the loss is too big—I'll have to wait for it to come back up," and then it doesn't. So I ended up staying with it and losing even more.

I've also been on the other side where a trade went up and then I couldn't decide when to get out. I was stressed that I would lose the profit I had but didn't want to miss out if it kept going up. Being caught between the conflicting and stressful emotions of fear and greed at the same time is very uncomfortable.

The way to avoid stress is to have a proven trading system. A system that you *know*, based on testing and experience, will produce predictable results over a wide variety of market conditions. This system *must* include risk control and signals for you to take profit and close the trade. The system must provide a basis for making decisions that are based on the realities of the price action on the chart—not emotions about what you think the price *should* do.

THE PROS AND CONS OF TRADING ON NEWS

News is a funny thing for a trader. I think that to be successful as a trader, you have to pay attention to the news. But it is a two-edged sword. On one hand, the trader needs to be aware of what is going on in the world that is affecting the markets. Particularly when big events and announcements are planned.

Once a month the Federal Open Market Committee (FOMC) releases its meeting minutes and reveals its plans for stimulus, interest rates, and its take on the economy. The market is usually very stagnant leading up to the release of the minutes and then gets volatile afterward. That is very useful to know if you are placing short-term day-trades on intraday time frames. It may be wise to sit things out for a while and let them stabilize and wait for a clear pattern to form. Or it may cause you to scrutinize your stops and targets on existing, open trades.

There are other important reports that come out on a regular basis, things like GDP, employment reports, housing reports, etc. There are free websites that show the economic calendar and which reports are scheduled to be released (for example, see http://www.bloomberg.com/markets/economic-calendar/). I think it is important for a trader, particularly a day trader, to be aware of these news events and to exercise some caution around the times that they are planned to be released.

There are also unscheduled news events that can cause disruption in the markets. Events like this cannot be planned for, but it is helpful, at least for me, to have an idea of why the markets are suddenly moving or becoming unstable. It satisfies some curiosity at least and helps provide some context about what is going on.

For example, as I am writing this, I see a headline on my other monitor. OPEC just released a statement on its decision to continue current production levels in the midst of an oil glut. The article reported that oil futures (which I trade) dropped 8 percent on the news. Eight percent is a *huge* move for the most heavily traded commodity on the planet.

If I hadn't been aware of that news, when I logged into my trading platform and started looking at the oil futures contract I would have been confused and started checking my chart settings and data feed to see if there was some mistake. Now, I know to expect a really dramatic looking chart.

But the other side of the sword is that news can create expectations of what the market should do, what I expect it to do, and it can cause confusion and even stress if the market doesn't do what I expect it to do. Having an expectation of what a particular trading instrument will do is not bad. In fact, I think that is what Elliott Wave analysis helps the trader do.

Analyzing waves is essentially creating a thesis or hypothesis about what the instrument will do next. If I see a clear Wave 1-2-3-4 pattern, and price action then confirms the beginning of Wave 5, I can draw Fibonacci retracement and extension lines and have a solid, data- and reality-based projection of a target where price will go.

This is a healthy expectation and is one of the key patterns that my trading system is based on.

What is not so healthy is when a news story comes out—a company getting FDA approval for a drug, an earnings report, an analyst's upgrade or downgrade for a company—and the news creates an expectation in me about what the stock should do. Before learning Elliott Wave and having a proven trading system and the discipline to follow it, I would be heavily influenced by the news and by my expectations. I would jump into a trade based on the news and then be bewildered when the stock didn't do what it was "supposed" to do.

Think of News as Peripheral Information

Paying attention to the news and staying informed with what is going on in the markets is helpful and I would say necessary for a successful trader. The key that I have learned is to let the news be peripheral information, information that may explain what the market is doing. But all of my trading decisions have to be based on the realities on the chart in front of me, based on my analysis of the chart and my established trading rules.

One of the hardest things for me, still, is when the market doesn't do what I expect. Sometimes I see a report that affects a particular trading instrument, and the report creates an expectation that the market will go down. But the realities on the chart in front of me show a very clear long trade. This creates confusion.

What I've learned is this: I don't have to take every trade. If something about it makes me uncomfortable, I can just move on. If I've been tracking a stock for a while, looking for a short setup, and then things change and the chart shows a long setup, and I just can't believe it, I can just move on. There are thousands of stocks to trade, and I don't have to trade one that is going to cause me stress or confusion because of the news.

The Phenomenon of Target Fixation

There is a phenomenon called *target fixation*. Wikipedia defines it this way:

> The phenomenon is common amongst racing drivers, fighter pilots, motorcyclists, mountain bikers, and surfers, amongst others. When individuals target fixate, they are prone to steer in the direction of their gaze, which is often the ultimate cause of a collision.[2]

I think traders can suffer from a form of target fixation. For example, I could be totally enamored with Apple, Inc. Apple could have a great earnings report, and the newest iPhone is coming out soon and the reviews are awesome. AAPL has to go up, and I want a long position in it. I study the chart and fixate on finding the signs for a good long entry.

What I may miss because of my fixation, my expectation, and my desire to go long on AAPL is that there is no long setup. There may even be a clear short setup, but I can't see it because of my fixation. That is a recipe for a collision! I've learned that I have to keep news and expectations in perspective and to stay focused on the realities on the chart and on the trading system that I trust.

"STALKING" TRADES REQUIRES PATIENCE

I like the term *stalking*. Stalking your ex-wife or girlfriend is bad. Stalking a stock or ETF is good! Last year I read the book *American Sniper* by Chris Kyle, the most successful military sniper in U.S. history. What does that have to do with trading?

Well, in the book, Chris talks about the patience that is needed to be a successful sniper. Sure, you need to be able to shoot well, to understand ballistics and all that. But according to Chris, the most important skill for a sniper is patience. You have to be willing and able to spend hour upon hour waiting in your "hide" for your target. The setup has to be perfect because you usually only get one shot.

Once you take your shot, there is no more surprise; your presence is revealed and you have to hustle out of there. For a sniper, all of the preparation is done up front, and once the shot is taken, it cannot be taken back. Sound familiar? Hunting deer is similar as well. (Sorry if I'm using too many gun references—I'm not a gun nut, but these are good analogies!) I have friends who are passionate about deer hunting. We live in western Washington State. These guys will spend their weekends prior to hunting season driving four to five hours each way over to eastern Washington to walk the hills where they will be hunting during the season. They know the habits of deer, and they study the tracks and all the signs, way in advance of the actual hunt. When the season opens, these guys are in place, and they have a plan and a very good idea about where the prize deer will be and how they will hunt them.

I've been listening to Bennett on conference calls and webinars for about three years now. The most common phrase you will hear him say is "We'll have to wait and see." Another very frequent phrase you will hear is "Let's put that on a watch list." Most of the work of trading is done long before any buy or sell orders are entered on your trading platform.

Most of the time we are "stalking" a trade. We see the beginnings of a pattern, but all of the rules have not been met yet.

It is actually pretty rare to log into your trading platform and have a pattern in front of you that is immediately tradable. The normal thing is to see a pattern that is setting up but needs time to prove itself. So we stalk the trade.

As I go through lists of stocks, ETFs, and futures markets and analyze the charts, I typically reject most of them. But 5 to 10 percent of them are interesting, and I put them on a watch list. I set an automated alert for a particular price level and add a few notes about what I am looking for. When (and if) the alert goes off, I look at the chart and see if what I was expecting to happen, is happening.

Many times I have a two-stage watch list. If a stock is clearly in an impulsive Wave 3 move that looks like it is maturing, I will project what the Wave 4 retracement should be and set an alert for that. Once the Wave 4 alert is triggered, I then calculate the Wave 5 extensions and set an alert for a level that I think will confirm Wave 5 is under way. When (and if) that alert is triggered, I look at the chart again and evaluate whether my rules have been met and decide whether or not to place a trade.

It is not uncommon at all for a stock to sit on my watch list for weeks or even months waiting to trigger. Sometimes they never do, and I occasionally go through and clean up my watch list and remove stocks that didn't pan out. For me, it is much more comfortable to scan for possibilities and add them to my watch list and to stalk them than it is to feel like I have to find a trade, right now.

Just like a sniper or a hunter doesn't just walk in and expect to find targets and start shooting right away, successful traders don't expect trades to magically appear in front of them every time they sit down at the computer. We stalk the trades, and when the conditions are right, when the rules are met, then we pull the trigger.

This was hard for me to learn at first. For most of my working career, I got up in the morning, went to my job, and worked hard. The harder and smarter and longer I worked, the more I succeeded. Trading is not really like that. How many jobs will you have where you will make more money if you take time off? Certainly, to succeed at trading you will have to work hard. But that hard work is in the learning and practicing and then in stalking good trades. The actual amount of time spent "trading" can be very minimal. This is hard to accept for someone with a strong work ethic.

When I first started trading, I would get up very early (I'm on the West Coast, so the market open is at 6:30 a.m. here) at least an hour before the market open, log onto my trading platform, and begin analyzing charts. I expected to start placing trades and making money, just like a "real" job. The problem is, the market didn't really care if I was up out of bed, showered and shaved and ready for work. Good day-trade setups might come right away, or they might be hours away, or they might not come at all during the day. I could spend an entire day staring at charts and not find any good trades.

I felt like I wasn't being productive and that I must be doing something wrong. After all, this is my job, I'm working, why am I not doing anything? Well, welcome to the world of trading!

SOMETIMES THE BEST TRADE IS *NO* TRADE

Because sometimes the most profitable day that day traders can have is the day when they place no trades. Because preserving capital and not losing it on bad trades is *way* more profitable than the alternative. Success as a trader has to be measured on your overall win ratio, your payout ratio and your profitability, not on how often or how many trades you place. A master trader finds satisfaction in following an established trading system, not in being "busy" during the day.

For me, one of the keys is in finding other productive things that I can do at my desk while I'm keeping an eye on the markets. I have reading material, bills to pay, e-mails to answer, webinars to attend, etc., that will keep me completely productive during the trading session if no trades are there. But I have alerts and triggers set up, and I am ready if a good setup appears, and I am ready to give my full attention to the market and the trade if one presents itself.

DAY-TRADING VERSUS LONG-TERM TRADING

This is a good time to talk about the difference between day-trading and other, longer-term trading. My discussion about being at my desk and being ready for a trade is related to day-trading. Day-trading is its own beast.

The same tools, analysis, and rules can be applied to any time frame. The markets have fractal symmetry and follow the same patterns regardless of the time frame. But day-trading happens pretty fast, and you have to be at your computer for a good part of the trading session to take part in it. Day-trading takes a lot of energy and attention, and you have to approach it with that in mind.

You can multitask on other things while waiting for triggers and setups, but you have to be able to drop what you are doing and focus completely on the market and your trade when the setups appear. Longer time frame trading is completely different.

Here is a funny dichotomy. I have 80 percent of my money in my longer-term trading account—mainly daily charts trading stocks, ETFs, and options. I make 90 percent of my profit from this trading account, and I only spend about 10 percent of my time on this.

Ninety percent of my time is spent day-trading about 20 percent of my money on intraday trades on futures contracts, and this accounts for 10 percent of my earnings. As I write this, it makes me question what I am doing a little bit.

I'm not crazy. Day-trading has tremendous potential, and I keep at it in the hope that I will continue to mature as a trader and get more profitable. But it raises a good point. I know from experience that day-trading is harder than trading longer time frame charts. When day-trading there is more volatility, things happen faster, you have to spend more time in front of the screen, you get transfixed watching every tick of the charts, etc.

Only about four hours per week is spent working on my trades on longer time frames—daily and 60-minute charts. And this accounts for 90 percent of my profits.

I think that most people could do this as well. You don't have to day-trade. It takes an investment of time to learn Elliott Wave and to develop and test a trading system. But once you've made that investment of time and hard work, I believe that you can spend about four hours per week and have really, really good success in trading your account if that is what you want to do.

If you don't want to spend four hours per week looking at charts, you could even reduce that. Once you learn Elliott Wave and develop a trading system and set of trading rules, you can apply it to any time frame. That is part of the beauty of Elliott Wave and the fractal symmetry of the markets: you can apply them to any time frame. If you want to trade the markets and increase your account, but don't want to spend much time in front of your computer, use longer time frames!

For example, you could trade stocks, indexes, and ETFs on weekly charts. If you are trading weekly charts, the investment of time is very minimal. It is totally possible to spend a few hours doing your analysis, finding the instruments that you want to trade, and looking for your setups, and then only check in on your trades for a few minutes every week or so.

It takes a week for a single bar to form on a weekly chart, and it takes several weeks for meaningful signals to develop. You could literally spend 10 minutes looking at your charts every other week and be doing a thorough, responsible job of managing your trades.

Continuing your trading education

If you want to be a successful trader and to consistently make money over time, and to increase your success, continuing education is important. I've been "trading" for over 20 years, but only doing it using Elliott Wave and with a defined trading plan for about 2 years. I've learned a lot in that time. I've been successful and have demonstrated enough results and competence that Bennett invited me to write this chapter in his book.

But I don't feel like I know everything that I need to know or that I have reached some plateau where I don't need to continue to learn. There is so much to learn about the markets and about trading that I don't think I will ever be done. For me that is exciting.

I want to learn more. I enjoy trading, and I enjoy learning more about it, and I am always looking to improve my edge, to make my trading more efficient and more profitable. There are many ways to continue your education as a trader. Reading a book like this is an excellent example. Bennett provides a clear, understandable, and repeatable way to learn and use Elliott Wave to analyze charts and to make trading decisions.

There are many other resources available. Continuing your education as a trader means not only finding good resources like this one, but also sometimes going down paths that have no fruit. Whatever trading system you end up using, it is important to find a system that works for you, one that makes sense that fits your personality and one that you thoroughly understand and can use, on your own, without help and without confusion, doubt, and stress.

Bennett's Elliott Wave and ART system are that for me, and I believe that it can be for many, many people as well. As you pursue continuing education, it is important to find things that complement the major trading system that you have chosen.

THE VALUE AND THE RISK OF EDUCATION

Most of the major trading platforms like TradeStation, NinjaTrader, eSignal, etc. provide educational literature and webinars. I think it is valuable to make use of these resources, to sit in on the webinars and to hear different traders and experts talk about their systems and approaches.

There is both value and some degree of risk in this. A mature approach is to have already decided on the major trading system that you are going to use and then to look for information that enhances your knowledge and use of that system.

The unhealthy, immature approach is to let every webinar or article you read cause you to switch systems or to change your trading system. Chasing strategies because some expert showed his system getting amazing results on a few charts is not continuing education, it is chaos, no different really than gambling. Mature and successful traders are not gamblers; they have a defined and proven edge that ensures predictable results over time and with limited risk.

So, therein lies the possible risk in education, and exposing yourself to new viewpoints and ideas. It is important to expose yourself to education with a mature approach so that you do not risk creating chaos and deviating from your core and primary system.

And it is crucial that you do not spend your trading and investing career as a "system hopper," never focusing on one approach long enough to solve the puzzle and create a profitable consistent edge.

I sit in on two or three webinars per month, and the first question I ask myself is, "Does this complement my system, or does it conflict with my system?" I recently watched a webinar in which the presenter talked about Dow Theory and the analysis of Higher Highs–Higher Lows and Lower Lows–Lower Highs. This information fit nicely with Elliott Wave and gave me some additional tools to use in my trading system, a way to refine my analysis. This information was complementary.

I've also sat through some recent sessions where the expert was focused on stochastics, MACD, and "squeezes" (whatever that means). This information was contradictory to Elliott Wave theory, and I logged off of the session pretty quickly after realizing that.

Indicators like stochastics and MACD are focused on completely different approaches than Elliott Wave, and trying to combine them will only create confusion and trading paralysis. When I look at a chart and put an MACD or stochastic indicator on it, I see an oversold or overbought condition being indicated just when Elliott Wave is telling me a new impulse wave is starting. If I tried to combine those systems, it would yield nothing but stress and confusion. Who needs that?

I'm sure there are good, profitable trading systems that use these indicators, but they are completely different than Elliott Wave. Those systems don't speak to me and I cannot replicate them, so I stick with something that does work for me.

Indicators and Information Overload

This leads to a discussion about indicators. There are literally hundreds of indicators available. Most trading platforms provide, for free, lots and lots of indicators to put on your charts. There are also hundreds of vendors selling indicators. I've been in webinars or trading rooms where people will show their charts and you can barely see price action for all the indicators on the screen. I'm always amazed by this. How can people make trading decisions with that much data coming at them? I have no idea.

Indicators are important, I firmly believe this. But indicators should help you analyze price action, not be a substitute for it. One of the first things I learned from Bennett was the idea of market realities.

Bennett teaches that there are only two realities on a chart, in a particular market, and those are price and volume. This is incredibly important. This was like a light clicking on for me.

The price open, high, low, and close of a particular bar on a chart and the number of shares or contracts traded are indisputable realities—they are actual truths of the market and cannot be distorted. This reality of price and volume actually happened, and the pattern formed by a series of historical bars is equally indisputable.

All indicators lag the current reality; they are calculated based on what happened previously and make some attempt to predict what will happen, but they are all derivatives of reality, they are not reality itself. I cannot count the number of indicators that I have tried and have put on my charts. It's embarrassing, actually, when I think about the indicators that I have looked at and the excitement I felt when I thought that I had found the magical indicator that would guide me.

Pretty much every indicator will show promise when you find a chart to fit its pattern. Every indicator publisher will be more than happy to show you charts where its indicator caught trends early and triggered trades with amazing profit. The problem is that the market doesn't care what indicator you are using, and it doesn't realize that it is supposed to conform to your new, cool indicator.

I've found that Elliott Wave and the ART system provide a way of interpreting the reality of the markets. I have a few indicators on my charts, indicators that help me to interpret price action. As I wrote this, I looked over at my trading platform. My chart has the indicators on it; ART pyramids, the OWL (Optimum Wave Locator), and the PTF (Precision Trend Filter). This is all I need.

These indicators help me to interpret reality, to determine wave counts, and to make probability-based predictions about the future. I use additional tools including trend lines, Fibonacci retracement and extensions, and horizontal lines for support and resistance, but my charts are very clean and I can see the most important thing, price action, very clearly. My charts are not cluttered up with unneeded, confusing, and contradictory indicators.

Testing Builds Confidence and Gets Results

Testing is a critical part of developing a trading system. Testing can be interesting and even fun if you are an analytical type of person and if you like conducting experiments. But it is also hard work and can get a little tedious. Regardless of whether you enjoy it or not, spending real time testing and proving your trading system is essential—there is no shortcut around this.

Here's why there are no shortcuts. Your trading system has to be one that you develop, that suits your personality, your strengths and weaknesses, etc. It is fine to base your system on someone else's as a starting point. But, I am convinced that you won't be successful trading someone else's system.

If you noticed, Bennett doesn't offer a fully defined trading system with rigid rules and everything defined for you that you can just follow blindly. He provides tools and instructions and support on how to use the tools to develop and trade your own system. That is really important.

Testing is important for a few reasons. First, you have to prove that the system is profitable. The only way to know if a trading system is profitable is to test it. That just makes sense, right?

The second major reason for testing is for you to develop skill and most important confidence in using your system. You will inevitably have losing trades, maybe even several in a row. If you haven't thoroughly tested your system and developed confidence in it, when you encounter some losses (which are totally normal for any system), you will start having doubts, fears, and stress.

This will cause you to start changing your system on the fly or to start breaking your own trading rules. You will jump out of trades too early, stop taking good trades, or start taking bad trades to "make up" for losses. This is all really unhealthy.

If you have done sufficient testing of your system, you will have the confidence to stick with it and to follow your rules—you can do this because you have firsthand proof, proof that your system works, proof that you have generated on your own and that is indisputable.

Lots and lots has been written about testing trading systems. A lot of articles on the Internet talk about how to test an automated trading system. In many cases the term *back-testing* has become synonymous with using software to "back-test" an automated system. I'll use the term *back-testing*, but I am not talking about automated testing at all.

As I said earlier, I'm very skeptical about automated trading systems, and I'm not interested in them. Back-testing for me is looking at historical charts and seeing if the trading system and rules that you have developed would have generated entries, exits, and profits. This is a somewhat laborious process where you look at a chart, see if an entry was indicated, and then walk through the price action and see what your rules would have had you do as the trade played out. You need to keep detailed notes on these historical paper trades and then evaluate the system's performance.

It is really important to use the same account size and risk control that you plan to use in your live trading. Sometimes it can be really hard to be honest with yourself when doing paper analysis of historical trades. Why? Because you can "see the future"!

You can already see what happened, and there can be a temptation to fudge things and make up an entry for a stock that really took off. Equally tempting is the desire to pass on a trade that may have met your entry criteria and looked great, but it tanked and would have been a loser. Your results are only as good as the integrity that you bring to the testing process.

If you really want to have results that you are confident in, you have to trade the system, even on paper, just the way you would in live trading.

The second method of testing is to trade the live market using a SIM (simulation) account on your trading platform. This is the best testing. Paper trading historical charts is good and should be done to validate that the system and the rules are profitable, but the real test is in live markets using your SIM account.

Just as in paper trading, you have to treat your SIM trading like it is real, using the same account size, trade size, and risk control that you plan to use in live trading with real money. You have to mimic everything about your live trading in your SIM trading, otherwise the testing is not really valid. Doing this takes real time and real discipline, but it pays off well.

One of the mistakes that I made early on was to jump out of SIM trading and into live trading too soon, without enough testing. This is an easy mistake to make, particularly with day-trading. If you day-trade futures a couple of days in SIM and make some really good money, it is easy to start thinking, "This works, and I'm missing out on profit—I'm wasting my time!"

Here is the truth: if your system is great and profitable, there will be plenty of time to trade it and make money. But if you jump into live trading too soon and find out that you just had a couple of good days, but your system has problems, not only are you going to lose real money, you're going to lose a lot of time having to figure things out and retest, etc. Not to mention the discouragement and frustration that you will probably experience.

Working with a good coach can really help with your testing, help you keep your testing legitimate, and help you make good decisions about when to start trading real money in your live account. It is great to have an experienced and objective person looking at your results and keeping emotion out of it.

I talked earlier about how important I think it is to have continuing education. One of the things that comes from education, as you learn new concepts, is the desire to make changes to your trading system. This is good and healthy. I think it is important to continue to refine my trading system, and I hope I'm not doing exactly the same thing five years from now that I am doing today. I hope I have learned more and am even better at this as time goes by.

But here is the hard part. Every time you make a change to your trading system, guess what? You have to do the hard work of testing again. A change to your trading system shouldn't be implemented in your live trading until it has been thoroughly tested. That takes a lot of time and effort, so I have to think that the change is worth it before I invest my time and energy in a new change.

Scanning for New Opportunities

Finding stocks to trade is an interesting process for me. The *Wall Street Journal* reports that there are 5,008 companies traded on major U.S. stock exchanges. That doesn't count the hundreds of ETFs, ETNs, or futures or forex. There are a lot of trading choices to filter through.

So how do I find charts to analyze? I've tried lots of different methods. I started looking at sector lists. You can google "stock sectors" and will find that there are lots of quality lists of stocks organized by a wide variety of sectors. I found that using this method, I was looking at a lot of charts without finding very many good candidates.

Sector lists are still useful to me, but only when something in the news has drawn my attention to the sector. Recently there has been a lot of chatter about the retail sector, so I go look at the stocks in that sector and scan for good candidates. What I primarily do now is follow the news, and let the news lead me to stocks and sectors to scan.

There are a handful of free newsletters and trading news services that I subscribe to. When articles are being written about companies or if analysts are making upgrades or downgrades, there is usually something going on, some kind of new information that the market may be responding to. I don't read the articles—I couldn't really care less what the analyst or author has to say. I'm really only interested in the fact that they are writing about it.

I then take a quick look at the chart. If it is not interesting, I move on. If it is interesting, I spend a few minutes doing some analysis. If it has promise but needs to play out a bit, I put it on a watch list with an alert and a few notes. If the alert is triggered, I go look at it again, and then make my trading decision.

Using TradeStation's RadarScreen scanner tool, I also run scans and look for breakout stocks. My thinking is that something, some news or some event, caused traders and investors to move the stock quickly. I look at the top 25 breakout stocks each day. Out of these 25, I usually find one or two interesting candidates to analyze and put on my watch list.

Uncovering the "Non-Marquee" Stocks

I also attend a few market outlook webinars each week. TradeStation hosts a free premarket briefing each morning before the open. A different expert presents material in a live webinar format each morning and offers his or her outlook and usually some stocks that he or she is watching. Usually there is a time when the expert takes questions and analyzes stocks for the participants. Bennett has been presenting the Wednesday TradeStation premarket briefing every week for years, and he gives out trade pick suggestions each week.

Sometimes a good pick is identified this way. The only caveat is that the pick has to meet my criteria. I'm not jumping in just because the expert likes it, based on his or her system. I have to like it based on my system, I just use what the expert is sharing to draw my attention to stocks to take a look at. Being in these webinars is pretty interesting.

One of the things I've noticed is that a lot of traders seem to be enamored with the same small set of what I call "marquee" stocks. It is pretty much guaranteed that in a webinar like this the expert will be asked to look at Apple, Google, Amazon, and Netflix.

These are great stocks, and I've traded them all when they had good setups, but I think it is more fun to uncover a "non-marquee" stock that no one is talking about in the webinars.

MY TOP 11 TRADING TIPS

Many years ago, I was in the navy. I remember that my shipmates and I would grumble about the seemingly endless safety regulations that we had to comply with as we did our work. They seemed to get in the way and slow us down.

When we grumbled, our chief would often remind us that each of those safety rules was "written in blood," meaning that in many cases someone had been injured or killed doing what we were doing. The rules were there to keep it from happening to us.

The chief was also fond of reminding us that we were floating around in a metal container full of nothing but fuel, high explosives, and electronic gear, and that a small accident could turn catastrophic very quickly. Those comments usually managed to capture the attention of overconfident 19-year-olds who otherwise knew everything.

My top 11 trading tips are similar.

They are not written in blood, but in many cases they are written in red ink. Several of these items are things that I have personally learned through painful lessons, from either taking losses or going through unnecessary stress. I share these items in hope that others can use them and avoid some of the mistakes that I've made and benefit from the lessons that I have learned. (The tips appear in no particular order.)

MY TOP 11 TRADING TIPS

- **Always review open orders before logging off of your trading platform for the day.** This only takes a minute but can save you a lot of money and grief. If you are trading multi-leg orders during the day, it is possible that you lost track of some of the legs, that they didn't get filled, etc. It is a real bummer to log on in the morning and find a fill that you didn't want. It is also good to check that stop-loss and limit orders are in place for your longer-term trades. Depending on your default platform settings, it is possible to place day orders that expire at the end of the session, when you really wanted GTC (good till cancelled) orders. Having a stock blow through a stop you thought was in place, but wasn't, will wipe the smile right off of your face—this I know.

- **Always use stops when placing trades.** This forces the discipline of determining the correct trade size and maximum loss that you will be at risk for during the trade. Having the stop order in place ensures that the order will execute if the trade goes against you, and it takes the emotion out of the execution.
- **Never, ever move your stop for a bigger loss after taking the trade.** Get your stops in the right place before taking the trade. It can be tempting to move them, to think that things will turn around. You may get away with it occasionally, but it is a really bad habit and can get you into trouble. It is possible to keep nudging the stop until you have far exceeded your risk control parameters, and then you feel trapped into staying with the trade no matter what. Get the stops right in the first place, and if the trade loses, just take the loss in stride and move on.
- **Don't trade if you are upset about something.** Counselors use the acronym HALT (hungry, angry, lonely, tired) and advise people not to make important decisions when they are upset, but rather to HALT and wait until things are stable. I think this applies to trading. If I am mad at my wife, kid, or neighbor, or something in my life has me really upset, it is a bad time to try to trade. It takes discipline and maturity to recognize this and to just walk away for a while. Better to take a walk or do something else than to sit at the computer and make mistakes and feel even worse.
- **Don't trade for income you need in the short term.** If you need your trades to make money so you can pay

your bills, so your family can survive right now, you are setting yourself up for unbelievable stress. I think it is possible to make a good living trading, but in order to do that, to trade your system in a calm and disciplined way, you have to have other income or deep reserves to live on. If you need the current trade to win so you can make your mortgage or car payment, that pressure is going to cause you to make bad decisions and cause stress and depression if it doesn't go your way.

- **Keep your focus on the most important thing—the trade.** When day-trading, there can be lots of things to distract you. Alerts going off from the watch list, news headlines from feeds, a webinar, the UPS guy banging on the door, the dog barking—any number of distractions. If you are watching multiple charts and trying to keep your trading log up to date while you have an active trade on, it is possible to lose track of it and to make mistakes. Pilots have a saying, "Aviate—Navigate—Communicate." This helps pilots keep their attention in the right place during a crisis. The first order of business is to fly the airplane, then to be on course, and then to tell people what is going on. Losing track of the priorities can mean losing control of the airplane and crashing. Day-trading is the same—the first order of business when you have a trade on is to monitor and manage the trade.
- **Know what you are trading.** Elliott Wave theory applies to all instruments in all time frames. But I think it is important to know a little bit about the instrument you are trading. I'm not talking about fundamentals or earning or analyst reports, but know *what* the instrument is. Stocks are pretty clear. ETFs are usually based on some underlying thing. I want to know what this thing is. Sometimes it matters a lot. For example, the ETF USO is based on crude oil futures. Crude oil is active and trades around the clock and around the globe. USO

only trades during U.S. market hours and lags the crude oil futures. Before I take a position in USO, I'm going to have a look at the oil futures and see if things are in sync. Futures contracts trade on a variety of exchanges. Different exchanges have different trading hours. Imagine the shock if you are watching a futures day-trade and the exchange closes on you before you get out of the position. You get to spend a long night wondering if the thing will gap past your stop and open with a big loss in the morning. Also, some futures contracts settle in physical goods rather than cash. I have no desire to have a shipping container of soybeans delivered to my driveway, so I pay attention to how the contracts settle and the settlement dates and make sure I am out of positions well in advance of their expiration.

- **Understand your platform and brokerage order system.** Are your stop and limit orders sitting on your broker's servers, or are they sitting on your PC? This is critical if you lose your Internet connection or your PC locks up or crashes—especially for highly leveraged instruments like futures contracts. It is uncomfortable, to say the least, to suddenly be blind and have no idea what the price is doing and whether or not your orders will be filled. Many platforms hold the orders on your PC and then send them once the criteria are met. If you are not sure, ask your broker and have a backup plan. It is a good idea to have your broker's number and your account number and password written somewhere where you can get to it if your PC is down and you need to call and manage your trade.
- **Don't let small mistakes turn into big mistakes.** If you make a mistake in placing your trade, wrong direction (yeah, I've done that), wrong quantity, etc., don't "wait and see what happens." Just get out, even if it means a loss. Learn from it and move on.

- **For day-trading: set a daily loss limit.** This is a rule I heard from another trader, and I like it and use it in my trading. You have to be a pretty seasoned and mature trader not to let a series of losers bother you, at least a little bit. On longer time frame trading, you have time to let those emotions settle out. In day-trading, not so much. So, if I hit the daily loss limit that I have established (about three trades at my max risk for each one), I log off and am done for the day. Otherwise, I know that I run the risk of starting to trade a bit more aggressively and trying to "make it back." At that point, I'd rather walk away and do something fun or relaxing than sit at my computer and take more losses. If you really want to keep going and think there is something to learn, switch to your SIM account and carry on.
- **Evaluate each trade independently.** Avoid playing head games like "my first two trades were winners today, so I can take more risk now" and stuff like that. It will just make you more inconsistent. I played racquetball competitively for years and noticed that more inexperienced players only seemed to remember their great shots. They remember how great it felt to hit a good kill shot and make the ball roll out from the wall. They don't remember the four shots before that one that were skips and made them lose the rally. Experienced players only take high probability shots and are happy to win the rally with a simple pass shot rather than risking a kill shot. Trading is the same: treat each trade as its own and only take high probability trades that meet your rules, regardless of how the other ones went.

IN CLOSING

I am honored that Bennett asked me to write this chapter in his new book. Getting to know Bennett and his wife Jean has been a true blessing for me. Both Bennett and Jean are great folks, and they genuinely care about helping people become successful traders.

I'm convinced that most people can take the material that Bennett is teaching in this book and put it to use in their own trading system. I have shared my own story and what I have learned in this chapter. I hope you find it useful and interesting and that it helps you make a decision about whether or not to become a trader.

And if you do, I hope that I've added something that will help you. It takes hard work and perseverance and you will go through some ups and downs, but stick with it. It's worth it.

APPENDIX A

Resources

Charting Platforms, Data, and More

This resources appendix has a wealth of information for both the "newbie" and the seasoned professional alike. With your finances, as in life, very often it is who you know and what you know that can make or break the outcome of any situation. This is why we wanted to give you our personal "little black book" or "yellow pages" of terrific organizations that can speed you along on the path to greater profitability.

Keep in mind that we do not make any guarantees that you will be successful using the following resources. As in the markets, your success with these kinds of professional relationships depends entirely on you and how you manage and cultivate them. For the categories listed you will see that we have a variety to choose from. This gives you choices to select from when it comes to a charting platform, market data, and so forth.

It's essential that you interview potential resources prior to signing up with them and be sure that they are a good fit for your personality, trading and investing needs, and budget. This means you are in the driver's seat and you will need to do your homework in order to obtain the best results.

Keep us posted and give us your feedback with regard to the following resources. And of course let us know if you find any outstanding firms or individuals that we can add to the list. Contact us via e-mail: Info@TradersCoach.com.

CHARTING PLATFORMS

We encourage you to visit each charting platform's website to gather as much current information as possible. This will enable you to develop a custom plan perfectly suited for you.

TradeStation
www.TradeStation.com
888-853-9743 (toll free)
954-652-7417 (local)
(0808) 234-1049, ext. 7417 (U.K. residents)

TradeStation is a premier and first-class broker, data provider, and charting platform. It provides a variety of services, products, and tools for virtually every trading and investing market. It is *not* compatible with other brokers or data vendors. Call today for more information.

eSignal
www.eSignal.com
E-mail: ray.fitzgerald@interactivedata.com
800-322-0940 (toll free)
510-723-1671 (local)
Contact: Ray Fitzgerald

eSignal is a premier and first-class data provider and charting platform. It is *not* a broker but is compatible with many other brokers. Some of the brokers eSignal is compatible with are MB Trading, Interactive Brokers, Infinity Futures, GAIN Capital, and R. J. O'Brien. Check out the eSignal website for a current listing of compatible brokers.

Trade Navigator (Genesis Financial Technologies)
www.tradenavigator.com
E-mail: sales@tradenavigator.com
800-808-3282 (toll free)
719-884-0244 (local)

Trade Navigator is a premier and first-class charting platform. It is *not* a broker and *not* a data provider. Some of the brokers Trade Navigator is compatible with are Interactive Brokers, TransAct Futures, and Infinity Futures.

NinjaTrader
www.NinjaTrader.com
E-mail: orders@ninjatrader.com
800-496-1683 (toll free)
312-423-2230 (local)

NinjaTrader is a premier and first-class trading and investing charting platform, broker, and data provider. Call or visit the website for more information.

Market Analyst
www.Market-Analyst.com
E-mail: support@market-analyst.com

Market Analyst is a premier and first-class charting platform. Market Analyst can connect to eSignal, Interactive Brokers, GFT, and IQFeed. Contact Market Analyst for more information.

Data sources

eSignal
www.eSignal.com
E-mail: ray.fitzgerald@interactivedata.com
800-322-0940 (toll free)
510-723-1671 (local)
Contact: Ray Fitzgerald

Kinetick
www.kinetick.com

IQFeed (DTN Markets)
www.iqfeed.net
E-mail: sales@iqfeed.net
800-475-4755 (toll free)
402-255-8435

Current resources

For the absolute latest, most current list of quality resources visit the TradersCoach.com website.

TradersCoach.com
www.TradersCoach.com
E-mail: info@traderscoach.com
800-695-6188 (toll free)
858-695-0592 (local)

APPENDIX B

Suggested Reading and Education

Elliotticians Past and Present, Books, and More

The significance of Elliott's work is proven by the number of individuals that continue to successfully use his theories to this very day. Granted, each Elliottician interprets the initial theory in his or her own unique way, but had it not been for Ralph Nelson Elliott bringing these ideas forward and sharing them with the world in 1938, we would have a vast emptiness in the current field of technical analysis.

We can learn a lot about how we might personally interpret the wave theory by understanding how others before us have done so. And we can understand more about the theory itself by looking at some of the work that influenced Elliott in the first place.

Below is a list of individuals you can read about to further your Elliott Wave studies and it's worth finding out more about them:

- Pythagoras
- Leonardo Fibonacci
- William Delbert Gann
- Charles Henry Dow
- Robert Rhea
- Charles J. Collins
- Robert R. Prechter Jr.
- A. J. Frost
- Robert C. Beckman

Suggested Books

A Trader's Money Management System, How to Ensure Profit and Avoid the Risk of Ruin. McDowell, Bennett A., John Wiley & Sons, Hoboken, New Jersey, 2008.

The ART of Trading, Combining the Science of Technical Analysis with the Art of Realty-Based Trading. McDowell, Bennett A., John Wiley & Sons, Hoboken, New Jersey, 2008.

Survival Guide For Traders, How to Set Up and Organize Your Trading Business. McDowell, Bennett A., John Wiley & Sons, Hoboken, New Jersey, 2012.

The Elliott Wave Principle: Key to Stock Market Profits. Frost, A. J. and Prechter, Robert R. Jr., New Classics Library, New York, New York, 1978.

The Major Works of R. N. Elliott. Prechter, Robert R. Jr., New Classics Library, Georgia, 1980.

Elliott Wave Explained, A Real-World Guide to Predicting & Profiting from Market Turns. Beckman, Robert C., McGraw-Hill, New York, New York, 1995.

The Wave Principle. Elliott, R. N. and Collins, Charles J., 1938.

Nature's Law: The Secret of the Universe. Elliott, R. N., 1946.

The Dow Theory. Rhea, Robert, Barron's, 1932.

Continuing Education

Consider the development of your skills and techniques as an ongoing education and remember, we are here to help you. We have a variety of support products and services ranging from webinars and courses to software tools. Visit the TradersCoach.com website to learn more.

TradersCoach.com
www.TradersCoach.com
E-mail: info@traderscoach.com
800-695-6188 (toll free)
858-695-0592 (local)

Available Software from TradersCoach.com

- ART (Applied Reality Trading) for entries, exits and risk control
- ART Scanner for scanning
- OWL (Optimum Wave Locator) for identifying Wave 3 and filtering
- PTF (Precision Trend Filter) for determining trends and filtering
- TLM (Trend Line Master) for drawing trend lines and filtering
- TSC (Trade Size Calculator) for optimum trade size and risk control
- TA (Traders Assistant) for record keeping

ELLIOTT WAVE "CHEAT SHEET" STATISTICS

	FIBONACCI TARGET ZONES	APPROXIMATE % PROBABILITY
WAVE 2 Price Retracement	23.6%–38.2% of Wave 1 length	15%
	38.2%–61.8% of Wave 1 length	70%
	61.8%–100% of Wave 1 length	15%
WAVE 3 Price Extension	100%–161.8% of Wave 1 length	15%
	161.8%–175% of Wave 1 length	45%
	175%–261.8% of Wave 1 length	30%
	Greater than 261.8% of Wave 1 length	10%
WAVE 4 Price Retracement	23.6%–38.2% of Wave 3 length	15%
	38.2%–61.8% of Wave 3 length	70%
	61.8%–76.40% of Wave 3 length	15%
WAVE 5 Price Extension	38.2%–61.8% (see guidelines below)	15%
	61.8%–100% (see guidelines below)	70%
	100%–161.8% (see guidelines below)	15%

NOTE: Most charting platforms have "Fibonacci" drawing software tools that when properly used will show these "Fibonacci Target Zones" on your charts. It is important you understand where to place the multiple anchoring points when using the Fibonacci software drawing tools.

GUIDELINES FOR ANCHORS WHEN USING FIBONACCI DRAWING TOOLS

- **WAVE 2:** Anchor the drawing tool at the beginning of Wave 1 and at the end of Wave 1.
- **WAVE 3:** Anchor the drawing tool at the beginning of Wave 1 and the end of Wave 1. (To use three anchors, anchor the drawing tool at the end of Sub-Wave 2, the end of Sub-Wave 3 and the end of Sub-Wave 4.)
- **WAVE 4:** Anchor the drawing tool at the end of Wave 2 and at the end of Wave 3.
- **WAVE 5:** Anchor the drawing tool at the end of Wave 2, the end of Wave 3 and the end Wave 4.

List of Important Financial Terms and Definitions

ABC correction This is a simple corrective pattern also know as a zigzag correction. It is made up of three-waves and is the most common and easy to spot correction.

accumulation/distribution (A/D) A momentum indicator that attempts to gauge supply and demand by determining whether traders or investors are accumulating (buying) or distributing (selling) a certain financial instrument by identifying divergences between price and volume flow.

American Stock Exchange (AMEX) The third-largest stock exchange in the United States, renamed NYSE Amex Equities. Generally, the listing rules are more lenient than those of the NYSE, and therefore it has a larger representation of stocks and bonds issued by smaller companies. It is located in New York City.

annual percentage rate (APR) The periodic rate times the number of periods in a year. Example: A 5 percent quarterly return has an APR of 20 percent.

Applied Reality Trading® (ART) A technical analysis system developed by Bennett A. McDowell that focuses on trading the realities of the financial markets. The ART software works on any time frame and in any market for both investors and day traders. The software generates charts that illustrate clear entry and exit signals and sound money management rules.

APR See *annual percentage rate.*

ART bear price bar When prices close on the *lower* half of the bar, it is an ART bear price bar. The bar is defined by the relationship between the *close* and the price bar interval. The bears are in control at the close of the price bar. (ART determines bear and bull differently than other systems.)

ART bull price bar When prices close on the *upper* half of the bar, it is an ART bull price bar. The bar is defined by the relationship between the *close* and the price bar interval. The bulls are in control at the close of the price bar. (ART determines bear and bull differently than other systems.)

ART elongated price bar A price bar that is at least one-third longer than the previous three to five price bars.

ART inside price bar A compressed price bar forming directly after the signal bar in an ART reversal. It can be used to aggressively enter an ART reversal trade.

ART neutral price bar On this price bar, the open and the close are at the 50 percent point on the bar when it closes. Bulls and bears are in a stalemate at the close of the price bar.

ART one-bar reversal (1B) This scalp signal identifies exact entries and exits, and can also be used for scaling in and scaling out of trends. This reversal signal requires only one price bar that is the signal bar, which determines both the entry and also the stop-loss exit. It can be used on all markets and all time frames.

ART signal price bar The price bar used for a trade entry when making an ART reversal trade. The ART trading software designates the ART signal bar with a 1B or 2B directly above or below the price bar.

ART two-bar reversal (2B) This scalp signal identifies exact entries and exits, and can also be used for scaling in and scaling out of trends. This reversal signal requires two price bars; the first price bar is used for the stop-loss exit, and the second price bar or signal bar is used for the entry. It can be used on all markets and all time frames.

ask price The price a seller is willing to accept. It is also known as the offer. The difference between the bid and ask is known as the bid-ask spread.

asset Any possession that has value in an exchange.

asset allocation The process of deciding what types of assets you want to own, and the percentage of each. As conditions change, the percentage allotted to each asset class changes.

at-the-money An option is at-the-money if the strike price of the option is equal to the market price of the underlying asset.

average true range (ATR) An indicator that helps determine a market's volatility over a given period. It is calculated by taking an average of the true ranges over a set number of previous periods. It is the moving average of the true range for a given period.

back-testing The use of historical data to test technical or fundamental theories or systems to determine the historical performance of a given set of rules. Back-testing can give information on what the performance would have been but does not guarantee future results. eSignal has a playback feature that enables you to test your trading skills using historical data and playing it forward to determine what your performance would have been. The value of the playback is that you do not see the right side of the chart, so you are testing your own ability to make decisions without knowing what the next price bar will bring.

balance sheet A listing of all assets and liabilities for an individual or a business. The surplus of assets over liabilities is the net worth, or what is owned free of debt.

basis The cost of the asset. If you pay $10 per share for a stock plus $1 per share for commission, your basis is $11 per share.

bear Someone who believes prices will decline and is generally pessimistic about future market returns.

bear market A market characterized by prolonged broadly declining prices. Some negative information has entered the market to create this condition. Generally the downturn in prices is in excess of 20 percent. It is not to be confused with a correction. Less than 30 percent of historic periods have been bear markets.

bid-ask spread The difference between the bid and the ask. The spread narrows or widens according to the supply of and demand for the security being traded.

bid price The price a buyer is willing to pay.

black box system A 100 percent mechanical system that requires absolutely no discretion. The concern with these systems is that they are unable to adapt to ever-changing market cycles. The reality is that over time, all systems require some form of discretionary decision making to be consistently profitable. ART is not a black box system.

Black Monday Refers to October 19, 1987, when the Dow Jones Industrial Average fell 508 points after sharp drops the previous week.

blue chip company A large, nationally recognized, financially sound firm with a long track record, usually selling high-quality and widely accepted goods and services. Examples: General Electric and IBM.

bond A debt investment. Investors lend money to an institution by buying bonds and receiving fixed interest payments in return. When the bond matures, the investor receives the principal back.

bond market The bond market, also known as the debt, credit, or fixed income market, is a financial market where participants buy and sell debt securities.

bracketed market This is also known as a consolidating, range-bound, sideways, nontrending, choppy, channeling, sleepy, or drunk market. When a market is bracketed, it is stuck in a price range between identifiable resistance and support levels. On a chart, a bracket will be seen as a sideways horizontal line. Some of the most powerful and profitable trends come out of markets that have been bracketed for more than 20 price bars.

breakout A sharp change in price movement after the market has traded sideways for at least 20 price bars. This is beyond a previous high (or low) or outside the boundaries of a preceding price bracket.

broker An individual or online firm that is paid a commission for executing customer orders; an agent specializing in stocks, bonds, commodities, or options. The broker must be registered with the exchange where the securities are traded.

bull Someone who believes that prices will rise and is generally optimistic about future market returns.

bull market A market characterized by prolonged broadly rising prices. Positive information has entered the market to create this condition. Over 70 percent of historic periods have been bull markets.

buy To purchase an asset.

buyer's market A market in which the supply exceeds the demand, creating lower prices.

call option An options contract with the right to buy a specific number of shares of a stock at a specified price (the strike price) on or before a specific expiration date, regardless of the underlying stock's current market price. A call option writer sells the right to a buyer.

candlestick chart A type of bar chart developed by the Japanese, in which the price range between the open and the close is either a white rectangle (if the close is higher) or a black rectangle (if the close is lower).

capital The money you need to trade or invest. This should be risk capital, meaning that you can afford to lose this money.

cash per share The amount of cash divided by the total number of common stock shares outstanding for a given stock. A corporation with high cash per share ratio is said to be cash rich and may be considered low-risk or undervalued.

central bank The institution in each country responsible for setting monetary policy, printing money, managing reserves, and controlling inflation. In the United States, the central bank is the Federal Reserve System, also known as the Fed.

channeling market This is also known as a bracketed, consolidating, range-bound, sideways, or nontrending market. See *bracketed market*.

chart A graph that depicts the price movement of a given market. The most common type of chart is the bar chart, which denotes each interval's open, high, low, and close for a given market with a single price bar.

chart analysis The study of price charts in an effort to find patterns that in the past preceded price advances or declines. The basic concept is that the development of similar patterns in a current market can signal a probable market move in the same direction. Practitioners of chart analysis are often referred to as *technical analysis* traders or investors.

Chicago Board of Trade (CBOT) Established in 1848, the CBOT is a leading exchange for futures and options on futures. More than 3,600 CBOT members trade 50 different futures and options products at the exchange through open auction and/or electronically. CME Group is a combined entity formed by the 2007 merger of the Chicago Mercantile Exchange (CME) and the Chicago Board of Trade (CBOT).

Chicago Board Options Exchange (CBOE) Founded in 1973, the CBOE is an exchange that focuses on options contracts for individual equities, indexes, and interest rates. The CBOE is the world's largest options market. It captures a majority of the options traded. It is also a market leader in developing new financial products and technological innovation, particularly with electronic trading.

Chicago Mercantile Exchange (CME) Founded in 1898 as the Chicago Butter and Egg Board, this is an American financial exchange based in Chicago. Originally the exchange was a not-for-profit organization. The exchange demutualized in November 2000, went public in December 2002, and merged with the Chicago Board of Trade in July 2007. CME trades several types of financial instruments: interest rates, equities, currencies, and commodities. CME has the largest options and futures contracts open interest (number of contracts outstanding) of any futures exchange in the world. Trading is conducted in two methods: an open outcry format and the CME Globex® electronic trading platform. Approximately 70 percent of total volume at the exchange occurs on CME Globex.

choppy market See *bracketed market.*

churning When a broker excessively trades an account for the purpose of increasing his or her commission revenue. This practice is entirely unethical and does not serve the customer's investment or trading goals.

close The period at the end of the trading session; sometimes refers to the closing price.

CME Group The world's largest and most diverse exchange. Formed by the 2007 merger of the Chicago Mercantile Exchange (CME) and the Chicago Board of Trade (CBOT), CME Group serves the risk management needs of customers around the globe. As an international marketplace, CME Group brings buyers and sellers together on the CME Globex electronic trading platform and on its trading floors.

commission Fee paid to a brokerage house to execute a transaction.

commission ratio Total dollars of commission paid divided by total dollars of profit earned equals the commission ratio. This formula is not applicable to traders who are not generating a profit or who have a payoff ratio of less than 1 to 1.

commodities Physical goods that are traded at a futures exchange, such as grains, foods, meats, metals, and so on.

complex correction These types of corrections are known to form channels, pennants, and flags. They are difficult to trade. There are three types: flat; irregular; and triangular.

consolidating market This is also known as a bracketed, range-bound, sideways, nontrending, choppy, or channeling market. See *bracketed market.*

consumer price index (CPI) Issued by the U.S. Bureau of Labor Statistics, this figure is a popularly used measure of inflation. It measures the relative change in prices of a basket of consumer products and services.

contract A single unit of a commodity or future. This is similar to shares in stocks.

contrarian One who trades or invests on contrary opinion using the theory that one can profit by doing the opposite of the majority of traders or investors in the market.

correction A short, sharp reverse in prices during a longer market trend.

corrective Elliott Wave This is a wave that points in the opposite direction of the current trend. In a five wave pattern, the two waves that are corrective are Wave 2 and Wave 4.

countertrend trade A trading strategy where an investor or trader attempts to make small gains through a series of trades against the current trend.

cover To liquidate an existing position (such as sell if one is long; buy if one is short).

covered call To sell a call option at the same time you own the same number of shares represented by the option in the underlying stock.

covered put To sell a put option at the same time you are holding a short position in the underlying stock.

data Live streaming market data is provided to the trader or investor by data providers and brokerage houses. This data is used to conduct technical analysis and provide price and volume information. Real-time data is sent by the minute during the trading day. Generally data providers charge more for real-time data because it is more labor-intensive to provide. Real-time data is used by day traders. End-of-day data is provided at the end of the day and gives you final price and volume information for the market you are analyzing. Data providers charge less for end-of-day data, and this type of data is used more by investors and position traders.

day-trade A trade that is liquidated on the same day it is initiated.

day trader Refers to the practice of buying and selling financial instruments within the same trading day such that all positions will usually (not necessarily always) be closed before the market close. Traders who participate in day-trading are day traders.

debt-to-equity ratio Ratio demonstrating an institution's debt relative to its equity. It is just one component used by corporations in assessing optimal capital structures.

decimal Increment of movement in the stock market.

deflation A drop in average product and services price levels, usually caused by excessive tightening of the money supply. Deflation can lead to reduced economic demand and higher unemployment. It is not to be confused with disinflation.

discretionary trader A trader who makes decisions based on his or her own analysis of the market, rather than in response to signals generated by a computerized black box system. The best discretionary traders are those who develop a systematic approach and then use discretion in their entries, exits, and position sizing to improve performance.

disinflation The slowing growth of average product and services price levels. This can be thought of as the slowing of inflation and is not to be confused with deflation.

divergence The failure of a market or an indicator to follow suit when a related market or indicator sets a new high or low. Some analysts look for divergences as signals of impending market tops and bottoms.

diversification Trading or investing in a variety of markets and sectors to reduce risk. Don't put all your eggs in one basket!

dividend A payment made to stockholders, usually quarterly, out of a firm's current or retained earnings.

DJIA See *Dow Jones Industrial Average.*

dollar cost averaging Averaging the cost per share of a particular security by investing a fixed sum regularly.

double witching A term used for the day when both options and futures expire.

doubling down Adding onto a losing position.

Dow Jones Industrial Average (DJIA) A price-weighted index of 30 blue-chip U.S. stocks. This index is also known as the Dow.

downtrend A general tendency for declining prices in a given market.

drawdown A decrease in the value of an account because of losing trades or because of paper losses, which may occur simply because of a decline in the value of open positions. No or low drawdown is a desirable performance feature of a trader or investor.

earnings per share (EPS) A firm's total after-tax net earnings divided by the number of common shares outstanding.

earnings-to-price (E/P) ratio Ratio of a company's earnings per share to its share price. This is the reverse of the price-to-earnings ratio.

edge The advantage you and your system give you over the market by dollars earned. See *payoff ratio*.

efficient market The theory that the financial markets quickly and efficiently compensate and price in all widely known information.

Elliott Wave analysis A method of market analysis based on the theories of Ralph Nelson Elliott. Although relatively complex, the method is based on the concept that markets move in waves, forming a general pattern of five waves (or market legs) in the direction of the main trend.

e-mini Used in the futures market to represent a smaller trading market of its parent market.

entry The point at which you place or open your trade or investment. This is the opposite of your exit. When placing your entry, you should already know what your initial exit will be—see *stop-loss exit*. The distance between your entry and your exit will determine what your trade size will be.

equities markets Stock markets.

equity The total dollar value of an account.

equity curve The value of your account over time, illustrated in a graph.

exchange-traded fund (ETF) A security that tracks a specific index, equity category, or other basket of assets but is traded on an exchange like a single stock.

exercise To buy or sell a call or put option by the expiration date on the option contract.

exit The point at which you close your trade or investment. This is the opposite of your entry. It can also be known as your *stop-loss exit*. It is a crucial part of your money management risk control plan. The distance between your entry and your exit will determine what your trade size will be.

expiration date The last day on which an option may be exercised. For stock options, this date is the third Friday of the expiration month.

extension See *Fibonacci time extension* and *Fibonacci price extension.*

false breakout A short-lived price move that penetrates a prior high or low before succumbing to a pronounced price move in the opposite direction. For example, if the price of a stock that has been trading between $18 and $20 rises to $21 and then quickly falls below $18, the move to $21 can be termed a false breakout.

Federal Open Market Committee (FOMC) A 12-member committee responsible for setting credit and interest rate policy for the Federal Reserve System. The members set the discount rate directly and control the federal funds rate by buying and selling government securities impacting the rate. They meet eight times a year under the direction of a chairman.

Federal Reserve Board of Governors The governing arm of the Federal Reserve System, which seeks to regulate the economy through the implementation of monetary policy. The seven members of the Board of Governors are appointed by U.S. presidents to serve 14-year terms.

Federal Reserve System (Fed) The central banking system of the United States, responsible for regulating the flow of money and credit. It serves as a bank for other banks and the U.S. government.

Fibonacci price extension The concept that extensions of price movements will often approximate 38.2 percent and 61.8 percent—numbers derived from the Fibonacci sequence. This enables you to determine price targets.

Fibonacci price retracement The concept that price retracements of prior trends will often approximate 38.2 percent and 61.8 percent—numbers derived from the Fibonacci sequence. See *retracement.*

Fibonacci sequence A sequence of numbers that begins with 1, 1, and progresses to infinity, with each number in the sequence equal to the sum of the preceding two numbers. Thus, the initial numbers in the sequence would be 1, 1, 2, 3, 5, 8, 13, 21, 34, 55, 89, and so on. The ratio of consecutive numbers in the sequence converges to 0.618 as the numbers get larger. The ratio of alternate numbers in the sequence (for example, 21 and 55) converges to 0.382 as the numbers get larger. These two ratios—0.618 and 0.382—are commonly used to project retracements of prior price swings.

Fibonacci time extension The concept that time extensions will often approximate 38.2 percent and 61.8 percent—numbers derived from the Fibonacci sequence. These extensions appear as vertical lines on your chart.

fill The price at which an order is executed. For example, if a trade was placed at $32.00 and executed at $32.25, the fill price would be $32.25.

filter An indicator that selects only data that meet specific criteria. Too many filters can lead to overoptimization.

financial instrument A term used to denote any form of funding medium. Financial instruments can be categorized by whether they are cash instruments or derivative instruments. Cash instruments are financial instruments whose value is determined directly by markets. They can be divided into securities, which are readily transferable, and other cash instruments such as loans and deposits, where both borrower and lender have to agree on a transfer. Derivative instruments are financial instruments that derive their value from some other financial instrument or variable. They can be divided into exchange-traded derivatives and over-the-counter (OTC) derivatives. If it is debt, it can be further categorized into short-term (less than one year) or long-term debt. Foreign exchange instruments and transactions are neither debt nor equity based and belong in their own category.

flat When you are not in the market with a live position or when you close out all your positions before the end of the trading day, you are considered flat.

floor trader A member of the exchange who trades on the floor for personal profit.

forecasts Individuals who attempt to predict future market behavior are said to be forecasting the market. They tend to use indicators such as moving average convergence/divergence (MACD), stochastics, and Elliott Waves to determine their forecasts. Forecasting the markets is often like forecasting the weather; it is difficult to do with any consistent accuracy.

forex market The foreign exchange (forex) market exists wherever one currency is traded for another. It is by far the largest financial market in the world and includes trading between large banks, central banks, currency speculators, multinational corporations, governments, and other financial markets and institutions.

fractal symmetry This is the relationship of waves within waves on different time frames, meaning that the same patterns exist from a macro level down to a micro level.

fundamental analysis The use of economic data and news data to analyze financial markets. For example, fundamental analysis of a currency might focus on such items as relative inflation rates, interest rates, economic growth rates, and political factors. In evaluating a stock, a fundamental analyst would look at financials, value, earnings, debt, management, operations, competition, and other relative data. Fundamental analysis is often contrasted with technical analysis, and some investors and traders use a combination of the two.

futures When commodity exchanges added stock index contracts and currency contracts, the term *futures* was developed to be more inclusive.

futures market An auction market in which participants buy and sell commodity/futures contracts for delivery on a specified future date. Trading is carried on through open outcry and hand signals in a trading pit.

Gann analysis Market analysis based on a variety of technical concepts developed by William Gann, a famous stock and commodity trader during the first half of the twentieth century.

gap A price zone at which no trades occur. For example, if a market that has previously traded at a high of $20 per share opens at $22 on the following day, the price zone between $20 and $22 is referred to as a gap up. If the price zone were to go from $22 to $20, it would be a gap down. Sometimes Fed announcements or corporate earnings announcements can create an immediate gap even in the middle of a trading day.

Globex® Today the CME Globex trading system operates at the heart of CME. Proposed in 1987, it was introduced in 1992 as the first global electronic trading platform for futures contracts. This fully electronic trading system allows market participants to trade from booths at the exchange or while sitting in a home or an office thousands of miles away.

good till canceled (GTC) order By choosing GTC, you ensure that your order will remain open until it is executed or canceled, regardless of the number of trading days.

gross domestic product (GDP) The monetary value of all products and services produced in a country over a certain time period. In the United States, GDP growth is a popularly used indicator of overall economic health.

grounded assessments Trading and investing rules that are based on reality versus forecasts or predictions. For example, trade and investment entries based on price and volume would be considered grounded assessments. The ART signals are all grounded assessments.

hedge To reduce risk in an investment or trade by offsetting it with another investment or trade.

hedge fund A managed portfolio of investments that is generally unregulated (unlike a mutual fund) and may invest in any highly speculative markets, including options.

hedger A market participant who implements a position to reduce price risk. The hedger's risk position is exactly opposite that of the speculator, who accepts risk in implementing positions to profit from anticipated price moves.

higher time frame filter A filter technique used to look at the market you are trading or investing in on a higher time frame to see if it confirms your primary time frame.

high probability Refers to trades or investments that statistically are more likely to succeed.

hyperbolic move A sharp and significant move to the upside or downside of your position. You might decide to scale out of a position to lock in profit if this type of move occurs. See *scaling out.*

immediate or cancel (IOC) order By choosing IOC, you ensure that your order will have immediate execution of all or part of the quantity of stock you specified. Any portion of the order that is not executed immediately is automatically canceled.

impulsive Elliott Wave This is a wave that points in the same direction of the current trend. In a five wave pattern, the three waves that are impulsive waves are Wave 1, Wave 3, and Wave 5.

index fund A mutual fund that tracks a stated market index.

individual retirement account (IRA) A retirement account that any employed person (or spouse of an employed person) can open and contribute to. Assets in the account grow tax deferred, and contributions may be tax deductible. Distributions taken before age 59 are subject to penalty.

inflation Rate of increase in average product and service price levels. Different indexes use different baskets of products and services to compute the average prices. A popular index is the consumer price index.

initial public offering (IPO) The first sale of equities (stocks) to the public by a private firm. In making an IPO, a private firm has gone public.

insider trading Trading by officers, directors, major stockholders, or others who hold private inside information allowing them to benefit from buying or selling stock. It is a misuse of inside information to profit more quickly than the average shareholder would.

institutional investor A bank, mutual fund, pension fund, or other corporate entity that trades financial instruments in large volumes.

in-the-money When an option's current market price is above the strike price of a call or below the strike price of a put. An in-the-money option would produce a profit if exercised.

intraday time frame A shorter time frame (from the one-minute to the 60-minute) that day traders use in making their entry and exit decisions.

investing A term with several closely related meanings in business management, finance, and economics, related to saving or deferring consumption. An asset is usually purchased, or equivalently a deposit is made in a bank, in hopes of getting a future return or interest from it. Think of it as using financial instruments to invest savings for future gain; it usually is not considered a short-term endeavor.

investor Generally, one who favors a buy-and-hold approach using weekly and monthly charts to evaluate the market. An investor can be a trader when timing long-term investments. Investors are more likely to incorporate fundamental analysis into their approach than a day trader would.

Kelly formula See *optimal* f *formula*.

large cap Refers to the size of a firm's market capitalization. Generally, any firm with a market cap above $10 billion is referred to as large cap.

left brain The human brain is divided into two hemispheres, the left and the right, each of which is responsible for specific functions in human behavior and existence. The left brain is responsible primarily for speech, logic, planning, and analytical abilities. It tends to think in words as opposed to pictures and looks at the details as opposed to the big picture. Those who are analytical and scientific in nature are generally referred to as left-brain thinkers.

leverage The ability to control a dollar amount of a commodity or financial instrument greater than the amount of personal capital employed. This ability is obtained by using borrowed money, such as a margin account. The greater the leverage of the position, the greater the potential profit or loss.

limit order An order in which you set the maximum price you will pay for your purchase, or a minimum price you will accept as a seller.

limit position For many futures contracts, government regulations specify a maximum position size (such as number of contracts) that a speculator may hold.

limit price move For many futures contracts, the exchanges specify a maximum amount by which the price can change on a single day. A market that increases in price by this specified maximum is said to be limit-up, while a market that declines by the maximum is said to be limit-down.

liquidity The degree to which a given market is liquid. When volume is high, there is usually a lot of liquidity. Low liquidity in markets can result in poor fills.

liquidity risk The risk when you enter a trade that you may not have sufficient liquidity to exit at your desired exit point.

liquid market A market in which there are a large number of trades daily so that most buy and sell orders can be executed without dramatically moving prices. In other words, a liquid market allows you ease of entry and exit.

long A position established with a buy order, which profits in a rising price market. The term is also used to refer to the person or entity holding such a position.

long call To buy a call option.

long put To buy a put option.

lot The quantity of shares in which stocks are bought or sold. In futures markets, a lot is called a *contract.*

MACD See *moving average convergence/divergence.*

margin To borrow money from a financial provider (broker or bank) to purchase certain financial instruments.

margin call A Federal Reserve Board and financial service provider requirement that you deposit additional funds or sell some of your holdings to increase the equity in your margin account if it has fallen below the minimum.

margin debit The amount of money borrowed from a financial service provider.

margin risk The risk that you can lose more than the dollar amount in your margined trading account.

market index The weighted average of companies composing an index. The index represents a category or market (such as the S&P 500 or the NASDAQ).

market maker A broker, bank, or firm such as Goldman Sachs or Merrill Lynch that buys or sells a security, currency, or futures contract.

market order An order to execute a purchase or sale at the best price available at the time the order is received.

market risk Uncontrolled risk possibilities that are always present in open trade and investment positions. Economic and world events can cause market risk where the market could move so quickly that you may not be able to exit at your stop-loss exit point.

Minneapolis Grain Exchange (MGEX) This exchange was founded as a not-for-profit membership organization and maintains that structure today with a membership base of 390 outstanding seats or memberships. In 1883, MGEX launched its first futures contract, hard red spring wheat, which is the exchange's most heavily traded product today.

Minor Pyramid Trading Point® (MP) An MP indicates a correction in the dominant trend.

momentum investing and trading Momentum represents the change in price now from some fixed time period in the past. This strategy attempts to capture short-term price movements based on the belief that price patterns are indicative of future results.

money flow index (MFI) A volume-weighted momentum indicator that measures the strength of money flowing in and out of a financial instrument. It compares *positive* money flow to *negative* money flow to create an indicator that can be compared to price in order to identify the strength or weakness of a trend. The MFI is measured on a 0 to 100 scale and is often calculated using a 14-day period.

money management The use of various methods of risk control in trading and investing. These methods include: (1) using proper trade size, (2) not risking more than 2 percent of your risk account on any one trade, and (3) diversifying your trading or investing account over a number of markets and sectors. This is also known as risk management.

moving average (MA) An average of data for a certain number of time periods. It moves because for each calculation we use data from the latest number of time periods. By definition, a moving average lags the market. An exponentially smoothed moving average (EMA) gives greater weight to the more recent data in an attempt to reduce the lag time.

moving average convergence/divergence (MACD) This indicator, developed by Gerald Appel, is calculated by subtracting the 26-period exponential moving average of a given financial instrument from its 12-period exponential moving average. By comparing moving averages, MACD displays trend-following characteristics, and by plotting the difference between the moving averages as an oscillator, MACD displays momentum characteristics. The MACD histogram is the visual representation of the difference between the MACD line and the MACD signal line.

mutual fund An investment company investing in a variety of securities as dictated by the specific fund's prospectus. Investors do not own the underlying investments; they buy shares of the fund itself.

naked option A short option position by a trader who does not own the underlying commodity or financial instrument.

naked put A put option in which the seller does not own the short position. Loss potential is total except for the premium.

narrowing the spread Reducing the difference between the bid and ask prices of a security.

NASDAQ See *National Association of Securities Dealers Automated Quotations System.*

NASDAQ-100 index A modified capitalization-weighted index designed to track the performance of the 100 largest and most actively traded nonfinancial domestic and international securities listed on the NASDAQ.

National Association of Securities Dealers Automated Quotations System (NASDAQ) An American stock market founded in 1971 by the National Association of Securities Dealers (NASD), which divested it in a series of sales in 2000 and 2001. It is owned and operated by the NASDAQ Stock Market, Inc., the stock of which was listed on its own stock exchange in 2002. NASDAQ is the largest electronic screen–based equity securities market in the United States. With approximately 3,200 companies, it lists more companies and on average trades more shares per day than any other U.S. market.

National Association of Securities Dealers, Inc. (NASD) This self-regulatory organization of the securities industry is responsible for the regulation of the NASDAQ stock market and the over-the-counter markets.

nearest month The expiration date of an option or future that is closest to the present.

net asset value (NAV) An increment of movement in the mutual fund market.

net worth Total assets minus total liabilities.

New York Cotton Exchange (NYCE) Founded in 1870 by a group of 100 cotton brokers and merchants in New York City, the NYCE is the oldest commodities exchange in the city. Well into the twentieth century, cotton was a leading American commodity for both export and domestic consumption.

New York Futures Exchange (NYFE) An exchange on which trading occurs for Treasury bond futures and some currency futures.

New York Mercantile Exchange (NYMEX) The world's largest physical commodity futures exchange, located in New York City. Its two principal divisions are the NYMEX and the New York Commodities Exchange (COMEX), which were once independent companies but are now merged.

New York Stock Exchange (NYSE) Known as the Big Board, this is a New York City–based stock exchange. The NYSE provides an efficient method for buyers and sellers to trade shares of stock in companies registered for public trading. The exchange provides efficient price discovery via an auction environment designed to produce the fairest price for both parties. As of January 24, 2007, NYSE stocks can be traded via its electronic hybrid market (except for a small group of very high-priced stocks). Customers can now send orders for immediate electronic execution or route orders to the floor for trade in the auction market. In excess of 50 percent of all order flow is now delivered to the floor electronically.

nontrending market This is also known as a bracketed, consolidating, range-bound, sideways, choppy, or channeling market. See *bracketed market.*

NYSE Composite index A capitalization-weighted index designed to track the performance of all common stocks listed on the New York Stock Exchange.

OBV See *on balance volume.*

on balance volume (OBV) A method is used in technical analysis to detect momentum, the calculation of which relates volume to price change. OBV provides a running total of volume and shows whether this volume is flowing into or out of a given financial instrument. It attempts to detect when a stock, bond, or other instrument is being accumulated by a large number of buyers or sold by many sellers. Joe Granville developed this indicator.

opening price guaranteed (OPG) order By choosing OPG at the opening, you ensure that your order will be executed at the opening price. If it is not executed at the opening, it will be canceled automatically.

open interest In futures markets, the total number of long and short positions is always equal. This total is called the open interest. By definition, when a contract month first begins trading, the open interest is zero. The open interest builds to a peak and then declines as positions are liquidated as the contract approaches its expiration date.

open order An order to buy or sell a security that remains in effect until it is either canceled by the customer or executed.

optimal *f* formula A formula that calculates for you the optimum fraction of capital, or percent of capital, to risk on any one trade based on your win ratio and payoff ratio. It gives you a more aggressive calculation than the risk of ruin tables do. It is sometimes referred to as the Kelly formula.

optimization Refers to optimizing software and the process of discovering what impact is the result of varying a particular parameter across different values, and then using that information to make an informed decision about which specific parameter values to use in actual trading or investing.

Optimum Wave Locater (OWL) Elliott Wave software created by Bennett A. McDowell to determine where Wave 3 appears. Also used as a filter to weed out lower probability trades.

option The right to buy or sell an underlying asset at a fixed price up to some specified date in the future. The right to buy is a *call option*, and the right to sell is a *put option*.

options market An open market to trade options.

oscillator A technical analysis tool that is a trend indicator for discovering short-term overbought and oversold conditions. Most oscillators go from 0 to 100. Analysts believe that when the indicator is near zero the price is oversold and when it is near 100 it is overbought.

out-of-the-money When an option's current market price is below the strike price of a call or above the strike price of a put.

overbought/oversold indicator An indicator that attempts to define when prices have risen (or fallen) too far, too fast, and hence are vulnerable to a reaction in the opposite direction.

overtrading You are overtrading when your commission fees are eating into your profit or when you feel out of control. Stop and reverse (SAR) traders can overtrade because of the speed of their entries and exits.

Pacific Exchange (PCX) Originally a regional stock exchange located in San Francisco, California. Its history began with the founding of the San Francisco Stock and Bond Exchange in 1882. Seven years later, the Los Angeles Oil Exchange was founded. In 1957, the two exchanges merged to form the Pacific Coast Stock Exchange, though trading floors were kept in both original cities. A name change to the Pacific Stock Exchange took place in 1973. Options trading began three years later. In 1997, *Stock* was dropped from the exchange's name. In 1999, the Pacific Exchange was the first U.S. stock exchange to demutualize. In 2001, the Los Angeles trading floor was closed, and the next year the San Francisco trading floor was closed as well. Pacific Exchange equities trading now takes place exclusively through NYSE Arca (formerly known as ArcaEx), an electronic communication network. In 2003, the Pacific Exchange launched PCX Plus, an electronic options trading platform.

paper gain Unrealized capital gain on securities held based on a comparison of the current market price to the original cost.

paper loss Unrealized capital loss on securities held based on a comparison of the current market price to the original cost.

pattern recognition A price-forecasting method that uses historical chart patterns to draw analogies to current situations.

payoff ratio Average winning trade divided by average losing trade equals the payoff ratio. For example, a 2 to 1 payoff ratio means that you are winning two dollars for every dollar you lose.

P/E ratio See *price-to-earnings (P/E) ratio.*

percentage in point (PIP) The increment of movement in the forex market.

percentage price oscillator (PPO) histogram An indicator based on the difference between two moving averages; it is expressed either as a percentage or in absolute terms. The plot is presented as a histogram so that the centerline crossovers and divergences are easily identifiable. The same principles apply to the MACD histogram.

pit The area where a futures contract is traded on the exchange floor.

playback feature See *back-testing*.

position A trader's or investor's financial stake in a given financial instrument or market.

position trader A trader who uses daily and weekly charts on which to base decisions and holds positions for days, weeks, or months.

Precision Trend Filter (PTF) Software created by Bennett A. McDowell to determine if a trend will continue in its current direction. Also used as a filter to weed out lower-probability trades.

price In trading and investing, *price* refers to the last trade price.

price bar The price bar represents the high and low price behavior in a measured time interval, such as a one-minute, five-minute, 60-minute, daily, or weekly time frame.

price gap See *gap*.

price-to-earnings (P/E) ratio The current price of a stock divided by the company's annual earnings. One of the most commonly used stock valuation ratios.

Primary Pyramid Trading Point® (P) This ART signal indicates entries into and exits out of a primary trend trade or investment.

profit margin An indicator of profitability, determined by dividing net income by revenue for the same 12-month period. Also known as net profit margin.

put-call ratio The ratio of the volume of put options traded to the volume of call options traded, which is used as an indicator of investor sentiment (bullish or bearish).

psychology Mastering the psychology of trading and investing is a crucial part of becoming successful. The *trader's mindset* is our definition of what you will attain when you have mastered your financial psychology. Some of the challenges in developing strong psychology are overcoming fear, greed, ego, and anger when trading and investing.

PTP apex The PTP apex is the point of the pyramid (triangle) and always points in the direction of the trend. It tells you where to enter based on current market dynamics.

PTP base leg The base leg is the flat base of the pyramid (triangle) and tells you where to set your stop-loss exit based on current market dynamics.

PTP confirmed When the market moves beyond the PTP apex in the direction of the trend, it will be confirmed. At that moment, the triangle will turn either *green* or *red*, depending on whether it is a bull or a bear trend.

PTP MinScore This adjustable setting on the ART software determines the number of pyramids you will see on your chart.

PTP potential When the pyramid is potential, it will be *yellow* in color. Once the market moves beyond the apex of the pyramid, it will then be confirmed and will turn either *green* or *red*, depending on whether it is a bull or a bear trend. If the market does not confirm the pyramid by exceeding the apex, the yellow pyramid (triangle) will disappear.

PTP voided If a potential *yellow* pyramid is not confirmed, it will be voided and will disappear.

put option An options contract with the right to sell a security at a specified exercise price (the strike price) on or before a specific expiration date. A put option writer sells the right to a buyer. If the option exercises, the buyer puts the stock to the writer, and the writer must buy it.

Pyramid Trading Point® (PTP) This ART trend trading signal was developed by Bennett A. McDowell and identifies exact entries and exits. It enables you to trade and invest utilizing the realities of the markets. It can be used on all markets and in all time frames.

rally (recovery) An upward movement of prices.

range-bound market See *bracketed market.*

reality-based trading Living in reality is to be seeing and reacting to the environment as events are occurring, without attempting to predict future events. When traders are living in reality, they are dealing with what is actually occurring at any given moment. When trading and investing in reality, they are focusing on the current moment. They are free of opinions and other past or future distractions or thoughts. Reality-based trading and investing involve looking at what is real in the market, such as *price* and *volume.*

recession A contraction in the business cycle, usually manifesting in slow or negative GDP growth.

relative strength index (RSI) An indicator developed by J. Welles Wilder Jr. that is used to ascertain overbought and oversold conditions. It works on a scale of 99 to 1, with 99 being the strongest and 1 being the weakest. In the stock market, it is a measure of a given stock's price strength relative to a broad index of stocks. The term can also be used in a more general sense to refer to an overbought/oversold type of indicator.

resistance level In technical analysis, a price area at which a rising market is expected to encounter increased selling pressure sufficient to stall or reverse the advance.

retracement A price movement in the opposite direction of the previous trend. A retracement is usually a price correction. For example, in a rising market, a 55 percent retracement would indicate a price decline equal to 55 percent of the prior advance. Also known as a pullback. See *Fibonacci price retracement.*

return on investment (ROI) Book income as a proportion of net book value.

reward-to-risk ratio The average winning trade divided by the size of the average losing trade. This formula will enable you to determine the estimated potential loss or gain of future transactions. Provided that you have more winners than losers, a ratio of 3:1 is excellent.

right brain The human brain is divided into two hemispheres, the left and the right, each of which is responsible for specific functions in human behavior and existence. The right brain is considered to be primarily responsible for feelings, emotions, and creativity. The right brain tends to think in pictures as opposed to words and is able to look at the big picture as opposed to minute detail. Those who are more creative tend to be considered right-brain thinkers.

right side of the chart When trading the live market, the right side of the chart is the unknown. Hindsight is 20/20, and when in the live market there is always uncertainty as to where the market actually will go. It is the not knowing that is on the right side of the chart.

risk The price of being wrong about an investment or trade.

risk control See *money management.*

ROI See *return on investment.*

RSI See *relative strength index.*

Russell 2000 index A capitalization-weighted index designed to track the performance of the 2,000 smallest U.S. stocks included in the Russell 3000 index.

Russell 3000 index A capitalization-weighted index designed to track the performance of the 3,000 largest and most liquid U.S. stocks.

S&P See *Standard & Poor's Corporation.*

S&P 500 composite stock price index A capitalization-weighted index designed to track the performance of 500 stocks that are included in the index based on their liquidity, market capitalization, and sector. While not necessarily the 500 largest U.S. companies, these are generally the 500 most widely held.

S&P 500 E-mini Designated by the commodity ticker symbol ES and often abbreviated as E-mini, this is a stock market index futures contract traded on the Chicago Mercantile Exchange's Globex electronic trading platform.

SAR See *stop and reverse.*

scaling in Refers to adding onto your current trade position to increase your *trade size*. Scale in only if the trade or investment is already profitable.

scaling out Exiting 30 percent of your position when your trading rules tell you to. This is a technique that is effective in reducing stress and locking in profit.

scalper A trader who seeks to profit from very small price fluctuations. Scalpers buy and sell quickly to make a quick profit. They often use *stop and reverse* (SAR) techniques. They can trade larger trade sizes than trend traders and still maintain proper risk control.

seasonal trading Trading based on consistent, predictable changes in price during the year due to production cycles or demand cycles.

SEC See *Securities and Exchange Commission.*

sector Used to characterize a group of securities that are similar with respect to maturity, type, rating, and/or industry.

securities Also known as *stocks*. There are a number of categories of securities, including debt securities such as bonds, equity securities such as common stock, and derivative contracts such as futures, options, and swaps.

Securities and Exchange Commission (SEC) The federal agency that is designed to promote full public disclosure and protect the investing public against fraudulent practices in the securities markets.

seller's market A market in which demand exceeds supply. As a result, the seller can dictate the price and terms of a sale.

sell-off The sale of securities under pressure.

setup When your trading rules identify certain criteria that must be present prior to entering the market.

share A unit of measure for financial instruments, including stocks, mutual funds, limited partnerships, and real estate investment trusts (REITs).

shareholder A person or entity that owns shares or equity in a corporation.

short When you sell before you have bought the item, you are *shorting* the market. This position is implemented with a sale that profits from a declining price market. The term also refers to the trader or entity holding such a position.

short call Refers to selling a *call option* that you don't already own.

short put Refers to selling a *put option* that you don't already own.

sideways market Also known as a bracketed, consolidating, range-bound, nontrending, choppy, or channeling market. See *bracketed market.*

simple correction See *ABC correction.*

slippage The difference in price between what you expect to pay when you enter the market and what you actually pay. For example, if you attempt to buy at 20 and you end up buying at 20.5, you have a half point of slippage.

small cap Refers to the relative size of a firm's market capitalization. Traditionally, any firm with a market cap under $10 billion is referred to as small cap.

speculator A person who willingly accepts risk by buying and selling financial instruments or commodities in hopes of profiting from anticipated price movements.

split The division of outstanding shares of a corporation into a larger or smaller number of shares. For example: in a three-for-one split, each holder of 100 shares before would now have 300 shares.

spread The difference between the bid price and the ask price.

Standard & Poor's Corporation (S&P) A company well known for its ratings of stocks and bonds according to investment risk (the Standard & Poor's rating) and for compiling the Standard & Poor's 500 index.

stochastic An overbought/oversold indicator, made popular by George Lane, that is based on the observation that prices tend to close near the high of the day in an uptrend, and in a downtrend they tend to close near the low of the day.

stock A financial instrument that signifies an ownership position in a corporation. Stock is the capital raised by a corporation through the issuance of shares. A person who holds at least a partial share of stock is called a *shareholder.*

stock market A market for trading and investing in company stock that is listed on a stock exchange.

stop and reverse (SAR) order An order that is used to close the current trade and open a new trade in the opposite direction.

stop limit order An order that is triggered when the stop price is reached but can only be executed at the limit price.

stop-loss exit Also referred to as a stop, stop loss, initial stop, or trailing stop. It is your designated price level where you have determined you must exit your trade if it goes against you. It is used to help control your *trade risk*. This is the worst-case scenario if the trade or investment does go against you. It is important to determine the exit point *before* entering the trade or investment.

stop order A buy order placed above the market (or sell order placed below the market) that becomes a market order when the specified price is reached.

stopped out A purchase or sale executed under a stop order at the stop price specified by the customer.

straddle The purchase or sale of an equal number of puts and calls with the same terms at the same time.

strike price The fixed price of an option.

supply equals demand When supply equals demand, the seller and buyer agree on price but disagree on value. This is the relationship between the availability of a good or service and the need or desire for it among consumers.

support level In technical analysis, a price area at which a falling market is expected to encounter increased buying pressure sufficient to stall or reverse the decline.

swing trading A short-term trading approach designed to capture quick moves in the market.

technical analysis Price forecasting methods based on a study of price itself (and volume) as opposed to the underlying fundamental (such as economic) market factors. Technical analysis traders and investors use charts to detect price patterns in the market. Technical analysis is often contrasted with fundamental analysis, and some investors and traders use a combination of the two.

tick The increment of movement and price fluctuation up or down in a market is called a tick. The value of a tick movement will vary from market to market.

ticker symbol Standard abbreviation used to refer to a stock when placing orders or conducting research.

time extension See *Fibonacci time extension.*

time frame The length of time represented by a price bar interval, such as a two-minute chart, 60-minute chart, or daily chart.

trade risk The risk that traders attempt to control through money management and risk control.

The Trader's Assistant™ (TA) A complete trade posting and trade record-keeping system created by Bennett A. McDowell to streamline trading and keep a trader organized by recording all trade information on trade posting cards and in trade ledgers.

trader's mindset See *psychology.*

trade size Also known as position size, this is the size of your trade or investment represented in the number of units (shares, contracts, etc.) of the market you are trading or investing in. Selecting optimal trade size is important in maintaining solid risk control.

Trade Size Calculator™ (TSC) Risk control software created by Bennett A. McDowell to determine a trader's maximum *trade size* based on certain variables such as percent risk and equity account size.

trading Opening a position in a financial market, either long or short, with the plan of closing it out at a substantial profit. If the trade goes against you, the plan is to cut losses quickly by using effective risk control.

trailing stop A stop-loss exit that moves in the direction of a trend trade, locking in profit in either a long or a short trend.

transaction The delivery of a security by a seller and its acceptance by the buyer.

trend The tendency of prices to move in a given general direction (up or down).

trend channel A trend line or series of trend lines used to identify upward-sloping or downward-sloping trends by placing the trend lines on the highs and lows of the channel.

trend exhaustion When a trend ends, it has reached trend exhaustion. With the ART system, trend exhaustion generally occurs after four to five consecutive *Primary Pyramid Trading Points* in the same direction.

Trend Line Master (TLM) Software created by Bennett A. McDowell to automatically draw in trend lines. Also used as a filter to weed out lower probability trades.

trending day A day that continued primarily in one trend direction, either up or down, from open to close.

trend trader A trader who trades or invests in the direction of the overall trend.

true range The greatest difference, either between the current high and the current low, between the current high and the previous close, or between the current low and the previous close.

ungrounded assessments Trading and investing rules that try to forecast or predict the market. For example, MACD, stochastics, and Elliott Wave analysis are ungrounded assessments.

unrealized gain The appreciation in value of an asset that has not been sold—paper gain.

unrealized loss The depreciation in value of an asset that has not been sold—paper loss.

uptrend A general tendency for rising prices in a given market.

volatility Refers to the range of prices in a given time period. A highly volatile market has a large range in daily prices, whereas a low-volatility market has a small range of daily prices. This is a measure of price variability in a market. A volatile market is a market that is subject to wide price fluctuations.

volume The total number of shares or contracts traded during a given period.

whipsaw A price pattern characterized by repeated, abrupt reversals in trend. The term is often used to describe losses resulting from a choppy or trendless market.

win ratio The number of winning trades divided by the total number of trades equals the win ratio. For example, if you have 6 winning trades out of a total of 10 trades, the result is a win ratio of 60 percent, meaning you have 60 percent winning trades.

NOTES

CHAPTER 1

1. *R. N. Elliott's Masterworks*, edited by Robert R. Prechter Jr. (New Classics Library, 1994), 18.
2. Ibid., 21–22.
3. Ibid., 37.
4. http://www.bls.gov/data/inflation_calculator.htm.
5. Biography of Elliott provided by George A. Schade Jr., CMT, 1996, Market Technician's Association, http://knowledgebase.mta.org/?fuseaction=kb.resource&kbResourceID=13C3A11D-F6C9-9E9D-DBB6B724D1DB22B9.
6. Ibid.
7. *R. N. Elliott's Masterworks*, 26.
8. Ibid., 27.
9. This was reported in the *New York Times* per George A. Schade, Jr., CMT MTA.
10. *R. N. Elliott's Masterworks*, 44.
11. Ibid.
12. Ibid.
13. Ibid., 42–43.
14. Ibid., 46.
15. http://www.bls.gov/data/inflation_calculator.htm.
16. http://www.bls.gov/data/inflation_calculator.htm.
17. K. J. Ryan and C. G. Ray, editors, *Sherris Medical Microbiology*, 4th ed. (McGraw Hill, 2004), 733–738; http://en.wikipedia.org/wiki/Entamoeba_histolytica.
18. *R. N. Elliott's Masterworks*, 47–48.
19. Ibid., 49-50.
20. http://ww1.dowtheoryletters.com/dtlol.nsf/Robert+Rhe+Calls+the+Turn?OpenPage.
21. *R. N. Elliott's Masterworks*, 51.

22. Ibid., 55.
23. Ibid., 57.
24. Ibid., 58.

CHAPTER 9

1. Graham, Benjamin, Wikipedia, http://en.wikipedia.org/wiki/Benjamin_Graham.
2. Target Fixation, Wikipedia. http://en.wikipedia.org/wiki/Target_fixation.

INDEX

Page numbers followed by f or t indicate figures or tables, respectively.

ABOUT THE AUTHOR

Bennett A. McDowell, founder of TradersCoach.com®, began his financial career on Wall Street and later became a registered securities broker and financial advisor for Prudential Securities and Morgan Stanley. As a financial advisor, Bennett's niche was active trading and investing for a community of high net worth clients using his own proprietary trading system. This system later became known as the Applied Reality Trading® or ART® system.

In answer to numerous requests for Bennett to share his successful trading and investing techniques, he brought the ART software to the public in 2003. Today the ART system is used in over 70 countries around the world by sophisticated hedge fund managers, individual investors, and active traders alike.

An expert in technical analysis and Elliott Wave analysis, Bennett speaks at trade shows including the Trader's Expo and writes articles for leading trading publications including *Technical Analysis of Stocks & Commodities* magazine. Internationally recognized as a leader in trading education, Bennett teaches trading to students worldwide through his company TradersCoach.com.

He is honored to be included as a member of the eSignal "Trading with the Masters" team and also to present the TradeStation "Morning Market Briefing" every Wednesday. In addition, TradersCoach.com, Applied Reality Trading, and The Trader's Assistant® record-keeping system have received numerous *Stocks & Commodities* magazine Readers' Choice Awards.

McDowell has also written three bestselling books published by John Wiley & Sons, *The ART® of Trading*, *A Trader's Money Management System*, and *Survival Guide for Traders*.

Bennett resides in San Diego, California, with his wife and two children. He can be reached by e-mail via Team@TradersCoach.com.

Lightning Source UK Ltd.
Milton Keynes UK
UKHW022346150722
405923UK00004B/255

9 780071 819305